THE INQUISITION OF THE MIDDLE AGES

THE INQUISITION

OF

THE MIDDLE AGES.

Its Organization and Operation

BY

HENRY CHARLES LEA

BARNES
&NOBLE
BOOKS
NEW YORK

This edition published by Barnes & Noble, Inc.,
by arrangement with The Citadel Press.

1993 Barnes & Noble Books

ISBN 1-56619-223-4

Printed and bound in the United States of America

M 9 8 7 6 5 4 3 2

CONTENTS

CHAPTER I.—THE INQUISITION FOUNDED.

CHAPTER II.—ORGANIZATION.

CHAPTER III.—THE INQUISITORIAL PROCESS.

CHAPTER IV.—EVIDENCE.

CHAPTER V.—THE DEFENCE.

CHAPTER VI.—THE SENTENCE.

CHAPTER VII.—CONFISCATION.

CHAPTER VIII.—THE STAKE.

INTRODUCTION

In the Preface to his monumental *A History of the Inquisition of the Middle Ages*, published in 1887, Henry Charles Lea wrote: "At the commencement of my historical studies I speedily became convinced that the surest basis of investigation for a given period lay in an examination of its jurisprudence, which presents without disguise its aspirations and the means regarded as best adopted for their realization. I have accordingly devoted much space to the origin and development of the inquisitorial process, feeling convinced that in this manner only can we understand the operations of the Holy Office and the influence which it exercised on successive generations."

It is this all-important section from Lea's three-volume work that is included in the present volume. In these chapters, Lea traces the gradual organization of the courts of the Inquisition to the middle of the thirteenth century. By this time the Inquisition was fully established, and the persecution of heresy, or freedom of individual thought, was under way. Then follows the fullest account yet published of the machinery of the Inquisition: its formal organization, its officers and jurisdiction, its method of trial, its treatment of evidence, and its varieties of sentence and punishment.

The first chapter in the present volume opens: "The gradual organization of the Inquisition was simply a process of evolution arising from the mutual reaction of the social forces which we have described." Lea is here referring to the chapters in the first volume of his work which presented the background for the founding of the Inquisition. These chapters, not included in the present volume, open with an explanation of the domination of the Church at the end of the twelfth century. "The vicissitudes of a hundred and fifty years, skillfully improved, had rendered it the mistress of Christendom." Its control over the souls, minds and actions of all Christians, accomplished by an admirably centralized organization, had given it a power unequaled by any other institution. But even at this time, the height of the Church's power, forces were· arising to challenge its authority. "As the twelfth century drew to a close, the Church was approaching a crisis in its career."

Lea briefly depicts the social forces which led to the growth of this opposition. He describes the corrupt political conditions within the Church, citing the election of Bishops, the martial character of Prelates, the prostitution of the Episcopal Office, the burdening of the people by tithes, by the sale of the Sacraments, and by various methods of extortion, the sexual disorders among sections of the clergy, and the claims to clerical immunity. These conditions provide the fertile soil for the growth of revolt and heresy.

Lea describes the intellectual awakening of the twelfth century that accelerated the rise of various heresies. He then describes the heresies and the leading heretical thinkers. Special attention is paid to the Albigensians and Waldenses in southern France who wished to restore the simple apostolic life as commanded by Christ, and to the Cathari in the south of Europe who sought to cast aside all the machinery of the Church.

The struggle of the church against heresy is then traced from early attempts, such as the unsuccessful crusades of 1181, and the independent efforts of individuals, like Pope Innocent III, through the Albigensian crusades, until the success of the Church was recognized in the Treaty of Paris in 1229. Here heresy was denounced and doomed to an established system of persecution.

Lea then describes the development of the mendicant orders, which started as zealous missionaries, and gradually were transformed into trained and itinerant inquisitors. The work of converting and persecuting heretics thus became the special field of activity of the Mendicants, especially the Dominicans.

This brings Lea's account to the founding, organization, and operation of the Inquisition—the eight chapters which are presented in this volume.

The second volume of Lea's work deals with the inquisition in the several lands of Christendom, France, the Spanish Peninsula, Italy, Germany, and Bohemia, and the third volume with special fields of Inquisitorial activity, sorcery and witchcraft.

In February, 1887, a month before his *History of the Inquisition of the Middle Ages* went to the press, Lea wrote to his publisher from Philadelphia: "Mine is the result of many years of labor and research and covers nearly the whole spiritual and intellectual development of the medieval period, offering much variety of subject. I have endeavored to make it interesting both to the general reader and the special student, for which the theme offers abundant opportunity. I have exhausted all original sources of information, and have had the libraries and archives of Europe ransacked for unprinted material, much of which is of high value . . ."

The reception to the work when published was enthusiastic. It was recognized as the most important contribution to a sadly neglected field of research and was soon translated into French, Italian, and German. Lord Acton, the noted Catholic historian, greeted the British edition with the comment: "Lea has made the most important contribution of the new world to the religious history of the old. . . . Nothing in European literature can compare with this. . . ."

Lea's great work has stood the test of time. "It has been built upon but not superseded," correctly notes Edward S. Bradley, Lea's biographer. The *Dictionary of American Biography* points out: "The great work on which he had long been engaged, *A History of the Inquisition of the Middle Ages* . . . is still the one indispensable work on the subject."

CHAPTER I.

THE gradual organization of the Inquisition was simply a process of evolution arising from the mutual reaction of the social forces which we have described. The Albigensian Crusades had put an end to open resistance, yet the heretics were none the less numerous, and, if less defiant, were only the more difficult to discover. The triumph of force had increased the responsibility of the Church, while the imperfection of its means of discharging that responsibility was self-confessed in the enormous spread of heresy during the twelfth century. We have seen the confused and uncertain manner in which the local prelates had sought to meet the new demands upon them. When the existence of hidden crime is suspected there are three stages in the process of its suppression—the discovery of the criminal, the proof of his guilt, and finally his punishment. Of all others the crime of heresy was the most difficult to discover and to prove, and when its progress became threatening the ecclesiastics on whom fell the responsibility of its eradication were equally at a loss in each of the three steps to be taken for its extermination.

Immersed, for the most part, in the multiplied troubles connected with the overgrown temporalities of their sees, the bishops would await popular rumor to designate some man or group of men as heretical. On seizing the suspected persons, there was rarely any external evidence to prove their guilt, for except where numbers rendered repression impossible, the sectaries were assiduous in outward conformity to orthodox observance, and the slender theological training of episcopal officials was generally unequal to the task of extracting confessions from thoughtful and keen-witted men, or of convicting them out of their own mouths. The judicial use of torture was as yet happily unknown, and the current substitute of a barbarous age, the Ordeal, was resorted to with a frequency which shows how ludicrously helpless were the ecclesiastics called upon to perform functions so novel. Even St. Bernard approved of this expedient, and in 1157 the Council of Reims prescribed it as the rule in all cases of suspected heresy. More enlightened churchmen viewed its results with well-grounded disbelief, and Peter Cantor mentions several cases to prove its injustice. A poor woman accused of Catharism was abandoned to die of hunger, till in confession to a religious dean she protested her innocence and was advised by him to offer the hot-iron ordeal in proof, which she did with the result of being burned first by the iron and then at the stake. A good Catholic, against whom the only suspicious evidence was his poverty and his pallor, was ordered by an assembly of bishops to undergo the same ordeal, which he refused to do unless the prelates would prove to him that this would not be a mortal sin in tempting God. This tenderness of conscience was sufficient, so without further parley they unanimously handed him over to the secular authorities, and he was promptly burned. With the study of the Roman law, however, this mode of procedure gradually fell into disfavor with the Church, and the enlightenment of Innocent III. peremptorily forbade its use in 1212, when it was extensively employed by Henry of Vehringen, Bishop of Strassburg, to convict a number of heretics; while in 1215 the Council of Lateran, following the example of Alexander III. and Lucius III., formally prohibited all ecclesias. tics from taking part in the administration of ordeals of any kind. How great was the perplexity of ignorant prelates, debarred from this ready method of seeking the judgment of God, may be guessed by the expedient which had, in 1170, been adopted by the good Bishop of Besançon, when the religious repose of his diocese was troubled by some miracle-working heretics. He is described as a learned man, and yet to solve his doubts as to whether the strangers were saints or heretics, he summoned the assistance of an ecclesiastic deeply skilled in necromancy and ordered him to ascertain the truth by consulting Satan. The cunning clerk deceived the devil into a confidential mood and learned that the strangers were his servants; they were deprived of the satanic amulets which were their protection, and the populace, which had previously sustained them, cast them pitilessly into the flames.*

---

* S. Bernard. Serm. LXVI. in Cantic. c. 12.—Hist. Vizeliacens. Lib. IV.—Concil.

When supernatural means were not resorted to, the proceedings were far too cumbrous and uncertain to be efficient against an evil so widely spread and against malefactors so numerous. In 1204 Gui, Archbishop of Reims, summoned Count Robert, cousin of Philip Augustus, the Countess Yolande, and many other laymen and ecclesiastics to sit in judgment on some heretics discovered at Brienne, with the result of burning the unfortunate wretches. In 1201, when the Knight Everard of Châteauneuf was accused of Catharism by Bishop Hugues of Nevers, the Legate Octavian summoned for his trial at Paris a council composed of archbishops, bishops, and masters of the university, who condemned him. All this was complicated by the supreme universal jurisdiction of Rome, which enabled those who were skilful and rich to protract indefinitely the proceedings and perhaps at last to escape. Thus in 1211 a canon of Langres, accused of heresy, was summoned by his bishop to appear before a council of theologians assembled to examine him. Though he had sworn to do so and had given bail, he failed to come forward, and was, after three days' waiting, condemned in default. His absence was accounted for when hé turned up in Rome and asserted to Innocent that he had been forced to take the oath and give security after he had appealed to the Holy See. The pope sent him back to the Archbishop of Sens, to the Bishop of Nevers, and Master Robert de Corzon, with instructions to examine into his orthodoxy. Two years later, in 1213, he is again seen in Rome, explaining that he had feared to come before his judges at the appointed time, because the popular feeling against heresy was so strong that not only were all heretics burned, but all who were even suspected, wherefore he craved papal protection and permission to perform due purgation at Rome. Innocent again sent him back with orders to the prelates to give him a safe-conduct and protection until his case should be decided. Whether he was innocent or guilty, whether absolved or condemned, is of little moment. The case sufficiently shows the im-

---

Remens. ann. 1137 c. 1.—Cæsar. Heisterb. Dial. Mirac. III. 16, 17; v. 18.—Guibert. Noviogent. de Vita sua Lib. III. c. 18.—Pet. Cantor. Verb. abbrev. c. 78.—Innoc. PP. III. Regest. XIV. 138.—Alex. PP. III. Epist. 74.—C. 8 Extra v. xxxiv.—C. Lateran. IV. c. 18.

possibility of efficient suppression of heresy under the existing system.*

Even after conviction had been obtained there was the same uncertainty as to penalties. In the case of the Cathari who confessed at Liége in 1144, and were with difficulty rescued from the mob who sought to burn them, the church authorities applied to Lucius II. for instructions as to what disposition should be made of them. Those who were captured in Flanders in 1162 were sent to Alexander III., then in France, for judgment, and he sent them back to the Archbishop of Reims. William Abbot of Vezelai possessed full jurisdiction, but when, in 1167, he had some confessed heretics on his hands, in his embarrassment he asked the assembled crowd what he should do with them, and the ready sentence was found in the unanimous shout, "Burn them! burn them!" which was duly executed, although one who recanted and was yet condemned by the water ordeal was publicly scourged and banished by the abbot in spite of a popular demand for concremation. In 1114 the Bishop of Soissons, after convicting some heretics by the water ordeal, went to the Council of Beauvais to consult as to their punishment; but during his absence the people, fearing the lenity of the bishops, broke into the jail and burned them.†

It was not that the Church was absolutely devoid of the machinery for discharging its admitted function of suppressing heresy. It is true that in the early days of the Carlovingian revival, Zachary's instructions to St. Boniface show that the only recognized method at that time of disposing of heretics was by summoning a council, and sending the convicted culprits to Rome for final judgment. Charlemagne's civilizing policy, however, made efficient use of all instrumentalities capable of maintaining order and security in his empire, and the bishops assumed an important position in his system. They were ordered, in conjunction with the secular officials, zealously to prohibit all superstitious observances and remnants of paganism; to travel assiduously throughout their

---

* Chron. Laudunens. Canon. ann. 1204 (D. Bouquet, XVIII. 713).—Chronolog. Roberti Autissiodor. ann. 1201.—Innocent PP. III. Regest. xiv. 15; xvi. 17.

† Martene Ampl. Collect. I. 776-8.—Alex. PP. III. Epist. 118, 122; Varior. ad Alex. III. Epist. 16.—Hist. Vizeliacens. Lib. iv.—Guibert. Noviogent. l. c.

dioceses making strict inquiry as to all sins abhorred of God, and thus a considerable jurisdiction was placed in their hands, although strictly subordinated to the State. During the troubles which followed the division of the empire, as the feudal system arose on the ruins of the monarchy, gradually the bishops threw off not only dependence on the crown, but acquired extensive rights and powers in the administration of the canon law, which now no longer depended on the civil or municipal law, but assumed to be its superior. Thus came to be founded the spiritual courts which were attached to every episcopate and which exercised exclusive jurisdiction over a constantly widening field of jurisprudence. Of course all errors of faith necessarily came within their purview.*

The organization and functions of these courts received a powerful impetus through the study of the Roman law after the middle of the twelfth century. Ecclesiastics, in fact, monopolized to such an extent the educated intelligence of the age that at first there were few besides themselves to penetrate into the mysteries of the Code and Digest. Even in the second half of the thirteenth century Roger Bacon complains that a civil lawyer, even if wholly untrained in canon law and theology, had a much better chance of high preferment than a theologian, and he exclaims in bitterness that the Church is governed by lawyers to the great injury of all Christian folk. Thus long before the feudal and seignorial courts felt the influence of the imperial jurisprudence, it had profoundly modified the principles and practice of ecclesiastical procedure. The old archdeacon gave way, not without vituperation, before the formal episcopal judge, known as the Official or Ordinary, who was usually a doctor of both laws—an LL.D. in fact—learned in both civil and canon law; and the effect of this was soon seen in a systematizing of ecclesiastical jurisprudence which gave it an immense advantage over the rude processes of the feudal and customary law. These episcopal courts, moreover, were soon sur-

---

* Hartzheim Concil. German. I. 76, 85–6.—Capit. Car. Mag. ann. 769, c. 6; Capit. II. ann. 813, c. 1.—Gratiani Decret. P. I. Dist. x. I have elsewhere considered in some detail the growth of the spiritual jurisdiction of the Church, through the False Decretals, in the anarchy accompanying the fall of the Carlovingian empire. See "Studies in Church History," 2d Ed. pp. 81–7, 326–39.

rounded by a crowd of clerkly advocates, whose zeal for their cli-
ents often outran their discretion, furnishing the first mediæval
representatives of the legal profession.*

Following in the traces of the civil law, there were three forms
of action in criminal cases—*accusatio, denunciatio,* and *inquisitio.*
In *accusatio* there was an accuser who formally inscribed himself
as responsible and was subject to the *talio* in case of failure. *Denunciatio* was the official act of the public officer, such as the *testis
synodalis* or archdeacon, who summoned the court to take action
against offenders coming within his official knowledge. In *inquisitio* the Ordinary cited the suspected criminal, imprisoning him if
necessary; the indictment, or *capitula inquisitionis,* was communicated to him, and he was interrogated thereupon, with the proviso that nothing extraneous to the indictment could be subsequently brought into the case to aggravate it. If the defendant
could not be made to confess, the Ordinary proceeded to take testimony, and though the examination of witnesses was not conducted in the defendant's presence, their names and evidence were
communicated to him, he could summon witnesses in rebuttal, and
his advocate had full opportunity to defend him by argument, exception, and appeal. The Ordinary finally gave the verdict; if
uncertain as to guilt, he prescribed the *purgatio canonica,* or oath
of denial shared by a given number of peers of the accused, more
or less, according to the nature of the charge and degree of suspicion. In all cases of conviction by the inquisitorial process, the
penalty inflicted was lighter than in accusation or denunciation.
The danger was recognized of a procedure in which the judge was
also the accuser; a man must be popularly reputed as guilty before the Ordinary could commence inquisition against him, and
this not by merely a few men or by his enemies, or those unworthy
of belief. There must be ample ground for esteeming him guilty
before this extraordinary power vested in the judge could be exercised. It is important to bear in mind the equitable provisions
of all this episcopal jurisdiction when we come to consider the

---

* S. Bernardi de Consideratione Lib. i. c. 4.—Rogeri Bacon Op. Tert. c.
xxiv.—Pet. Blesens. Epist. 202.—Concil. Rotomag. ann. 1231 c. 48. For the
rapidity with which the Church assimilated the Roman law see the collection of
decretals by Alexander III. *post Concil. Lateran.*

methods of what we call the Inquisition, erected on these foundations.*

Theoretically there also existed a thorough system of general inquisition or inquest for the detection of all offences, including heresy; and as it was only an application of this which gave rise to the Inquisition, it is worth our brief attention. The idea of a systematic investigation into infractions of the law was familiar to secular as well as to ecclesiastical jurisprudence. In the Roman law, although there was no public prosecutor, it was part of the duty of the ruler or proconsul to make perquisition after all criminals with a view to their detection and punishment, and Septimius Severus, in the year 202, had made the persecution of Christians an especial feature of this official inquisition. The Missi Dominici of Charlemagne were officials commissioned to traverse the empire, making diligent inquisition into all cases of disorder, crime, and injustice, with jurisdiction over clerk and layman alike. They held their assizes four times a year, listened to all complaints and accusations, and were empowered to redress all wrongs and to punish all offenders of whatever rank. The institution was maintained by the successors of Charlemagne so long as the royal power could assert itself; and after the Capetian revolution, as soon as the new dynasty found itself established with a jurisdiction that could be enforced beyond the narrow bounds set by feudalism, it adopted a similar expedient of "inquisitors," with a view of keeping the royal officials under control and insuring a due enforcement of the law. The same device is seen in the itinerant justiciaries of England, at least as early as the Assizes of Clarendon in 1166, when, utilizing the Anglo-Saxon organization, they made an inquest in every hundred and tithing by the lawful men of the vicinage to try and punish all who were publicly suspected of crime, giving rise to the time-honored system of the grand-jury—in itself a prototype of the incipient papal Inquisition. Similar in character were the "Inquisitors and Manifestors" whom we find in Verona in 1228, employed by the State for the detection and punishment of blasphemy; and a still stronger resemblance is seen in the *Jurados* of Sardinia in the fourteenth century—inhabi-

---

* Fournier, Les Officialités du moyen âge, Paris, 1880, pp. 256 sqq., 273-4.—Cap. 19, 21, §§ 1, 2, Extra v. 1.

tants selected in each district and sworn to investigate all cases of crime, to capture the malefactor, and to bring him before court for trial.*

The Church naturally fell into the same system. We have just seen that Charlemagne ordered his bishops to make diligent visitations throughout their dioceses, investigating all offences; and with the growth of ecclesiastical jurisdiction this inquisitorial duty was, nominally at least, perfected and organized. Already at the commencement of the tenth century we find in use a method (falsely attributed to Pope Eutychianus) which was subsequently imitated by the Inquisition. As the bishop reached each parish in his visitation, the whole body of the people was assembled in a local synod. From among these he selected seven men of mature age and approved integrity who were then sworn on relics to reveal without fear or favor whatever they might know or hear, then or subsequently, of any offence requiring investigation. These *testes synodales*, or synodal witnesses, became an institution established, theoretically at least, in the Church, and long lists of interrogatories were drawn up to guide the bishops in examining them so that no possible sin or immorality might escape the searching inquisition. Yet how completely these well-devised measures fell into desuetude, under the negligence of the bishops, is seen in the surprise awakened when, in 1246, Robert Grosseteste, the reforming Bishop of Lincoln, ordered, at the suggestion of the Franciscans, such a general inquisition into the morals of the people throughout his extensive diocese. His archdeacons and deans summoned both noble and commoner before them and examined them under oath, as required by the canons; but the proceeding was so unusual and brought to light so many scandals that Henry

---

* Fr. 13, Dig. I. (Ulpian.).—Allard, Histoire des Persecutions, Paris, 1885, p. iii. —Capit. Car. Mag. I. ann. 802; III. ann. 810; III. ann. 812.—Capit. Ludov. Pii v., vi. ann. 819; ann. 823, c. 28; Capit. Wormatiens. ann. 829.—Caroli Calvi Capit. apud Carisiacum ann. 857; Edict. Pistens. ann. 864.—Carolomanni Capit. ann. 884.—Guillel. Nangiac. Gest. S. Ludov. ann. 1255 (D. Bouquet, XX. 394, 400).—Ducange, s. v. *Inquisitores.*—Les Olim, T. III. pp. 169, 181, 211, 231, 358, 471, 501, 522, 529, 616.—Assisæ de Clarendon § 1 (Stubbs's Select Charters, p. 137, cf. p. 25).—Stubbs's Constitutional History, I. 99–100, 313, 530, 695–6.—Lib. Juris Civilis Veronæ c. 171 (Ed. 1728, p. 130).—Carta de Logu cap. xvi. (Ed. 1805, pp. 30–2).

III. was induced to interfere and ordered the sheriffs to put an end to it.*

The Church thus possessed an organization well adapted for the discovery and investigation of heretics. All that it lacked were the men who should put that organization to its destined use; and the progress of heresy up to the date of the Albigensian Crusades manifests how utterly neglectful were the ignorant prelates of the day, immersed in worldly cares, for the most part, and thinking only of the methods by which their temporalities could be defended and their revenues increased. Successive popes made fruitless efforts to arouse them to a sense of duty and induce them to use the means at their disposal for a systematic and vigorous onslaught on the sectaries, who daily grew more alarming. From the assembly of prelates who attended, in 1184, the meeting at Verona between Lucius III. and Frederic Barbarossa, the pope issued a decretal at the instance of the emperor and with the assent of the bishops, which if strictly and energetically obeyed might have established an episcopal instead of a papal Inquisition. In addition to the oath—referred to in a previous chapter—prescribed to every ruler, to assist the Church in persecuting heresy, all archbishops and bishops were ordered, either personally or by their archdeacons or other fitting persons, once or twice a year to visit every parish where there was suspicion of heresy, and compel two or three men of good character, or the whole vicinage if necessary, to swear to reveal any reputed heretic, or any person holding secret conventicles, or in any way differing in mode of life from the faithful in general. The prelate was to summon to his presence those designated, who, unless they could purge themselves at his discretion, or in accordance with local custom, were to be punished as the bishop might see fit. Similarly, any who refused to swear, through superstition, were to be condemned and punished as heretics *ipso facto*. Obstinate heretics, refusing to abjure and return to the Church with due penance, and those who after abjuration relapsed, were to be abandoned to the secular arm for fitting punishment. There was nothing organically new in all this—only a

---

* Reginon. de Eccles. Discip. Lib. II. c. 1-3.—Burchardi Decret. Lib. I. c. 91-4.—Gratiani Decret. P. II. c. xxxv. Q. vi. c. 7.—C. 7 Extra II. xxi.—Matt. Paris ann. 1246 (Ed. 1644, p. 480).

utilizing of existing institutions and an endeavor to recall the bishops to a sense of their duties; but a further important step was taken in removing all exemptions from episcopal jurisdiction in the matter of heresy and subjecting to their bishops the privileged monastic orders which depended directly on Rome. Fautors of heresy were, moreover, declared incapable of acting as advocates or witnesses or of filling any public office.*

We have already seen how utterly this effort failed to arouse the hierarchy from their sloth. The weapons rusted in the careless hands of the bishops, and the heretics became ever more numerous and more enterprising, until their gathering strength showed clearly that if Rome would retain her domination she must summon the faithful to the arbitrament of arms. She did not shrink from the alternative, but she recognized that even the triumph of her crusading hosts would be comparatively a barren victory in the absence of an organized system of persecution. Thus while de Montfort and his bands were slaying the abettors of heresy who dared to resist in the field, a council assembled in Avignon, in 1209, under the presidency of the papal legate, Hugues, and enacted a series of regulations which are little more than a repetition of those so fruitlessly promulgated twenty-five years before by Lucius III., the principal change being that in every parish a priest should be adjoined to the laymen who were to act as synodal witnesses or local inquisitors of heresy. Under this arrangement, repeated by the Council of Montpellier in 1215, there was considerable persecution and not a few burnings. In the same spirit, when the Council of Lateran met in 1215 to consolidate the conquests which then seemed secure to the Church, it again repeated the orders of Lucius. No other device suggested itself, no further means seemed either available or requisite, if only this could be carried out, and its enforcement was sought by decreeing the deposition of any bishop neglecting this paramount duty, and his replacement by one willing and able to confound heresy.†

This utterance of the supreme council of Christendom was as

---

* Lucii PP. III. Epist. 171.

† Concil. Avenionens. ann. 1209 c. 2.—Concil. Monspessulan. ann. 1215 c. 46.— Douais, Les sources de l'histoire de l'Inquisition (Revue des Questions Historiques, 1 Oct. 1881, p. 401).—C. Lateran. IV. c. 2.

ineffectual as its predecessors. An occasional earnest fanatic was found, like Foulques of Toulouse or Henry of Strassburg, who labored vigorously in the suppression of heresy, but for the most part the prelates were as negligent as ever, and there is no trace of any sustained and systematic endeavor to put in practice the periodical inquisition so strenuously enjoined. The Council of Narbonne, in 1227, imperatively commanded all bishops to institute in every parish *testes synodales* who should investigate heresy and other offences, and report them to the episcopal officials, but the good prelates who composed the assembly, satisfied with this exhibition of vigor, separated and allowed matters to run on their usual course. We hardly need the assurance of the contemporary Lucas of Tuy, that bishops for the most part were indifferent as to the matter of heresy, while some even protected heretics for filthy gain, saying, when reproached, "How can we condemn those who are neither convicted nor confessed?" No better success followed the device of the Council of Béziers in 1234, which earnestly ordered the parish priests to make out lists of all suspected of heresy and keep a strict watch upon them.*

The popes had endeavored to overcome this episcopal indifference by a sort of irregular and spasmodic Legatine Inquisition. As the papal jurisdiction extended itself under the system of Gregory VII. the legate had become a very useful instrument to bring the papal power to bear upon the internal affairs of the dioceses. As the direct representatives and plenipotentiaries of the vicegerent of God the legates carried and exercised the supreme authority of the Holy See into the remotest corners of Christendom. That they should be employed in stimulating languid persecution was inevitable. We have already seen the part they played in the affairs of the Albigenses, from the time of Henry of Citeaux to that of Cardinal Romano. In the absence of any systematic method of procedure they were even used in special cases to supplement the ignorance of local prelates, as when, in 1224, Honorius III. ordered Conrad, Bishop of Hildesheim, to bring before the Legate Cinthio, Cardinal of Porto, for judgment Henry Minneke, Provost of St. Maria of Goslar, whom he held in prison

---

* Concil. Narbonn. ann. 1227 c. 14.—Lucæ Tudens. de altera Vita c. 19.—Concil. Biterrens. ann. 1234 c. 5.

on suspicion of heresy. It was, however, in Toulouse, after the treaty of Paris, in 1229, that we find the most noteworthy case of the concurrence of legatine and episcopal action, showing how crude as yet were the conceptions of the nascent Inquisition. After Count Raymond had been reconciled to the Church, he returned in July to his dominions, followed by the Cardinal-Legate Romano, to see to the execution of the treaty and to turn back the armed "pilgrims" who were swarming to fight for the Cross, and who revenged themselves for their disappointment by wantonly destroying the harvests and creating a famine in the land. In September a council was assembled at Toulouse, consisting of all the prelates of Languedoc, and most of the leading barons. This adopted a canon ordering anew all archbishops, bishops, and exempted abbots to put in force the device of the synodal witnesses, who were charged with the duty of making constant inquisition for heretics and examining all suspected houses, subterranean rooms, and other hiding-places; but there is no trace of any obedience to this command or of any results arising from it. Under the impulsion of the legate and of Foulques of Toulouse, however, the council itself was turned into an inquisition. A converted "perfected" Catharan, named Guillem de Solier, was found and was restored to his legal rights in order to enable him to give evidence against his former brethren, while Bishop Foulques industriously hunted up other witnesses. Each bishop present took his share in examining these, sending to Foulques the evidence reduced to writing, and thus, we are told, a vast amount of business was accomplished in a short time. It was found that the heretics had mostly pledged each other to secrecy, and that it was virtually impossible to extract anything from them, but a few of the more timid came forward voluntarily and confessed, and of course each one of these, under the rules in force, was obliged to tell all he knew about others, as the condition of reconciliation. A vast amount of evidence was thus collected, which was taken by the legate for the purpose of deciding the fate of the accused, and with it he left Toulouse for Montpellier. A few of the more hardy offenders endeavored to defend themselves judicially, and demanded to see the names of the witnesses, even following the legate to Montpellier for that purpose; but he, under the pretext that this demand was for the purpose of slaying those who had testified against them, adroitly eluded it by exhibiting a combined list of all the witnesses, so that the culprits were forced to submit without defence. He then held another council at Orange, and sent to Foulques the sentences, which were duly communicated to the accused assembled for the purpose in the church of St. Jacques. All the papers of the inquisition were carried to Rome by the legate for fear that if they should fall into the hands of the evil-minded they would be the cause of many murders—and, in fact, a number of the witnesses were slain on simple suspicion.*

All this shows how crude and cumbrous an implement was the episcopal and legatine Inquisition even in the most energetic hands, and how formless and tentative was its procedure. A few instances of the use of synodal witnesses are subsequently to be found, as in the Council of Arles, in 1234, that of Tours, in 1239, that of Béziers, in 1246, of Albi, in 1254, and in a letter of Alphonse of Poitiers in 1257, urging his bishops to appoint them as required by the Council of Toulouse. An occasional example of the legatine Inquisition may also be met with. In 1237 the inquisitors of Toulouse were acting under legatine powers, as sub-delegates to the Legate Jean de Vienne; and in the same year, when the people of Montpellier asked the pope for assistance to suppress the growth of heresy, their bishop apparently being supine, he sent Jean de Vienne there with instructions to act vigorously. The episcopal office was similarly disregarded in 1239, when Gregory IX. sent orders to the inquisitors of Toulouse to obey the instructions of his legate. Yet this legatine function in time passed so completely out of remembrance that in 1351 the Signiory of Florence asked the papal legate to desist from a charge of heresy on which he had cited the Camaldulensian abbot, because the republic had never permitted its citizens to be judged for such an offence except by the inquisitors; and as early as 1257, when the inquisitors of Languedoc complained of the zeal of the Legate Zoen, Bishop of Avignon, in carrying on inquisitorial work, Alexander IV. promptly decided that he had no such power outside of his own diocese.†

---

* Potthast No. 7260.—Concil. Tolosan. ann. 1229 c. 1, 2.—Guill. de Pod. Laur. c. 40.—Guill. Pelisso Chron. Ed. Molinier, p. 18.

† Concil. Arelatens. ann. 1234 c. 5.—Concil. Turonens. ann. 1239 c. 1.—Concil. Biterrens. ann. 1246 c. 1.—Concil. Albiens. ann. 1254 c. 1.—Archives de l'Inq. de Carcassonne (Coll. Doat, XXX. 250).—Vaissette, III. Pr. pp. 385-6.—Raynald An-

The public opinion of the ruling classes of Europe demanded that heresy should be exterminated at whatever cost, and yet with the suppression of open resistance the desired end seemed as far off as ever. Bishop and legate were alike unequal to the task of discovering those who carefully shrouded themselves under the cloak of the most orthodox observance; and when by chance a nest of heretics was brought to light, the learning and skill of the average Ordinary failed to elicit a confession from those who professed the most entire accord with the teachings of Rome. In the absence of overt acts it was difficult to reach the secret thoughts of the sectary. Trained experts were needed whose sole business it should be to unearth the offenders and extort a confession of their guilt. As this necessity became more and more apparent two new factors contributed to the solution of the long-vexed problem.

The first of these was the organization of the Mendicant Orders, whose peculiar fitness for the work which had outgrown the capacity of the episcopal courts might well make their establishment seem a providential interposition to supply the Church of Christ with what it most sorely needed. As the necessity grew apparent of special and permanent tribunals devoted exclusively to the widespread sin of heresy, there was every reason why they should be wholly free from the local jealousies and enmities which might tend to the prejudice of the innocent, or the local favoritism which might connive at the escape of the guilty. If, in addition to this freedom from local partialities, the examiners and judges were men specially trained to the detection and conversion of the heretic; if, also, they had by irrevocable vows renounced the world; if they could acquire no wealth and were dead to the enticements of pleasure, every guarantee seemed to be afforded that their momentous duties would be fulfilled with the strictest justice—that while the purity of the faith would be protected, there would be no unnecessary oppression or cruelty or persecution dictated by private interests and personal revenge. Their unlimited popularity was also a warrant that they would receive far more efficient assistance in their arduous labors than could be expected by the

nal. ann. 1237, No. 32.—Archives de France, J. 430, No. 19-20.— Archivio di Firenze, Riformagioni, Classe v. fol. 80.—Archives de l'Inq. de Carcassonne (Doat, XXXI. 239).

bishops, whose position was generally that of antagonism to their flocks and to the petty seigneurs and powerful barons whose aid was indispensable. That the Mendicant Orders, to which this duty thus naturally fell, were peculiarly devoted to the papacy, and that they made the Inquisition a powerful instrument to extend the influence of Rome and destroy what little independence was left to the local churches, became subsequently doubtless an additional reason for their employment, but could scarce have been a motive in the early tentative efforts. Thus to the public of the thirteenth century the organization of the Inquisition and its commitment to the children of St. Dominic and St. Francis appeared a perfectly natural or rather inevitable development arising from the admitted necessities of the time and the instrumentalities at hand.

The other factor which promised success to the Church, in an organized effort to discharge the duty of persecution, was the secular legislation against heresy which at this period took form and shape. We have seen the spasmodic edicts of England and Aragon in the twelfth century, which have interest only as showing the absence of anterior penal laws. Frederic Barbarossa took no effective steps to give validity to the regulations which Lucius III. issued from Verona in 1184, though they purported to be drawn up with the emperor's sanction. The body of customary law which de Montfort adopted at Pamiers in 1212 of course disappeared with his short-lived domination. There had been, it is true, some fragmentary attempts at legislation, as when the Emperor Henry VI., in 1194, prescribed confiscation of property, severe personal punishment, and destruction of houses for heretics, and heavy fines for persons or communities omitting to arrest them ; and this was virtually repeated in 1210 by Otho IV., showing how soon it had been forgotten. How little uniformity, indeed, there was in the treatment of heresy is proved by such stray edicts of the period as chance to have reached us. Thus in 1217 Nuñez Sancho of Rosellon decreed outlawry for heretics, and in 1228 Jayme I. of Aragon followed his example, showing that this could not have previously been customary. On the other hand, the statutes of Pignerol in 1220 only inflict a fine of ten sols for knowingly giving shelter to Vaudois. Louis VIII. of France, just before his death, issued an *ordonnance* punishing this same crime with confiscation and deprivation of all legal rights, while the royal officials were ordered to inflict proper and immediate punishment on all who were convicted of heresy by the ecclesiastical judges. The statutes in force in Florence in 1227 required the bishop to act in conjunction with the podestà in all prosecutions for heresy, which was a serious limitation on the episcopal courts. In 1228 we hear of new laws adopted in Milan, at the instance of the papal legate, Goffredo, by which all heretics were banished from the territory of the republic, their houses torn down, the contents confiscated, their persons outlawed, with graduated fines for harboring them. A mixed secular and ecclesiastical inquisition was established for the discovery of heretics, and the archbishop and podestà were to co-operate in their examination and sentence; while the latter was bound to put to death within ten days all convicts. In Germany, as late as 1231, it required the decision of King Henry VII. to determine the disposition of property confiscated on heretics, and allodial lands were allowed to descend to the heirs, in contradiction, as we shall see, to all subsequent ruling.*

To put in action any comprehensive system of persecution, it evidently was requisite to overcome the centrifugal tendency of mediæval legislation, which finds its ultimate expression in free Navarre, where every town of importance had its special *fuero*, and almost every house its individual custom. Innocent III. endeavored, at the Lateran Council of 1215, to secure uniformity by a series of severe regulations defining the attitude of the Church to heretics, and the duties which the secular power owed to exterminate them under pain of forfeiture, and this became a recognized part of canon law; but in the absence of active secular co-operation its provisions for a while remained practically a dead letter. It was reserved for the arch-enemy of the Church, Frederic II., to break down, throughout the greater part of Europe, the particularism of local statutes, and place the population at the mercy of such emissaries as the popes might send to represent them. It was requisite for him to acquire the favor of Honorius III. to secure his coronation in 1220; and when the inevitable rupture took place, it was still necessary for him to meet the charge of heresy so freely brought against

---

* Lami, Antichità Toscane, pp. 484, 504, 524.—Muratori Antiq. Ital. Diss. LX. (T. XII. p. 447).—D'Achery Spicileg. III. 588, 598.—Charvaz, Origine dei Valdesi, Torino, 1838, App. No. xxii.—Isambert, Anc. Loix Fran. I. 228.—Corio, Hist. Milanese, ann. 1228-9.—Hist. Diplom. Frid. II. T. III. p. 466.

him by manifesting special zeal in the persecution of heretics, though doubtless, if left to himself, philosophic indifference would have led him to tolerate any form of belief that did not threaten disobedience to the ruler.*

In a series of edicts dating from 1220 to 1239 he thus enacted a complete and pitiless code of persecution, based upon the Lateran canons. Those who were merely suspected of heresy were required to purge themselves at command of the Church, under penalty of being deprived of civil rights and placed under the imperial ban; while, if they remained in this condition for a year, they were to be condemed as heretics. Heretics of all sects were outlawed; and when condemned as such by the Church they were to be delivered to the secular arm to be burned. If, through fear of death, they recanted, they were to be thrust in prison for life, there to perform penance. If they relapsed into error, thus showing that their conversion had been fictitious, they were to be put to death. All the property of the heretic was confiscated and his heirs disinherited. His children, to the second generation, were declared ineligible to any positions of emolument or dignity, unless they should win mercy by betraying their father or some other heretic. All " credentes," fautors, defenders, receivers, or advocates of heretics were banished forever, their property confiscated, and their descendants subjected to the same disabilities as those of heretics. Those who defended the errors of heretics were to be treated as heretics unless, on admonition, they mended their ways. The houses of heretics and their receivers were to be destroyed, never to be rebuilt. Although the evidence of a heretic was not receivable in court, yet an exception was made in favor of the faith, and it was to be held good against another heretic. All rulers and magistrates, present or future, were required to swear to exterminate with their utmost ability all whom the Church might designate as heretics, under pain of forfeiture of office. The lands of any temporal lord who neglected, for a year after summons by the Church, to clear them of heresy, were exposed to the occupancy of any Catholics who, after extirpating the heretics, were to possess them in peace without prejudice to the rights of

---

* De Lagrèze, La Navarre Française, I. xxi; II. 6.—Concil. Lateran. IV. c. 3 (C. 13 Extra v. vii.).

the suzerain, provided he had offered no opposition. When the papal Inquisition was commenced, Frederic hastened, in 1232, to place the whole machinery of the State at the command of the inquisitors, who were authorized to call upon any official to capture whomsoever they might designate as a heretic, and hold him in prison until the Church should condemn him, when he was to be put to death.*

This fiendish legislation was hailed by the Church with acclamation, and was not allowed to remain, like its predecessors, a dead letter. The coronation-edict of 1220 was sent by Honorius to the University of Bologna to be read and taught as a part of practical law. It was consequently embodied in the authoritative compilation of the feudal customs, and its most stringent enactments were incorporated in the Civil Code. The whole series of edicts was subsequently promulgated by successive popes in repeated bulls, commanding all states and cities to inscribe these laws irrevocably in their local statute-books. It became the duty of the inquisitors to see that this was done, to swear all magistrates and officials to enforce them, and to compel their obedience by the free use of excommunication. In 1222, when the magistrates of Rieti adopted laws conflicting with them, Honorius at once ordered the offenders removed from office; in 1227 the people of Rimini resisted, but were coerced to submission; in 1253, when some of the Lombard cities demurred, Innocent IV. promptly ordered the inquisitors to subdue them; in 1254 Asti peacefully accepted them as part of its local laws; Como followed the exam-

---

* Hist. Diplom. Frid. II. T. II. pp. 4–6, 422; T. IV. pp. 6–8, 299–302; T. V. pp. 201, 279–80. The coronation-edict, which formed the basis of all subsequent legislation against heresy, was drawn up by the papal curia, and sent, a fortnight before the ceremony, to the Legate Bishop of Tusculum, with orders to procure the imperial signature and return it, so that it could be published under the emperor's name in the church of St. Peter (Raynald. ann. 1220, No. 19.—Hist. Dipl. I. ii. 880). Nothing could seem a plainer duty to an ecclesiastic of the time than that the Church should stimulate the temporal ruler to the sharpest persecution of heresy.

It was doubtless the outlawry of heretics pronounced by the edicts of Frederic which enabled the Inquisition to establish the settled principle that the heretic could be captured and despoiled at any time and by any person, and that the spoiler could retain his goods—provided always that he was not an official of the Holy Office (Tract. de Inquisitione, Doat, XXXVI.).

ple, September 10, 1255; and in the recension of the laws of Florence made as late as 1355, they still appear as an integral part. Finally, they were incorporated in the latest additions to the Corpus Juris as part of the canon law itself, and, technically speaking, they may be regarded as in force to the present day.*

This virtually provided for a very large portion of Europe, extending from Sicily to the North Sea. The western regions made haste to follow the pious example. Coincident with the Treaty of Paris, in 1229, was an *ordonnance* issued in the name of the boy-king, Louis IX., giving efficient assistance. by the royal officials to the Church in its efforts to purge the land of heresy. In the territories which remained to Count Raymond his vacillating course gave rise to much dissatisfaction, until, in 1234, he was compelled to enact, with the consent of his prelates and barons, a statute drawn up by the fanatic Raymond du Fauga of Toulouse, which embodied all the practical points of Frederic's legislation, and decreed confiscation against every one who failed, when called upon, to aid the Church in the capture and detention of heretics. In the compilations and law books of the latter half of the century we see the system thoroughly established as the law of the whole land, and in 1315 Louis Hutin formally adopted the edicts of Frederic and made them valid throughout France. †

In Aragon Don Jayme I., in 1226, issued an edict prohibiting all heretics from entering his dominions, probably on account of the fugitives driven out of Languedoc by the crusade of Louis VIII. In 1234, in conjunction with his prelates, he drew up a

---

* Hist. Diplom. Frid. II. T. II. p. 7.—Post Libb. Feudorum.—Post constt. iv. xix. Cod. I. v. — Innoc. PP. IV. Bull. *Cum adversus*, 1243, 1252, 1254; Bull. *Orthodoxæ*, 27 Apr., 14 Maii, 1252.—Alex. PP. IV. Bull. *Cum adversus*, 1258.— Ejusd. Bull. *Cupientes*, 1260. — Clement. PP. IV. Bull. *Cum adversus*, 1265.— Wadding. Annal. Minor. ann. 1261, No. 3; ann. 1289, No. 20.—Urbani PP. IV. Bull. *Licet ex omnibus*, 1262, § 12. — Epistt. Sæculi XIII. No. 191 (Monument. Hist. German.).—Eymerici Direct. Inquis. Ed. Pegnæ, 1607, p. 392.—Innoc. PP. IV. Bull. *Ad aures*, 2 Apr. 1253.—Sclopis, Antica Legislazione del Piemonte, p. 440. — Bernardi Comens. Lucerna Inquisit. s. v, *Executio*, No. 3. — Archivio di Firenze, Riformagioni, Classe II. Distinz. 1, No. 14.—Potthast No. 7672.—C. 2 in Septimo, v. 3.

† Isambert, Anc. Loix Fran. I. 230–33; III. 126.—Harduin. Concil. VII. 203–8. —Guill. de. Pod. Laur. c. 42. — Établissements, Liv. I. ch. 85, 123. — Livres de Jostice et de Plet, Liv. I. Tit. iii. § 7.

series of laws instituting an episcopal Inquisition of the severest character, to be supported by the royal officials; in this appears for the first time a secular prohibition of the Bible in the vernacular. All possessing any books of the Old or New Testament, "in Romancio," are summoned to deliver them within eight days to their bishops to be burned, under pain of being held suspect of heresy. Thus, with the exception of farther Spain and the Northern nations, where heresy had never taken root, throughout Christendom the State was rendered completely subservient to the Church in the great task of exterminating heresy. And, when the Inquisition had been established, the enforcing of this legislation was the peculiar privilege of the inquisitors, whose ceaseless vigilance and unlimited powers gave full assurance that it would be relentlessly carried into effect.*

Meanwhile zeal or jealousy led, in the confusion and uncertainty of this transition period, to the experiment, in several parts of Italy, of a secular Inquisition. In Rome, in 1231, Gregory IX. drew up a series of regulations which was issued by the Senator Annibaldo in the name of the Roman people. Under this the senator was bound to capture all who were designated to him as heretics, whether by inquisitors appointed by the Church or other good Catholics, and to punish them within eight days after condemnation. Of their confiscated property one third went to the detector, one third to the senator, and one third to repairing the city walls. Any house in which a heretic was received was to be destroyed, and converted forever into a receptacle of filth. "Credentes" were treated as heretics, while fautors, receivers, etc., forfeited one third of their possessions, applicable to the city walls. A fine of twenty lire was imposed on any one cognizant of heresy and not denouncing it; while the senator who neglected to enforce the law was subject to a mulct of two hundred marks and perpetual disability to office. To appreciate the magnitude of these fines we must consider the rude poverty of the Italy of the period as described by a contemporary—the squalor of daily life

---

* Archives Nat. de France, J. 426, No. 4. — Martene Ampliss. Collect. VII. 123–4.—Bernard. Guidon. Practica P. IV. (Coll. Doat, XXX.).—Clem. PP. IV. Bull. *Præ cunctis*, 23 Feb. 1266.

In 1229 the Council of Toulouse had already prohibited all laymen from possessing any of the Scriptures, even in Latin (Concil. Tolosan. ann. 1229, c. 14).

and the scarcity of the precious metals, as indicated by the absence of gold and silver ornaments in the dress of the period. Not satisfied with the local enforcement of these regulations, Gregory sent them to the archbishops and princes throughout Europe, with orders to put them in execution in their respective territories, and for some time they formed the basis of inquisitorial proceedings. In Rome the perquisition was successful, and the faithful were rewarded with the spectacle of a considerable number of burnings; while Gregory, encouraged by success, proceeded to issue a decretal, forming the basis of all subsequent inquisitorial legislation, by which condemned heretics were to be abandoned to the secular arm for exemplary punishment, those who returned to the Church were to be perpetually imprisoned, and every one cognizant of heresy was bound to denounce it to the ecclesiastical authorities under pain of excommunication.*

At the same time Frederic II., who desired to give Rome as little foothold as possible in his Neapolitan dominions, placed the business of persecution there in the hands of the royal officials. In his Sicilian Constitutions, issued in 1231, he ordered his representatives to make diligent inquisition into the heretics who walk in darkness. All, however slightly suspected, are to be arrested and subjected to examination by ecclesiastics, and those who deviate ever so little from the faith, if obstinate, are to be gratified with the fiery martyrdom to which they aspire, while any one daring to intercede for them shall feel the full weight of the imperial displeasure. As the legislation of a freethinker, this shows the irresistible weight of public opinion, to which Frederic dared not run counter. Nor did he allow this to remain a dead letter. A number of executions under it took place forthwith, and two years later we find him writing to Gregory deploring that this had not been sufficient, for heresy was reviving, and that he therefore had ordered the justiciary of each district, in conjunction with some prelate, to renew the inquisition with all activity; the bishops were required to traverse their dioceses thoroughly, in company, when necessary, of judges delegated for the purpose; in

---

* Raynald. Annal. ann. 1231, No. 13, 18.—Ripoll I. 38.—Ricobaldi Ferrar. Hist. Impp. ann. 1234. — Paramo de Orig. Offic. S. Inq. p. 177. — Richardi di S. Germano Chron. ann. 1231. — C. 15 Extra v. vii. (In this canon "noluerint" is evidently an error for "voluerint").—Hartzheim Concil. German. III. 540.

each province the General Court held two assizes a year, when heresy was punished like any other crime. Yet, so far from praising this systematized persecution, Gregory replied that Frederic was using pretended zeal to punish his personal enemies, and was burning good Catholics rather than heretics.*

In this confused and irregular striving to accomplish the extirpation of heresy, it was inevitable that the Holy See should intervene, and through the exercise of its supreme apostolic authority seek to provide some general system for the efficient performance of the indispensable duty. The only wonder, indeed, is that this should have been postponed so long and have been at last commenced so tentatively and apologetically.

In 1226 an effort was made to check the rapid spread of Catharism in Florence by the arrest of the heretic bishop Filippo Paternon, whose diocese extended from Pisa to Arezzo. He was tried, in accordance with the existing Florentine statutes, by the bishop and podestà conjointly, when he cut short the proceedings by abjuration, and was released; but he speedily relapsed, and became more odious than ever to the orthodox. In 1227 a converted heretic complained of this backsliding to Gregory IX., and the pontiff, who had just ascended the papal throne, made haste to remedy the evil by issuing a commission, which may be regarded as the foundation of the papal Inquisition. Yet it was exceedingly unobtrusive, though the church of Florence was so directly under papal control. Bearing date June 20, 1227, it simply authorizes Giovanni di Salerno, prior of the Dominican house of Santa Maria Novella, with one of his frati and Canon Bernardo, to proceed judicially against Paternon and his followers and force them to abjuration; acting, in case of obstinacy, under the canons of the Lateran Council, and, if necessary, calling upon the clerks and laymen of the sees of Florence and Fiesole for aid. Thus, while there was no scruple in invading the jurisdiction of the Bishop of Florence, there was no legislation other than the Lateran canons to guide the proceedings. What the commissioners

---

* Constit. Sicular. Lib. I. Tit. 1.—Hist. Diplom. Frid. II. T. IV. pp. 435, 444. —Rich. de S. Germano Chron. ann. 1233.—Giannone, Istoria Civile di Napoli, Lib. XVII. c. 6; XIX. 5.

accomplished with regard to the inferior heretics is not known. They succeeded in capturing Bishop Paternon and cast him in prison, but he was forcibly rescued by his friends and disappeared, leaving his episcopate to his successor, Torsello.*

Frà Giovanni retained his commission until his death in 1230, when a successor was appointed in the person of another Dominican, Aldobrandino Cavalcanti. Still, their jurisdiction was as yet wholly undetermined, for in June, 1229, we hear of the Abbot of San Miniato carrying to Gregory IX., in Perugia, two leading heretics, Andrea and Pietro, who were forced to a public abjuration in presence of the papal court; and in several cases in 1234 we find Gregory IX. intervening, taking bail of the accused and sending special instructions to the inquisitor in charge. Yet the Inquisition was gradually taking shape, for shortly afterwards there were numerous heretics discovered, some of whom were burned, their trials being still preserved in the archives of Santa Maria Novella. Yet how little thought there could have been of founding a permanent institution is shown, in 1233, by the persecuting statutes drawn up by Bishop Ardingho, approved by Gregory, and ordered by him to be irrevocably inscribed in the statute-book of Florence. In these the bishop is still the persecuting representative of the Church, and there is no allusion to inquisitors. The podestà is bound to arrest any one pointed out to him by the bishop, and to punish him within eight days after the episcopal condemnation, with other provisions borrowed from the edicts of Frederic II. Frà Aldobrandino seems to have relied rather on preaching than on persecution; in fact he nowhere in the documents signed by him qualifies himself as inquisitor, and neither his efforts nor those of Bishop Ardingho were able to prevent the rapid growth of heresy. In 1235, when the project of an organized Inquisition throughout Europe was taking shape, Gregory appointed the Dominican Provincial of Rome inquisitor throughout his extensive province, which embraced both Sicily and Tuscany; but this seems to have proved too large a district, and about 1240 we find the city of Florence under the charge of Frà Ruggieri Calcagni. He was of a temper well fitted to extend the prerogatives of his office and to render it effective; but it was not until 1243 that

---

* Lami, Antichità Toscane, pp. 493–4, 509–10, 546.

he qualified himself as "*Inquisitor Domini Papœ in Tuscia*," and in a sentence rendered in 1245 he is careful to call himself inquisitor of Bishop Ardingho as well as of the pope, and recites the episcopal commission given him as authority to act. In the proceedings of this period the rudimentary character of the Inquisition is evident. One confession in 1244 bears only the names of two frati, the inquisitor not being even present. In 1245 there are sentences signed by Ruggieri alone, while other proceedings show him to be acting conjointly with Ardingho. He may be said, indeed, to have given the Inquisition in Florence form and shape when, about 1243, he opened for the first time his independent tribunal in Santa Maria Novella, taking as assessors two or three prominent friars of the convent and employing public notaries to make record of his proceedings.*

This is a fair illustration of the gradual development of the Inquisition. It was not an institution definitely projected and founded, but was moulded step by step out of the materials which lay nearest to hand fitted for the object to be attained. In fact, when Gregory, recognizing the futility of further dependence on episcopal zeal, sought to take advantage of the favorable secular legislation against heresy, the preaching friars were the readiest instruments within reach for the accomplishment of his object. We shall see hereafter how, as in Florence, the experiment was tried in Aragon and Languedoc and Germany, and the success which on the whole attended it and led to an extended and permanent organization.

The Inquisition has sometimes been said to have been founded April 20, 1233, the day on which Gregory issued two bulls making the persecution of heresy the special function of the Dominicans; but the apologetic tone in which he addresses the prelates shows how uncertain he felt as to their enduring this invasion of their jurisdiction, while the character of his instructions proves that he had no conception of what the innovation was to lead to. In fact, his immediate object seems rather the punishment of priests and other ecclesiastics, concerning whom there was a stand-

---

* Lami op. cit. 511, 519–22, 528, 531, 543–4, 546–7, 554, 557, 559.—Archiv. di Firenze. Prov. S. Maria Novella 1227, Giugn. 20; 1229, Giugn. 24; 1235, Agost. 23.—Ughelli, Italia Sacra, III. 146–7. Ripoll I. 69, 71.

ing complaint that they favored heretics by instructing them how to evade examination by concealing their beliefs and feigning ortho- doxy. After reciting the necessity of subduing heresy and the raising up by God of the preaching friars, who devote themselves in voluntary poverty to spreading the Word and extirpating mis- belief, Gregory proceeds to tell the bishops : " We, seeing you en- grossed in the whirlwind of cares and scarce able to breathe in the pressure of overwhelming anxieties, think it well to divide your burdens that they may be more easily borne. We have there- fore determined to send preaching friars against the heretics of France and the adjoining provinces, and we beg, warn, and exhort you, ordering you as you reverence the Holy See, to receive them kindly and treat them well, giving them in this, as in all else, favor, counsel, and aid, that they may fulfil their office." The other bull is addressed " to the Priors and Friars of the Order of Preach- ers, Inquisitors," and after alluding to the sons of perdition who defend heresy, it proceeds : " Therefore you, or any of you, wher- ever you may happen to preach, are empowered, unless they de- sist from such defence (of heretics) on monition, to deprive clerks of their benefices forever, and to proceed against them and all others, without appeal, calling in the aid of the secular arm, if necessary, and coercing opposition, if requisite, with the censures of the Church, without appeal." *

This experiment of investing all the Dominican preachers with legatine authority to condemn without appeal was inconsiderate. It could only lead to exasperation, as we shall see hereafter in Germany, and Gregory soon adopted a more practical expedient. Shortly after the issue of the above bulls we find him ordering the Provincial Prior of Toulouse to select some learned friars who should be commissioned to preach the cross in the diocese, and to proceed against heretics in accordance with the recent statutes. Though here there is still some incongruous mingling of duties, yet Gregory had finally hit upon the device which remained the ·permanent basis of the Inquisition—the selection by the provin- cial of certain fitting brethren, who exercised within their prov-

---

* Ripoll I. 45, 47.—C. 8 § 8, Sexto v. 2.—Gregor. PP. XI. Bull. *Ille humani generis; Licet ad capiendos.*—Potthast No. 9143, 9152, 9235.—Arch. de l'Inq. de Carcassonne (Doat, XXXI. 21, 25).

ince the delegated authority of the Holy See in searching out and examining heretics with a view to the ascertainment of their guilt. Under this bull the provincial appointed Friars Pierre Cella and Guillem Arnaud, whose labors will be detailed in a subsequent chapter. Thus the Inquisition, as an organized system, may be considered as fairly commenced, though it is noteworthy that these early inquisitors in their official papers qualify themselves as acting under legatine and not under papal authority. How little idea there was as yet of creating a general and permanent institution is seen when the Archbishop of Sens complained of the intrusion of inquisitors in his province, and Gregory, by a brief of February 4, 1234, apologetically revoked all commissions issued for it, adding a suggestion that the archbishop should call in the assistance of the Dominicans if he thought that their superior·skill in confuting heretics was likely to prove useful.*

As yet there was no idea of superseding the episcopal functions. About this time we find Gregory writing to the bishops of the province of Narbonne, threatening them if they shall not inflict due chastisement on heretics, and making no allusion to the new expedient; and as late as October 1, 1234, Pierre Amiel, Archbishop of Narbonne, exacted an oath from his people to denounce all heretics to him or to his officials, apparently in ignorance of the existence of special inquisitors. Even where the latter were commissioned, their duties and functions, their powers and responsibilities, were wholly undefined and remained to be determined. As they were regarded simply in the light of assistants to the bishops in the exercise of the immemorial episcopal jurisdiction over heresy, it was naturally to the bishops that were referred the questions which immediately arose. Many points as to the treatment of heretics had been settled, not only by Gregory's Roman

---

* Potthast No. 9263; cf. No. 9386, 9388.—Guill. de Pod. Laur. c. 43.—Coll. Doat, XXI. 143, 153.—Ripoll I. 66.

Guillem Arnaud generally qualifies himself as acting under commission from the legate, but sometimes as appointed by the Dominican provincial. In several sentences on the Seigneurs de Niort, in February and March, 1236, he acts with the Archdeacon of Carcassonne, both under legatine authority. As yet there was evidently no settled organization (Coll. Doat, XXI. 160, 163, 165, 166).

statutes of 1231, but by the Council of Toulouse in 1229, and those of Béziers and Arles in 1234, which were solely occupied with stimulating and organizing the episcopal Inquisition, yet matters of detail constantly suggested themselves in practice, and a new code of some kind was evidently required to render persecution effective.   The suspension of the Inquisition for some years at the request of Count Raymond postponed this, but when the Holy Office resumed its functions in 1241 the necessity became pressing, and the bishops were looked to as the authority from which such a code should emanate.   Sentences rendered in 1241 by Guillem Arnaud recite not only that Bishop Raymond of Toulouse acted as assessor, but that the special advice of the Archbishop of Narbonne had been asked.   It was evident that general principles for the guidance of the Inquisition must be laid down, and accordingly a great council of the three provinces of Narbonne, Arles, and Aix was assembled at Narbonne in 1243 or 1244, where an elaborate series of canons were framed, which remained the basis of inquisitorial action.   These were addressed to " Our cherished and faithful children in Christ the Preaching Friars Inquisitors;" and though the bishops discreetly say, " We write this to you, not that we wish to bind you down by our counsels, as it would not be fitting to limit the liberty accorded to your discretion by other forms and rules than those of the Holy See, to the prejudice of the business ; but we wish to help your devotion as we are commanded to do by the Holy See, since you, who bear our burdens, ought to be, through mutual charity, assisted with help and advice in our own business," yet the tone of the whole is that of absolute command, both in the definition of jurisdiction and the instructions as to dealing with heretics.   It is highly significant that, in surrendering control over the bodies of their flocks, these good shepherds strictly reserved to themselves the profits to be expected from persecution, for they straitly enjoined upon the new officials, " You are to abstain from these pecuniary penances and exactions, both for the sake of the honor of your Order, and because you will have fully enough other work to attend to."   While thus carefully preserving their financial interests, they abandoned what was vastly more important, the right of passing judgment and imposing sentence.   Sentences of this period are rendered in the name of the inquisitors, though if the bishop or other notable person took part, as was frequently the case, he is mentioned as an assessor.* The transfer of the old episcopal jurisdiction over heresy to the Inquisition naturally rendered the connection between bishop and inquisitor a matter of exceeding delicacy, and the ·new institution could not establish itself without considerable friction, revealed in the varying and contradictory policy adopted at successive periods in adjusting their mutual relations. This renders itself especially noticeable in the development of the Inquisition in the different lands of Europe. In Italy the independence of the episcopate had long since been broken down, and it could offer no efficient opposition to the encroachment on its jurisdiction. In Germany, on the other hand, the lordly prince-bishops looked with jealous eyes on the intruder, and, as we shall see hereafter, never allowed it to obtain a permanent foothold. In France, and more especially in Languedoc, although the prelates were far more independent than those of Italy, the prevalence of heresy required for its suppression a vigilance and an activity far beyond their ability, and they found themselves obliged to sacrifice a portion of their prerogatives in order to escape the more painful sacrifice of performing their long-neglected duties. Yet they did not submit to this without a struggle which may be dimly traced in the successive efforts to establish a *modus vivendi* between the respective tribunals.

We have just seen that at an early period the inquisitors assumed to render sentences in their own names, without reference to the bishops. This invasion of the latter's jurisdiction was evidently too great an innovation to be permanent; indeed, almost immediately we find the Cardinal Legate of Albano instructing the Archbishop of Narbonne to order the inquisitors not to condemn heretics or impose penances without the concurrence of the bishops. This order had to be repeated and rendered more absolute; and the question was settled in this sense by the Council of Béziers in 1246, where the bishops, on the other hand, surrendered the fines to be used for the expenses of the Inquisition, and drew

---

* Vaissette, III. Pr. 364, 370-1.—Concil. Tolosan. ann. 1229.—Concil. Biterrens. ann. 1234.—Concil. Arelatens. ann. 1234.—Concil. Narbonn. ann. 1244.— Coll. Doat, XXI. 143, 155, 158.

up another elaborate series of instructions for the inquisitors, "willingly yielding to your devout requests which you have humbly made to us." For a while the popes continued to treat the bishops as responsible for the suppression of heresy in their respective dioceses, and consequently as the real source of jurisdiction. In 1245 Innocent IV., in permitting inquisitors to modify or commute previous sentences, specified that this must be done with the advice of the bishop. In 1246 he orders the Bishop of Agen to make diligent inquisition against heresy under the rules prescribed by the Cardinal Legate of Albano, and with the same power as the inquisitor to grant indulgences. In 1247 he treats the bishops as the real judges of heresy in instructing them to labor sedulously for the conversion of the convict, before passing sentence involving death, perpetual imprisonment, or pilgrimages beyond seas; even with obstinate heretics they are to consult diligently with the inquisitor or other discreet persons whether to pass sentence or to postpone it, as may best subserve the salvation of the sinner and the interest of the faith. Still, in spite of all this, the sentences of Bernard de Caux, from 1246 to 1248, bear no trace of episcopal concurrence. There evidently was jealousy and antagonism. In 1248 the Council of Valence was obliged to coerce the bishops into publishing and observing the sentences of the inquisitors, by interdicting the entry into their own churches to those who refused to do so, showing that the bishops were not consulted as to the sentences and were indisposed to enforce them. In 1249 we find the Archbishop of Narbonne complaining to the pope that the inquisitor Pierre Durant and his colleagues had, without his knowledge, absolved the Chevalier Pierre de Cugunham, who had been convicted of heresy, whereupon Innocent forthwith annulled their proceedings. In fact the pardoning power seems to have been considered as specially vested in the Holy See, and about this period we find several instances in which it is conferred by Innocent on bishops, sometimes with and sometimes without injunctions to confer with the inquisitors. Finally this question of practice was settled by adopting the habit of reserving in every sentence the right to modify, increase, diminish, or abrogate it.*

---

* Vaissette, III. 452.—Concil. Biterrens. ann. 1246.—Berger, Les Registres

Inasmuch as the inquisitors in 1246 still expected the bishops to defray their expenses, they recognized themselves, at least in theory, as merely an adjunct to the episcopal tribunals. The bishops, moreover, were expected to build the prisons for the confinement of converts, and though they eluded this and the king was obliged to do it, the Council of Albi, held in 1254 by the papal legate, Zoen of Avignon, assumes that the prisons are under episcopal control. The same council drew up an elaborate series of instructions for the treatment of heretics, which marks the termination of episcopal control of such matters, for all subsequent regulations were issued by the Holy See. Even so experienced a persecutor as Bernard de Caux, notwithstanding his neglect of episcopal jurisdiction in his sentences, admitted in 1248 his subordination to the episcopate by applying for advice to Guillem of Narbonne, and the archbishop replied, not only with directions as to special cases, but with general instructions. Indeed, in 1250 and 1251 the archbishop was actively employed in making an inquisition of his own and in punishing heretics without the intervention of papal inquisitors ; and a brief of Innocent IV. in 1251 alludes to a previous intention, subsequently abandoned, of restoring the whole business to the bishops. In spite of these indications of reaction the intruders continued to win their way, with struggles, bitter enough, no doubt, in many places, and intensified by the hostility between the secular clergy and the Mendicants, but only to be conjectured from the scattered indications visible in the fragmentary remains of the period. There is an effort to retain vanishing authority in the offer made in 1252 by the bishops of Toulouse, Albi, Agen, and Carpentras to give full authority as inquisitors to any Dominicans who might be selected by the commissioners of Alphonse of Poitiers, only stipulating that their assent must be asked to all sen-

---

d'Innocent IV. No. 2043, 3867, 3868.—Arch. de l'Inq. de Carcass. (Doat, XXXI. 68, 74, 75, 77, 80, 152, 182).—Potthast No. 12744, 15805.—MSS. Bib. Nat., fonds latin, No. 9992.—Concil. Valentin. ann. 1248 c. 10.—Baluz. Conc. Narbonn. App. p. 100.

The system devised by the councils of Languedoc became generally current. In 1248 Innocent IV. ordered the Archbishop and Inquisitor of Narbonne to send a copy of their rules of procedure to the Provincial of Spain and Raymond of Pennaforte, to be followed in the Peninsula (Baluz. et Mansi I. 208) ; and their canons are frequently cited in the manuals of the mediæval Inquisition.

tences, and promising to observe in all cases the rules established by the Inquisition. This question of episcopal concurrence in condemnations evidently excited strong feeling and was long contested with varying success. If previous orders requiring it had not been treated with contempt, Innocent IV. would not have been obliged, in 1254, to reiterate the instructions that no condemnations to death or life-imprisonment should be uttered without consulting the bishops; and in 1255 he conjoined bishop and inquisitor to interpret in consultation any obscurities in the laws against heresy and to administer the lighter penalties of deprivation of office and preferment. This recognition of episcopal jurisdiction was annulled by Alexander IV., who, after some vacillation, in 1257 rendered the Inquisition independent by releasing it from the necessity of consulting with the bishops even in cases of obstinate and confessed heretics, and this he repeated in 1260. Then there was a reaction. In 1262 Urban IV., in an elaborate code of instructions, formally revived the consultation in all cases involving the death-penalty or perpetual imprisonment; and this was repeated by Clement IV. in 1265. Either these instructions, however, were revoked in some subsequent enactment or they soon fell into desuetude, for in 1273 Gregory X., after alluding to the action of Alexander IV. in annulling consultation, proceeds to direct that inquisitors in deciding upon sentences shall proceed in accordance with the counsel of the bishops or their delegates, so that the episcopal authority may share in decisions of such moment. Up to this period the Inquisition seems to have been regarded as merely a temporary expedient to meet a special exigency, and every pope on his accession had issued a series of bulls renewing its provisions. Heresy, however, was apparently ineradicable; the populations had accepted the new institution, and its usefulness had been proved in many ways besides that of preserving the purity of the faith. Henceforth it was considered a permanent part of the machinery of the Church, and its rules were definitely settled. Gregory's decision in favor of concurrent episcopal and inquisitorial action in all cases of condemnation consequently remained unaltered, and we shall see hereafter that when Clement V. endeavored to check the more scandalous abuses of inquisitorial power, he sought the remedy, insufficient enough, in some slight increase of episcopal supervision and responsibility, following in this an effort in the same direction which had been essayed by Philippe le Bel. Yet when bishop and inquisitor chanced to be on good terms, the slender safeguard thus afforded for the accused was eluded by one of them giving to the other power to act for him, and cases are on record in which the bishop acts as the inquisitor's deputy, or the inquisitor as the bishop's. The question as to whether either of them could render without the other a valid sentence of absolution was one which greatly vexed the canonists, and names of high repute are ranged on either side, with the weight of authority inclining to the affirmative.*

The control of the bishops was vastly increased, at least in Italy, over the vital question of expenditures, when Nicholas IV., in 1288, ordered that all moneys arising from fines and confiscations should be deposited with men selected jointly by the inquisitor and bishop, to be expended only with the advice of the latter, to whom accounts were to be rendered regularly. This was a serious limitation of inquisitorial independence, and it was not of long duration. The bishops soon made use of their supervisory power to demand a share of the spoils under pretext of conducting inquisitions of their own. The quarrel was an unseemly one, and Benedict XI., in 1304, put an end to it by annulling the regulations of his predecessor. The bishops were prohibited from requiring accounts, and these were ordered to be rendered to the papal camera or to special papal deputies.†

If there was this not unnatural vacillation in regulating the delicate relations of these competing jurisdictions, there was none whatever in regard to those between the Inquisition and society at large. Even in its early years of tentative existence and uncertain

---

* Concil. Biterrens. ann. 1246.—Arch. de l'Inq. de Carcass. (Doat, XXVII. 7, 156; XXX. 107-9; XXXI. 149, 180, 216).—Vaissette, III. Pr. 479, 496-7.—Martene Thesaur. I. 1045.—Ripoll I. 194.—Innoc. PP. IV. Bull. *Licet ex omnibus*, 30 Mai, 1254.—Concil. Albiens. ann. 1254 c. 24.—Alex. PP. IV. Bull. *Licet ex omnibus*, 20 Jan. 1257; Ejusd. Bull. *Ad capiendum*, ann. 1257.—Clement. PP. IV. Bull. *Licet ex omnibus*, 17 Sept. 1265.—Gregor. PP. X. Bull. *Præ cunctis mentis*, 20 Apr. 1273.—Lib. Sententt. Inq. Tolosan. *passim*.—C. 17 Sexto v. 2.—Eymeric. Direct. Inq. p. 580.—Albert. Repert. Inq. s. v. *Episcopus*.—Zanchini Tract. de Hæret. xv. —Isambert, II. 747.—Pegnæ Comment. in Eymeric. p. 578.

† Wadding. Annal. Minorum ann. 1288, No. 17.—C. 1 Extrav. Commun. v. iii.

organization it developed such abundant promise of usefulness in bringing the secular laws to bear upon heresy that means were sought to give it a fixed organization which should render it still more efficient in its functions both of detection and punishment. The death of Frederic II., in 1250, in removing the principal antagonist of the papacy, offered the opportunity of giving practical enforcement to his edicts, and accordingly, May 15, 1252, Innocent IV. issued to all the potentates and rulers of Italy his famous bull, *Ad extirpanda*, a carefully considered and elaborate law which should establish machinery for systematic persecution as an integral part of the social edifice in every city and every state, though the uncertain way in which bishop, inquisitor, and friar are alternately referred to in it shows how indefinite were still their respective relations and duties in the matter. All rulers were ordered in public assembly to put heretics to the ban, as though they were sorcerers. Any one finding a heretic could seize him, and take possession of his goods. Each chief magistrate, within three days after assuming office, was to appoint, on the nomination of his bishop and of two friars of each of the Mendicant Orders, twelve good Catholics with two notaries and two or more servitors whose sole business was to arrest heretics, seize their goods, and deliver them to the bishop or his vicars. Their wages and expenses were to be defrayed by the State, their evidence was receivable without oaths, and no testimony was good against the concurrent statement of any three of them. They held office for six months, to be reappointed or replaced then, or at any time, on demand of the bishop and friars; they were entitled to one third of the proceeds of all fines and confiscations inflicted on heretics; they were exempt from all public duties and services incompatible with their functions, and no statutes were to be passed interfering with their actions. The ruler was bound when required to send his assessor or a knight to aid them, and every inhabitant when called upon was obliged to assist them, under a heavy penalty. When the inquisitors visited any portion of the jurisdiction they were accompanied by a deputy of the ruler elected by themselves or by the bishop. In each place visited, this official was to summon under oath three men of good repute, or even the whole vicinage, to reveal any heretics within their knowledge, or the property of such, or of any persons holding secret conventicles or differing in life or manners from the ordinary faithful. The State was bound to arrest all accused, to hold them in prison, to deliver them to the bishop or inquisitor under safe escort, and to execute within fifteen days, in accordance with Frederic's decrees, all judgments pronounced against them. The ruler was further required, when called upon, to inflict torture on those who would not confess and betray all the heretics of their acquaintance. If resistance was made to an arrest, the community where it occurred was liable to an enormous fine unless it delivered up to justice within three days all who were implicated. The ruler was required to have four lists made out of all who were defamed or banned for heresy ; this was to be read in public thrice a year and a copy given to the bishop, one to the Dominicans and one to the Franciscans ; he was likewise to execute the destruction of houses within ten days of sentence, and the exaction of fines within three months, throwing in prison those who could not pay and keeping them until they should pay. The proceeds of fines, commutations, and confiscations were divisible into three parts, one enuring to the city, one to those concerned in the business, and the remainder to the bishop and inquisitors to be expended in persecuting heresy.

The enforcement of this stupendous measure was provided for with equally careful elaboration. It was to be inscribed ineffaceably in all the local statute-books, together with all subsequent laws which the popes might issue, under penalty of excommunication for recalcitrant officials, and interdict upon the city. Any attempt to alter these laws consigned the offender to perpetual infamy and fine, enforced by the ban. The rulers and their officials were to swear to their observance under pain of loss of office ; and any neglect in their enforcement was punishable as perjury with perpetual infamy, a fine of two hundred marks, and suspicion of heresy involving loss of office and disability for all official position in future. Every ruler, within ten days after assuming office, was required to appoint, on the nomination of the bishop or the Mendicants, three good Catholics, who under oath were to investigate the acts of his predecessor and prosecute him for any failure of obedience. Moreover each podestà at the beginning and end of his term was required to have the bull read in all places that might be designated by the bishop and inquisitors, and to erase from the statute-books all laws in conflict with them. At the same time

Innocent issued instructions to the inquisitors to enforce by excommunication the embodiment of this and of the edicts of Frederic in the statutes of all cities and states, and he soon after conferred on them the dangerous power of interpreting, in conjunction with the bishops, all doubtful points in local laws on the subject of heresy.

These provisions are not the wild imaginings of a nightmare, but sober matter-of-fact legislation shrewdly and carefully devised to accomplish a settled policy, and it affords us a valuable insight into the public opinion of the day to find that there was no effective resistance to its acceptance. Before the death of Innocent IV., in 1254, he made one or two slight modifications suggested by experience in its working. In 1255, 1256, and 1257 Alexander IV. revised the bull, explaining some doubts which had arisen, and providing for the enforcement in all cases of the appointment of examiners of rulers going out of office, and in 1259 he reissued the bull as a whole. In 1265 Clement IV. again went over it carefully, making some changes, principally in adding the words "inquisitors" in passages where Innocent had only designated the bishops and friars, thus showing that the Inquisition had during the interval established itself as the recognized instrumentality in the persecution of heresy; and the next year he repeated Innocent's emphatic order to the inquisitors to enforce the insertion of his legislation and that of his predecessors upon the statute-books everywhere, with the free use of excommunication and interdict. This shows that it had not been universally accepted with alacrity, but the few instances which we find recorded of refusal show how generally it was submitted to. Thus in 1256 Alexander IV. learned that the authorities of Genoa were recalcitrant, and he promptly ordered the censure and interdict if they did not comply within fifteen days; and in 1258 a similar course was observed with those of Mantua; while the retention of the bull in the statutes of Florence as late as the recension of 1355, even in the midst of incongruous legislation, shows how literally the papal mandates had been obeyed for a century.*

---

* Innoc. PP. IV. Bull. *Ad extirpanda*, ann. 1252 (Mag. Bull. Roman. I. 91).— Ejusd. Bull. *Orthodoxæ*, 1252 (Ripoll I. 208, cf. VII. 28).—Ejusd. Bull. *Ut commissum*, 1254 (Ibid. I. 250).—Ejusd. Bull. *Volentes*, 1254 (Ib. I. 251).—Ejusd. Bull.

In Italy this furnished the Inquisition with a completely organized *personnel* paid and sustained by the State, rendering it a substantive institution armed with all the means and appliances necessary for the thorough performance of its work. Whether the popes ever endeavored to render the bulls operative elsewhere does not appear, but if they did so they failed, for the measure was not recognized as in force beyond the Alps. Yet this was scarce necessary so long as public law and the conservative spirit of the ruling class everywhere rendered it the highest duty of the citizen of every degree to aid in every way the business of the inquisitor, and pious monarchs hastened to enforce the obligation of their subjects. By the terms of the Treaty of Paris all public officials were obliged to aid in the inquisition and capture of heretics, and all inhabitants, males over fourteen years of age and females over twelve, were to be sworn to reveal all offenders to the bishops. The Council of Narbonne in 1229 put these provisions in force; that of Albi in 1254 included inquisitors among those to whom the heretic was to be denounced, and it freely threatened with the censures of the Church all temporal seigneurs who neglected the duty of aiding the Inquisition and of executing its sentences of death or confiscation. The aid demanded was freely given, and every inquisitor was armed with royal letters empowering him to call upon all officials for safe-conduct, escort, and assistance in the discharge of his functions. In a memorial dated about 1317 Bernard Gui says that the inquisitors make under these letters full use of the baillis, sergeants, and other officials, both of the king and of the seigneurs, without which they would accomplish little. This was not confined to France, for Eymerich, writing in Aragon, in-

---

Cum venerabilis, 1253 (Mag. Bull. Roman. I. 93-4).—Ejusd. Bull. *Cum in constitutionibus*, 1254 (Pegnæ App. p. 19).—Alex. PP. IV. Bull. *Cum secundum*, 1255 (M. B. R. I. 106).—Ejusd. Bull. *Exortis in agro*, 1256 (Pegnæ App. p. 20).—Ejusd. Bull. *Exortis in agris*, 1256 (Ripoll I. 297).—Ejusd. Bull. *Delecti filii*, 1256 (Ripoll I. 312).—Ejusd. Bull. *Cum vos*, 1256 (Ripoll I. 314).—Ejusd. Bull. *Fœlicis recordationis*, 1257 (M. B. R. I. 106).—Ejusd. Bull. *Implacida*, 1257 (M. B. R. I. 113).— Ejusd. Bull. *Implacida*, 1258 (Potthast No. 17302).—Ejusd. Bull. *Ad extirpanda*, 1259 (Pegnæ App. p. 30).—Clement. PP. IV. Bull. *Ad extirpanda*, 1265 (M. B. R. I. 148-51).—Ejusd. Bull. *Ad extirpanda*, 1266 (Pegnæ App. p. 43).—Archivio di Firenze, Riformagioni, Classe II. Distinzione, 1, No. 14.

About 1330 Bernard Gui (Practica P. IV.—Coll. Doat, XXX.) quotes the provisions of the bull as still among the privileges of the Italian inquisitors.

forms us that the first act of the inquisitor on receiving his commission was to exhibit it to the king or ruler, and ask and exhort him for these letters, explaining to him that he is bound by the canons to give them if he desires to avoid the numerous penalties decreed in the bulls *Ad abolendam* and *Ut inquisionis.* His next step is to exhibit these letters to the officials and swear them to obey him in his official duties to the utmost of their power. Thus the whole force of the State was unreservedly at command of the Holy Office. Not only this, indeed, but every individual was bound to lend his aid when called upon, and any slackness of zeal exposed him to excommunication as a fautor of heresy, leading after twelve months, if neglected, to conviction as a heretic, with all its tremendous penalties.*

The right to abrogate any laws which impeded the freest exercise of the powers of the Inquisition was likewise arrogated on both sides of the Alps. When, in 1257, Alexander IV. heard with indignant emotion that Mantua had adopted certain damnable statutes interfering with the absolutism of the Inquisition, he straightway ordered the Bishop of Mantua to investigate the matter, and to annul anything which should impede or delay its operations, enforcing his action by excommunicating the authorities and laying an interdict on the city. This was simply in furtherance of the bull *Ad extirpanda*, but in 1265 Urban IV. repeated the order and made it universally applicable, and it was carried into the canon law as the expression of the undoubted rights of the Church. This rendered the Inquisition virtually supreme in all lands, and it became an accepted maxim of law that all statutes interfering with the free action of the Inquisition were void, and those who enacted them were to be punished; where such laws existed the inquisitor

---

* Bernard. Guidon. Gravamina (Coll. Doat, XXX. 90 sqq.).—Concil. Narbonn. ann. 1229 c. 1, 2.—Concil. Albiens. ann. 1254 c. 3, 5, 8.—Archives de l'Inq. de Carcass. (Doat, XXX. 110–11, 127; XXXI. 250).—Vaissette, III. Pr. 528–9, 536.— Archivio di Napoli, Registro 6, Lett. D. fol. 180.—Eymerici Direct. Inquis. pp. 390–1, 560–1.—Bernardi Guidon. Practica P. IV. (Doat, XXX.).

It was sometimes a work of some labor and time for the inquisitor to obtain his royal letters-patent. When, in 1269, the Franciscans Bertrand de Roche and Ponce des Rives were appointed inquisitors of Forcalquier, they were obliged to travel to Palermo, where Charles of Anjou happened to be residing, and whence he gave them letters, August 4, 1269, to his seneschal and other officials.—Archivio di Napoli, Registro 6, Lett. D, fol. 180.—Cf. Regist. 20, Lett. B, fol. 91.

was instructed to have them submitted to him, and if he found them objectionable the authorities were obliged to repeal or modify them. It was not the fault of the Church if a bold monarch like Philippe le Bel occasionally ventured to incur divine vengeance by protecting his subjects.*

Beyond the Alps there was no legal responsibility admitted, as in Italy, to defray the expenses of the Inquisition by the State. This is a subject which will be treated more fully hereafter, and meanwhile I may briefly state that royal generosity was amply sufficient to keep the organization in effective condition. Its necessary expenses were exceedingly small. The Dominican convents furnished buildings in which to hold its tribunals. The public officials were bound under royal order and the tremendous penalties involved in suspicion of heresy to render service whenever called upon. If the bishops had neglected the duty of establishing and maintaining prisons, the royal zeal had stepped in, had built them and had kept them up. In 1317 we learn that during the past eight years the king had spent the large sum of six hundred and thirty livres tournois on that of Toulouse alone, and he also regularly paid the jailers. Besides this, the inquisitors, whenever they needed aid and counsel, were empowered to summon experts to attend them and to enforce obedience to the summons. There was no exception of dignity or station. All the learning and wisdom of the land were made subservient to the supreme duty of suppressing heresy and were placed gratuitously at the service of the Inquisition; and any prelate who hesitated to render assistance of any kind when called upon was threatened in no gentle terms with the full force of the papal vengeance.†

That the powers thus conferred on the inquisitors were real and not merely theoretical we see in 1260 in the case of Capello di Chia, a powerful noble of the Roman province, who incurred the suspicion of heresy, was condemned, proscribed, and his lands confiscated. He refused to submit, when Frà Andrea, the inquisitor, called for assistance on the citizens of the neighboring town of

---

* Mag. Bull. Roman. I. 118.—C. 9 Sexto v. 1.—Zanchini Tract. de Hæret. c. xxxi.—Cf. Eymerici Direct. Inq. p. 561.—Bernardi Comens. Lucerna Inquisit. s. v. *Statutum*.

† Bernard. Guidon. Gravam. (Doat, XXX. 107–9).—Alex. PP. IV. Bull. *Cupientes*, 15 Apr. 1255; Ejusd. Bull. *Exortis in agro*, 15 Mar. 1256.

Viterbo, and they obeyed him by raising an army with which he marched to besiege Capello in his castle of Colle-Casale. Capello had craftily conveyed his lands to a Roman noble named Pietro Giacomo Surdi, and the pious enterprise of the Viterbians was arrested by a command from the senator of Rome forbidding violence to the property of a good Catholic Roman citizen. Then Alexander IV. intervened, ordering Surdi to withdraw from the quarrel, as his claim to the castle was null and void. He likewise commanded the senator to abandon his indefensible position, and warmly thanked the Viterbians for the zeal and alacrity with which they had obeyed the summons of Frà Andrea. Frà Andrea, in fact, had only exercised the power which Zanghino declares to be inherent in the office of inquisitor, of levying open war against heretics and heresy.*

In the exercise of this almost limitless authority, inquisitors were practically relieved from all supervision and responsibility. Even a papal legate was not to interfere with them or inquire into heresy within their inquisitorial districts. They were not liable to excommunication while in discharge of their duties, nor could they be suspended by any delegate of the Holy See. If such a thing were attempted, the excommunication or suspension was pronounced void, unless, indeed, it was issued by special command of the pope. Already, in 1245, they were empowered to absolve their familiars for any excesses, and in 1261 they were authorized to absolve each other from excommunication for any cause; which, as each inquisitor usually had a subordinate associate ready to perform this office for him, rendered them virtually invulnerable. Moreover, they were released from all obedience to their provincials and generals, whom they were even forbidden to obey in anything relating to the business of their office, and they were secured from any attempt to undermine them with the curia by the enormous privilege of being able to go to Rome at any time and to stay there as long as they might see fit, even in spite of prohibition by provincial or general chapters. At first their commissions were thought to expire with the death of the pope who issued them, but in 1267 they were declared to be continuously valid.†

---

* Pegnæ Append. ad Eymeric. pp. 37-8.—Zanchini Tract. de Hæret. c. xxxvii.
† Arch. Nat. de France, J. 431, No. 23.—Innoc. PP. IV. Bull. *Devotionis,* 2 Mai.

The question of the removability of inquisitors was one which bore directly upon their subordination or independence, and was the subject of much conflicting legislation. When the power of appointment was first conferred upon the provincials it carried with it authority to remove and replace them after consultation with discreet brethren; and in 1244 Innocent IV. declared that the provincials and generals of the Mendicant Orders had full power to remove, revoke, supersede, and transfer all members of their orders serving as inquisitors, even when commissioned by the pope. Some ten years later the vacillating policy of Alexander IV. indicates an earnest effort on the part of the inquisitors to obtain independence. In 1256 he asserted the removing power of the provincials; July 5, 1257, he withdrew their power, and December 9, of the same year, he reaffirmed it in his bull *Quod super nonnullis*, which was repeatedly reissued by himself and his successors. Later popes issued conflicting orders, until at length Boniface VIII. decided in favor of the removing power; but the inquisitors claimed that it could only be exercised for cause and after due trial, which practically reduced it to a nullity. It is true that in the reformatory effort of Clement V. *ipso facto* excommunication, removable only by the pope, was provided for three crimes of inquisitors—falsely prosecuting or neglecting to prosecute for favor, enmity, or profit, for extorting money, and for confiscating church property for the offence of a clerk—but these provisions, although they called forth the earnest protest of Bernard Gui, only amounted to a declaration of what was desirable, and were of no practical effect.*

1245 (Coll. Doat, XXXI. 70).—Berger, Registres d'Innoc. IV. No. 1963.—Ripoll I. 132; II. 594, 610, 644.—Alex. PP. IV. Bull. *Ut negotium*, 5 Mart. 1261.—Urbani PP. IV. Bull. *Ut negotium*, 4 Aug. 1262.—Mag. Bull. Roman. I. 116, 120, 126, 139, 267, 420.—C. 10 Sexto v. 2.—Potthast No. 13057, 18389, 18419, 19559.—Bern. Guidon. Practica P. IV. (Doat, XXX.).—Eymeric. Direct. Inquis. pp. 136, 137.

It is curious that the question whether the commission of an inquisitor did not expire with the death of the appointing pope was still considered in doubt as late as 1290, when it was settled in favor of permanence by Nicholas IV. in the bull *Ne aliqui* (Potthast No. 23302). In the earlier period Alexander IV. shortly after his accession, in 1255, considered it necessary to renew the commission of even so distinguished an inquisitor as Rainerio Saccone (Ripoll I. 275).

* Coll. Doat, XXXI. 73; XXXII. 15, 105.—Alex. PP. IV. Bull. *Odore suavi*, 13

The Franciscans endeavored to reduce their inquisitors to subjection by the expedient of issuing commissions for a limited term. Thus in 1320 the General Michele da Cesena adopted the term of five years, which seems to have long continued the rule, for in 1375 we see Gregory XI. requesting the Franciscan general to keep in office as inquisitor of Rome Frà Gabriele da Viterbo on account of his eminent merits. In 1439 a commission as inquisitor of Florence, issued to Frà Francesco da Michele, to take effect on the expiration of the term of the incumbent, Frà Jacopo della Biada, indicates that appointments were still for specified times, although in 1432 Eugenius IV. had conferred on the Franciscan general, Guglielmo di Casale, full power of appointment and removal. The Dominicans do not seem to have adopted this expedient, and no precautions of any kind were available to enforce subordination and discipline in view of the constant interference of the Holy See, which doubtless could always be obtained by those who knew how to approach it. Commissions were continually issued directly by the pope, and those who held them seem not to have been removable by any one else. Even when this was not done, it mattered little that the popes admitted the power of the provincials to remove, when they interposed to nullify its exercise. In 1323 John XXII. gave to Frà Piero da Perugia, inquisitor of Assisi, letters which protected him from suspension and removal. In 1339 we happen to hear of Giovanni di Borgo removed by the Franciscan general and replaced by Benedict XII. Even more subversive of discipline was the case of Francisco de Sala, appointed by the provincial of Aragon, removed by his successor, and reinstated by Martin V. in 1419, with a provision of inamovability by any superior of his Order. Yet in 1439 Eugenius IV., and in 1474 Sixtus IV. renewed the provisions of Clement IV. rendering inquisitors removable at will by both generals and provincials; and in 1479, Sixtus IV., to impress them with some sense of responsibility, adopted the expedient of requiring all complaints against them to be brought before the general of the Order to

---

Mai. 1256; Ejusd. Bull. *Catholicæ fidei*, 15 Jul. 1257; Ejusd. Bull. *Quod super nonnullis*, 9 Dec. 1257; Ejusd. Bull. *Meminimus*, 13 Apr. 1258.—Clem. PP. IV. Bull. *Licet ex omnibus*, 30 Sept. 1265.—C. 1, 2, Clementin. v. 2.—Bern. Guidon. Gravam. (Doat, XXX. 114).

which they belonged, to whom was confided power of punishment up to removal.*

The natural result of this conflicting legislation was that the inquisitors held themselves accountable to their superiors only for their actions as friars and not as inquisitors; in the latter capacity they acknowledged responsibility only to the pope, and they asserted that the power of removal could only be exercised in cases of inability to act through sickness, age, or ignorance. Their vicars and commissioners they held to be completely beyond any jurisdiction but their own, and any attempt on the part of a provincial to remove such a subordinate was to be met with a prosecution for suspicion of heresy, as an impeding of the Inquisition, to be followed by excommunication, when, if this was endured for a year, it was to be ended by condemnation for heresy. Men armed with these tremendous powers, and animated with this resolute spirit, were not lightly to be meddled with. The warmth with which Eymerich argues the subject suggests the character of the struggle continually going on between the provincials and their appointees, and the conclusions to which he arrives indicate the temper in which the latter vindicated their independence. The grave abuses and disorders to which this led obliged John XXIII. to intervene and declare that the inquisitors should in all things be subject and obedient to their superiors. The Great Schism, however, had weakened the papal authority, and this injunction met with scant respect, so that one of the first utterances of Martin V., in 1418, when the Church was reunited at Constance, was to repeat the order, and to prescribe implicit obedience to it. Yet, as in the matter of removals, the insatiable greed of the curia was a fatal obstacle to the enforcement of subordination, for those who were commissioned directly by the pope could not be expected to endure subjection to the officials of their Orders.†

From Eymerich's remarks we see that an inquisitor was bound

---

* Wadding. ann. 1323, No. 17; ann. 1327, No. 5; ann. 1339, No. 1; ann. 1347, No. 10, 11; ann. 1375, No. 30; ann. 1432, No. 10, 11; ann. 1474, No. 17–19.— Archivio di Firenze, Prov. del Convento di S. Croce 26 Ott. 1439.—Ripoll II. 324, 421, 570–1.—Sixti PP. IV. Bull. *Sacri*, 16 Jul. 1479, § 11.

† Eymeric. pp. 540–9, 553.—Archivio di Firenze, Prov. del. Conv. di. S. Croce, 16 Apr. 1418.

to have little hesitation in prosecuting his superior. His jurisdiction, in fact, was almost unlimited, for the dread suspicion of heresy brought, with few exceptions, all mankind to a common level, and suspicion of heresy was to be technically inferred from anything which affected the dignity or crossed the purposes of those who carried on the Inquisition. Even the jealously-guarded right of asylum in the churches was waived in its favor, and the immunities of the Mendicant Orders gave them no exemption from its jurisdiction. Kings, themselves, were subject to this jurisdiction, though Eymerich discreetly observes that in their case it is more prudent to inform the pope and await his instructions. Yet one exception there was. The episcopal office still retained enough of its earlier dignity to render its possessor exempt unless the inquisitor was furnished with special papal letters. It was his duty, however, in case a bishop was suspected of vacillating in the faith, to collect with diligence all the evidence procurable, and to forward it to Rome for examination and decision—a duty in the exercise of which he could render himself abundantly disagreeable, and even dangerous. The choleric John XXII., in 1327, introduced another exemption when provoked by the arrogance of the Sicilian inquisitor, Matthieu de Pontigny, who dared to excommunicate Guillaume de Balet, archdeacon of Fréjus, papal chaplain and representative of the Avignonese papacy in the Campagna and Maritima. The angry pope issued a decretal forbidding all judges and inquisitors to attack in any way the officials and nuncios of the Holy See without special letters of authority —but the mere audacity of the attempt shows the height of presumption to which the members of the Holy Office had attained. That laymen learned to address them as "your religious majesty" shows the impression made on the popular mind by their irresponsible supremacy.*

If bishops were exempt from judgment by the Inquisition they were not released from obedience to the inquisitors. In the ordinary papal commission issued to the latter, archbishops, bishops,

---

* Eymerici Direct. Inquis. p. 559.—Greg. PP. X. Bull. 20 Apr. 1273 (Martene Thes. V. 1821).—Zanchini de Hæret. c. viii.—Johann. PP. XXII. Bull. *Ex parte vestra*, 3 Jul. 1322 (Wadding. III. 291).—C. 16 Sexto v. 2.—C. 3 Extrav. Commun. v. 3.—Arch. de l'Inq. de Carcassonne (Doat, XXVII. 204).

abbots, and other prelates are commanded to obey them in all concerning their office, under pain of excommunication, suspension, and interdict. That this was not a mere idle form is manifest by the tone of arrogant domination in which the inquisitors issued their commands to episcopal officials. Though the papal superscription to the bishop was "venerable brother" and to the inquisitor "cherished son," yet the inquisitors held that they were superior to the bishops, as being direct delegates of the Holy See, and that if any one were cited simultaneously by a bishop and an inquisitor he must first attend to the summons of the latter. The inquisitor was to be obeyed as the pope himself, and this supremacy included the bishop. This formed part of the papal policy, for the inquisitor was a convenient instrument to reduce the episcopate to subjection. Thus in 1296 Boniface VIII., in giving directions to the bishops to suppress certain irregular and unauthorized hermits and mendicants, enclosed copies of the bull to the inquisitors with instructions to stimulate the bishops to their duty and to report to him all who showed themselves negligent. In spite of the assumed superiority of the inquisitor, however, the Inquisition was very commonly used as a stepping-stone to the episcopate. It is not easy to set bounds to the sources of influence which the office placed within reach of an ambitious man, and this influence was constantly employed to procure promotion into the ranks of the hierarchy. Instances of this are too frequent to be specified, commencing with the earliest inquisitors, Frà Aldobrandino Cavalcanti of Florence, who became Bishop of Viterbo, while his successor, Frà Ruggieri Calcagni, in 1245, was rewarded with the bishopric of Castro in the Maremma. I need only refer to the case of Florence, in 1343, where the inquisitor, Frà Andrea da Perugia was advanced to the episcopate and was succeeded by Frà Pietro di Aquila, who in 1346 was made Bishop of Santangelo dei Lombardi. His successor was Frà Michele di Lapo, and in 1350 we find the Signiory writing to the pope with the request that he be placed in the bishopric of Florence, which had become vacant. The office also afforded opportunities of promotion within the Orders which were not neglected. Thus in a list of Dominican provincials of Saxony in the latter half of the fourteenth century, three who occupied that post in succession from 1369 to 1382, Walther Kerlinger, Hermann Helstede, and Heinrich von Albrecht, are all described as having been previously inquisitors.*

It is not to be imagined that this gigantic structure which overshadowed Christendom was allowed to establish itself wholly without opposition, despite the favor of popes and kings. When we come to consider the details of its history we shall find numerous cases of popular resistance, desperate and isolated struggles, crushed remorselessly before revolt could so extend as to become dangerous. It required, indeed, courage to foolhardiness for any one to raise hand or voice against an inquisitor, no matter how cruel or nefarious were his actions. Under the canon law, any one, from the meanest to the highest, who opposed or impeded in any way the functions of an inquisitor, or gave aid or counsel to those who did so, became at once *ipso facto* excommunicate. After the lapse of a year in this condition he was legally a heretic to be handed over without further ceremony to the secular arm for burning, without trial and without forgiveness. The awful authority which thus shrouded the inquisitor was rendered yet more terrible by the elasticity of definition given to the crime of impeding the Holy Office and the tireless tenacity with which those guilty of it were pursued. If friendly death came to shield them, the Inquisition attacked their memories, and visited their offences upon their children and grandchildren.†

All unorganized efforts of insubordination were easily repressed. Had the bishops united in resistance, they could readily have prevented the serious encroachment on their jurisdiction and influence, and have saved their flocks from the horrors in store for them. There was no unity of action, however, among the prelates. Some

---

* Pegnæ App. ad. Eymeric. pp. 66–7.—Arch. de l'Inq. de Carcass. (Doat, XXXII. 143, 147).—Eymeric. Direct. Inq. pp. 537–8.—Albert. Repert. Inq. Ed. 1494, s. v. *Delegatus.*—Franz Ehrle, Archiv für Litteratur- u. Kirchengeschichte, 1886, p. 158.—Lami, Antichità Toscane, p. 583.—Archivio di Firenze, Riformagioni, Classe V. No. 129, fol. 46, 62–70.—Martene Ampl. Collect. VI. 344.

† MSS. Bib. Nat., fonds latin, No. 4270, fol. 146. In the trial of Friar Bernard Délicieux, in 1319, it was held that he was guilty of "impeding" the Inquisition because, among other acts, he had been concerned in enlarging somewhat the powers of the agents appointed by the city of Albi to prosecute their appeal to Pope Clement V. against their bishop and inquisitor (Ib. fol 165).

of them were honest fanatics who welcomed the Holy Office and assisted it in every way. Others were indifferent. Multitudes, engrossed in worldly cares and quarrels, were rather glad to be relieved of duties which were onerous and for which they had neither learning nor leisure. If any foresaw the end from the humble beginning, none dared to raise a voice against what was everywhere regarded by pious souls as supplying the most urgent need of the time. Still, that the episcopate at large looked with disfavor on these new functions and activities of the upstart Mendicants there can be no doubt, although jealousy could only manifest itself through a futile pretence to discharge the neglected duties in which the Mendicants had been summoned to replace them. Accordingly we find a certain bustling show of activity in ordering perquisition against heretics by the old device of the synodal witnesses, in the Council of Tours in 1239, that of Béziers in 1246, that of Albi in 1254; while that of Lille (Venaissin) in 1251 made a bolder effort to recover lost ground by not only ordering the bishops to make searching inquisition in their dioceses, but by demanding from the Inquisition the surrender of all its records to the Ordinaries; and when this failed the Council of Albi, in 1254, made a fruitless effort to obtain duplicate copies. The spirit in which the rival tribunals regarded each other is seen in the complaint of an inquisitor, not long after 1250, that heretics were encouraged and rendered audacious by the constant attacks and detraction to which the inquisitors were exposed, as being fools, and negligent and slow, and incapable of bringing any affair to a termination, as punishing the innocent and allowing the guilty to escape. These slanders, he says, proceed from judges, both secular and ecclesiastical, who profess great zeal for the extermination of heresy, but who are really impelled by covetousness for bribes, or who are secretly inclined to heresy, or have friends or relatives who are heretics or suspected of heresy. Evidently there was little love lost between the old organization and the new.*

If any thought existed of combined opposition, outside of Ger-

---

* Concil. Turonens. ann. 1239 c. 1.—C. Biterrens. ann. 1246 c. 1.—C. Albiens. ann. 1254 c. 1, 21. — C. Insulan. ann. 1251 c. 2.—Tract. de Paup. de Lugduno (Martene Thesaur. V. 1793).

many, it might well be thrown aside as impracticable after the spectacle of the defeat of the University of Paris on its own ground by the Mendicants. The jealousy perpetually fed by the constant encroachments of the inquisitors could only find vent in obscure squabbles wherein the final decision of the Holy See could always be confidently reckoned upon as against the episcopate. In 1330 we see the inquisitor, Henri de Chamay, complaining to John XXII. that the Bishop of Maguelonne was interfering with the free exercise of his office in Montpellier, on the ground of certain papal privileges granted him, when the pope at once instructs him to proceed without hesitation and to disregard the bishop's pretensions. Such a decision was a foregone conclusion, as the Archbishop of Narbonne and all his suffragans found in 1441, when they united in addressing Eugenius IV., complaining of the exorbitant pretensions of the Inquisition, and asking him to delay action till they should send him full details. Without waiting to hear their specific charges, he replied that the inquisitor had already accused them of impeding him in his office and with vexing him with proceedings and suits at law. There is no business, he added, of greater importance to the Church than the destruction of heresy, and no way to win his favor more efficacious than by aiding the Inquisition. It had been organized for the purpose of relieving bishops of a portion of their cares, and any interference with it would be visited with his displeasure. In the present case, for the sake of concord, the inquisitor would revoke the grievances complained of, and the pope pronounced all suits against him quashed and extinguished. Evidently in any contest the odds were too great against the episcopate, and the danger of systematic opposition too real, to render any organized antagonism feasible. How completely the papacy regarded the Inquisition as an instrumentality for furthering its schemes of aggrandizement is seen when, on the outbreak of the Great Schism, inquisitors were required to take a formal feudal oath of fidelity to the pope appointing him and to his successors.*

With so little to check and so much to stimulate, the spread of

---

* Arch. de l'Inq. de Carcass. (Doat, XXXV. 85, 184).—Ripoll II. 299, 311; III. 135.

the Inquisition was rapid throughout most of the lands of Christendom. I shall have occasion hereafter to trace its vicissitudes in
the principal centres of its activity, and need here only indicate the
limits of its extension.

The northern nations were too far removed from the focus of
heresy to be exposed to aberrations from the faith at the time
when papal supremacy found its most useful instruments in the
Mendicant inquisitors. Consequently the papal Inquisition cannot
be said to have had an existence in the British Islands, Denmark,
or Scandinavia. The edicts of Frederic II. had no currency there;
and when, in 1277, Robert Kilwarby, Archbishop of Canterbury,
and the masters of Oxford denounced certain errors springing
from the Averrhoist doctrines; when, in 1286, Archbishop Peckham
condemned the heresy of Friar Richard Crapewell, and in 1368
Archbishop Langham denounced as heretical thirty articles of
scholastic speculation, even had there been martyrs ready there
were no laws under which to punish them, although lawyers had
sought to introduce the penalty of the stake, and it had once been
inflicted by a council of Oxford, in 1222, on a clerk who had apostatized to Judaism. We shall see hereafter that in the affair of
the Templars the papal Inquisition was found necessary to procure
condemnation, but even then it was so opposed to the character of
English institutions that it worked defectively and disappeared as
soon as the occasion for its temporary introduction passed away.
When Wickliff came and was followed by Lollardry, the English
conceptions of the relations between Church and State had already
become such that there was no thought of applying to Rome for a
special tribunal with which to meet the threatened danger. The
statute of May 25, 1382, directs the king to issue to his sheriffs
commissions to arrest Wickliff's travelling preachers, and aiders
and abettors of heresy, and to hold them till they justify themselves " *selonc reson et la ley de seinte esglise;*" and, in the following July, royal letters ordered the authorities of Oxford to make
inquisition for heresy throughout the university. The weakness
of Richard II. allowed the Lollards to become a powerful political
as well as religious party, but their chances disappeared with the
revolution which placed Henry IV. on the throne. The support
of the Church was a necessity to the new dynasty, which lost no
time in earning its gratitude. After the burning of Sawtré by a

royal warrant confirmed by Parliament, in 1400, the statute "*de hæretico comburendo*" for the first time inflicted in England the death-penalty as a settled punishment for heresy. It restricted preaching to the beneficed curates and those *ex officio* privileged, it forbade the dissemination of heretical opinions and books, empowered the bishops to seize all offenders and hold them in prison until they should purge themselves or abjure, and ordered the bishops to proceed against them within three months after arrest. For minor offences the bishops were empowered to imprison during pleasure and fine at discretion—the fine enuring to the royal exchequer. For obstinate heresy or relapse, involving under the canon law abandonment to the secular arm, the bishops and their commissioners were the sole judges, and, on their delivery of such convicts, the sheriff of the county or the mayor and bailiffs of the nearest town were obliged to burn them before the people on an eminence. Henry V. followed this up, and the statute of 1414 established throughout the kingdom a sort of mixed secular and ecclesiastical inquisition for which the English system of grand inquests gave especial facilities. Under this legislation burning for heresy became a not unfamiliar sight to English eyes, and Lollardry was readily suppressed. In 1533 Henry VIII. repealed the statute of 1400, while retaining those of 1382 and 1414, and also the penalty of burning alive for contumacious heresy and relapse, and the dangerous admixture of politics and religion rendered the stake a favorite instrument of statecraft. One of the earliest measures of the reign of Edward VI. was the repeal of this law, as well as of those of 1382 and 1414, together with all the atrocious legislation of the Six Articles. With the reaction under Philip and Mary came a revival of the sharp laws against heresy. Scarce had the Spanish marriage been concluded when an obedient Parliament re-enacted the legislation of 1382, 1400, and 1414, which afforded ample machinery for the numerous burnings which followed. The earliest act of the first Parliament of Elizabeth was the repeal of the legislation of Philip and Mary and of the old statutes which it had revived; but the writ *de hæretico comburendo* had become an integral part of English law and survived until the desire of Charles II. for Catholic toleration caused him, in 1676, to procure its abrogation and the restraint of the ecclesiastical courts " in cases of atheism, blasphemy, heresy, and schism and other damnable doctrines and opinions" to the ecclesiastical remedies of "excommunication, deprivation, degradation, and other ecclesiastical censures not extending to death." Scotland was more tardy than England in humanitarian development, but the last execution for heresy in the British Islands was that of a youth of eighteen, a medical student named Aikenhead, who was hanged in Edinburgh in 1696.*

In Ireland the fiery temper of the Franciscan, Richard Ledred, Bishop of Ossory, led him into a prolonged struggle with presumed heretics—the Lady Alice Kyteler, accused of sorcery, and her accomplices. So little was known in Ireland of the laws concerning heresy that at first the secular officials refused contemptuously to take the oath prescribed by the canons to aid inquisitors in their persecuting duties, but Ledred finally obliged them to do so and had the satisfaction of burning some of the accused in 1325. He incurred, however, the enmity of the chief personages of the island, leading to a counter-charge of heresy against himself. For years he was obliged to live in exile, and it was not till 1354 that he was able to reside quietly in his diocese, though in 1335 we find Benedict XII. writing to Edward III., deploring the absence in England of so useful an institution as the Inquisition, and urging him to order the secular officials to lend efficient aid to the pious Bishop of Ossory in his struggles with the heretics, of whom the most exaggerated description is given. Even Alexander, Archbishop of Dublin, in 1347, was declared to have been a fautor of heresy because he interfered with Ledred's violent proceedings; and, in 1351, his successor, Archbishop John, was directed to take active measures to punish those who had escaped from Ossory and had taken refuge in his see.†

It is true that when the Hussite troubles became alarming and

---

* D'Argentré, Collect. Judic. I. r. 185, 234.—Harduin. Concil. VII. 1065-8, 1864.—Capgrave's Chronicle, ann. 1286.—Nic. Trivetti Chron. ann. 1222 (D'Achery III. 188).—Bracton. Lib. III. Tit. ii. cap. 9, § 2.—Myrror of Justice, cap. I. § 4, cap. II. § 22; cap. IV. § 14.—5 Rich. II. c. 5.—Rymer's Fœdera, VII. 363, 447, 458.—9 Henr. IV. c. 15.—Concil. Oxoniens. ann. 1408 c. 13.—2 Henr. V. c. 7.—25 Henr. VIII. c. 14.—1 Edw. VI. c. 12, § 3.—1 Eliz. c. 1, § 15.—29 Car. II. c. 9.—London Athenæum, May 31, 1873; Nov. 29, 1884.

† Wright, Proceedings against Dame Alice Kyteler, Camden Soc. 1843.— Wadding. Annal. ann. 1317, No. 56; ann. 1335, No. 5, 6.—Theiner Monument. Hibern. et Scotor. No. 531-2, p. 269; No. 570-1, p. 286; No. 599, p. 299.

there was danger that the disaffection might spread to the North, Martin V., in 1421, authorized the Bishop of Sleswick to appoint a Franciscan, Friar Nicholas John, as inquisitor for Denmark, Norway, and Sweden, but there is no trace of his activity in those regions, and the Inquisition may be considered as non-existent there.* As the mediæval missions for the conversion of schismatics and heathen were exclusively Dominican and Franciscan, the churches which they built up, however slender in membership, were nevertheless completely equipped with apparatus for preserving the orthodoxy of converts, and thus we read of Inquisitions in Africa and Asia. Friar Raymond Martius is honored as the founder of the Inquisition in Tunis and Morocco. About 1370 Gregory XI. appointed the Dominican Friar John Gallus as inquisitor in the East, who in conjunction with Friar Elias Petit planted the institution, as we are told, in Armenia, Russia, Georgia, and Wallachia, while Upper Armenia was similarly provided by Friar Bartolomeo Ponco. On the death of Friar Gallus, Urban VI., about 1378, applied to the Dominican general to select three brethren to serve as inquisitors, one in Armenia and Georgia, one in Greece and Tartary, and one in Russia and the two Wallachias; and in 1389 one of these, Friar Andreas of Caffa, obtained the privilege of appointing an associate in his extensive province of Greece and Tartary. In the fourteenth century an inquisitor seems to have been regarded as a necessary portion of the missionary outfit. Even in the fabled Ethiopian empire of Prester John we hear of an Inquisition founded in Abyssinia by the Dominican Friar, St. Pantaleone, and another in Nubia by Friar Bartolomeo de Tybuli, who was also honored as a saint in those regions. Grotesque as all this sounds, one cannot help honoring the unselfish zeal of the men who thus devoted themselves to the diffusion of the gospel among barbarous Gentiles, and one can find comfort in the conviction that their Inquisitions were comparatively harmless so long as they were not backed by the terrible laws of a Frederic II. or of a St. Louis.†

Even the decaying fragments of the Kingdom of Jerusalem

---

* Wadding. Annal. ann. 1421, No. 1.

† Paramo, pp. 252–3.—Monteiro, Historia da Santo Inquisição, P. I. Lib. I. c. 59.—Ripoll II. 299, 310; III. 9, 110.

could not be allowed burial without an inquisitor to attend the obsequies. The misfortunes of war, according to Nicholas IV., the first Franciscan pope, gave opportunity for the growth of heresy and Judaism. Therefore, in 1290, he granted full powers to his legate, Nicholas, Patriarch of Jerusalem, to appoint inquisitors, with the advice of the Mendicant provincials. This was accordingly done, but the fatherly care of Nicholas was a trifle tardy. The capture of Acre, May 19, 1291, drove the Christians finally from the Holy Land, and the career of the Syrian Inquisition was therefore of the briefest. It was revived, however, in 1375, by Gregory XI., who empowered the Franciscan provincial of the Holy Land to act as inquisitor in Palestine, Syria, and Egypt, to check the too prevalent apostasy of the Christian pilgrims who continued to flock to those regions.*

It is not to be supposed that the triumph of the Inquisition over the bishops gave to it a monopoly of persecution. The ordinary episcopal jurisdiction remained intact. About 1240 we see the Bishop of Toulouse and his provost conducting, without the aid of an inquisitor, an inquest for heresy upon the powerful seigneurs de Niort. Bishops who were zealous were frequently seen co-operating with inquisitors in the examination of heretics, as well as holding their own inquisitions. Thus, in a number of cases occurring at Albi in 1299, we find the trials held in the episcopal palace before the bishop, assisted sometimes by Nicholas d'Abbeville, inquisitor of Carcassonne, and sometimes by Bertrand de Clermont, inquisitor of Toulouse, and sometimes by both. At first, as we have seen, the inquisitor was only the assistant of the bishop, and the latter was by no means relieved of his duties and responsibilities in the extermination of heresy. In fact the bishops themselves sometimes appointed inquisitors of their own in order to operate more efficiently; and the names of such functionaries acting for the archbishops of Narbonne appear in documents of 1251 and 1325. There was nothing, moreover, to prevent a zeal-

---

* Wadding. ann. 1290, No. 2 ; ann. 1375, No. 27, 28.

It is worthy of note that in the Latin kingdom of Jerusalem heresy seems to have been justiciable by the lay court, and the heretic knight was entitled to be judged by his peers. — Assises de Jerusalem, Haute Court, c. 318 (Ed. Kausler, Stuttgart, 1838, p. 367–8).

ous prelate, who thought less of the dignity of his order than the suppression of heresy, from accepting a commission as inquisitor from the pope, as was the case with Guillem Arnaud, Bishop of Carcassonne, who, during his episcopate, lasting from 1249 to 1255, presided over the tribunal of Carcassonne with an energy that Dominicans might have envied.*

Yet, as the Inquisition achieved its independence of the episcopate, two concurrent jurisdictions could hardly coexist without jarring, even when both were animated by the desire of harmony: when jealousy and rivalry were strong, quarrels were inevitable. It was even hinted that bishops, desiring to preserve friends from the zeal of the inquisitors, would prosecute them in their own courts to preserve them from the rigorous impartiality of the Holy Office. To settle the questions which thus were constantly arising, Urban IV., in 1262, empowered the inquisitors to proceed in all cases at their discretion, whether or not these were also under examination by the bishops; and this was repeated in 1265 and 1266 by Clement IV., with strong injunctions to the inquisitors that they were not to allow their processes to be impeded by concurrent action of the bishops. In 1273 Gregory X. laid down the same rule; and it became the settled practice of the Church, embodied in the canon law, that both courts could simultaneously try the same case, communicating at intervals their proceedings to each other. Mutual conference, moreover, was necessary at the final sentence, and when they could not agree a full statement had to be submitted to the pope for decision. Even when proceeding alone and by his ordinary authority, the bishop was obliged to call in the concurrence of an inquisitor when he rendered sentence.†

---

* Trésor des Chartes du Roi en Carcassonne (Doat, XXI. 34–49).—Lib. Confess. Inquis. Albiæ (MSS. Bib. Nat., fonds latin, 11847).—Archives Nat. de France, J. 431, No. 22–29.—Vaissette, III. 446.—Coll. Doat, XXVII. 161.—Molinier, L'Inquisition dans le midi de la France, Paris, 1880, pp. 275–6.

† Mag. Bull. Roman. I. 122.—Wadding. Annal. ann. 1265, No. 3.—Arch. de l'Inq. de Carcassonne (Coll. Doat, XXXII. 32).—Martene Thesaur. V. 1818.—C. 17 Sexto v. 2. — C. 1 Extrav. Comm. v. 3. — Eymeric. Direct. Inquis. pp. 539, 580–1.—C. 1, § 1, Clement. v. 3.

Urban's bull of 1262 is virtually the same as his "*Præ cunctis*" of 1264, printed by Boutaric, Saint-Louis et Alph. de Toulouse, pp. 443 sqq.

During this period, at one time, it became a question whether the episcopal jurisdiction over heresy was not completely superseded by the papal commission given to an inquisitor to act in his diocese. Gui Foucoix, the foremost jurist of his day, in his " *Quæstiones,*" which long remained an authority in the inquisitorial tribunals, answered this question in the affirmative, and argued that the bishop was debarred from action by the special delegation of papal powers to the inquisitor. Yet, when Gui became pope, under the name of Clement IV., his bulls of 1265 and 1266, quoted above, show that he abandoned this position, and Gregory X. also expressly declared that the diocesan jurisdiction was not interfered with. Still the question was regarded as doubtful by canon lawyers, and for a period the episcopal jurisdiction sank almost into abeyance. There were few more active prelates in his day than Simon, Archbishop of Bourges, who, from 1284 to 1291, made repeated visitations of his southern dioceses, such as Albi, Rodez, Cahors, etc. Yet, in the records of these visitations, there is no allusion to his taking any cognizance of heresy, unless, indeed, his forcing, in 1285, a number of usurers of Gourdon to abjure be assumed as such, though usury was not justiciable by the Inquisition unless it became heresy by the assertion of its legality. About 1298, however, Boniface VIII. reasserted the jurisdiction of the episcopate, and we see Bernard de Castanet, Bishop of Albi, stirring up a revolt among his flock by the energy with which he scourged the heretics of Albi. Soon afterwards Clement V. enlarged the functions of the episcopate as a means of curbing the atrocities of the Inquisition, and the glossators argued that the appointment of inquisitors in no way relieved the bishop from the duty of investigating and suppressing heresy in his diocese—indeed, he was liable to deposition by the pope for negligence in this respect, though he was shielded by his position from prosecution by the inquisitor. Yet, even after the Clementines, Bernard Gui asserts it to be improper for the episcopal ordinary to cite any one who is already before the Inquisition. Still, if the power of the bishop had been limited by requiring him to consult with the inquisitor before rendering sentence, it had been enlarged in another direction by authorizing him to summon witnesses as well as offenders who had fled to other dioceses. There was one discrimination, however, against the bishop which handicapped him heavily. His attempts to get a share of the proceeds of fines and confiscations to meet the expenses of prosecution were ineffectual. He was told that he and his officials had revenues for the functions of the Church, and these must suffice to pay him for the service. Ingenious dialecticians reasoned this away as far as regards the bishop when he acted personally, but it held good against his officials. To the latter it was not encouraging to be urged to work and pay their own costs, while the inquisitor, at least in Italy, had control of the confiscations, without accountability to the bishop.*

Under the legislation of Boniface VIII. and Clement V. it was natural that the first quarter of the fourteenth century should witness a revival of the episcopal Inquisition. Even in Italy the provincial Council of Milan, held at Bergamo in 1311 under the Archbishop Gastone Torriani, organized a thorough system of inquisition on the model of the papal institution. The growing

---

* Vaissette, III. 515.—Archidiac. Gloss. sup. c. 17, 20 Sexto v. 2.—Harduin. VII. 1017-19.—C. 17, 19 Sexto v. 2.—C. 1, Clement. v. 3.—Concil. Melodun. ann. 1300, No. 4.—Bernard. Guidon. Hist. Conv. Albiens. (Bouquet, XXI. 767).—Albert. Repert. Inquis. s. v. *Episcopus.*—Guid. Fulcod. Quæst. I.—Ripoll I. 512; VII. 53.—Joann. Andreæ Gloss. sup. c. 13 § 8 Extra. v. vii.—Eymeric. Direct. Inquis. pp. 626, 637, 650.—C. 1 Extrav. commun. v. 3.—Bernard. Guidon. Practica P. IV. (Doat, XXX.).—Bernardi Comens. Lucerna Inquis. s. v. *Bona hæreticorum.*

As early as 1257 we find that the Inquisition had already extended its jurisdiction over usury as heresy (Alex. PP. IV. Bull. *Quod super nonnullis* [Arch. de l'Inq. de Carcass. Doat, XXXI. 244]—a bull which was repeatedly reissued. See Raynald. Annal. ann. 1258, No. 23; Potthast Regesta 17745, 18396; Eymeric. Direct. Inquis. Ed. Pegnæ, p. 133. Cf. c. 8 § 5 Sexto v. 2). The Council of Lyons, in 1274 (can. 26, 27), in treating of usury, alludes only to its punishment by the Ordinaries. The Council of Vienne, in 1311, directed inquisitors to prosecute those who maintained that usury is not sinful (c. 1 § 2 Clementin. v. 5); but Eymerich (Direct. Inquis. p. 106) deprecates attention to such matters as an interference with the real business of the Inquisition. Zanghino lays down the rule that a man may be a public usurer, or blasphemer, or fornicator without being a heretic, but if he, in addition, manifests contempt for religion by not frequenting divine service, receiving the sacrament, observing the fasts and other ordinances of the Church, he becomes suspect of heresy, and can be prosecuted by the inquisitors (Zanchini Tract. de Hæres. c. xxxv.).

We shall see that usury became a very profitable subject of exploitation by the Inquisition when the diminution of heresy deprived it of its legitimate field of action. As the offence was one cognizant by the secular courts (see Vaissette, IV. 164), there was really no excuse for the exercise of spiritual jurisdiction over it.

power of the Visconti, hostile to the papacy, had greatly crippled the Dominicans, and a vigorous effort was made to replace them. In every town the arch-priest or provost was instructed to raise an armed guard, whose duty was the ceaseless perquisition of heresy, and whose privileges and immunities were the same as those of the familiars of the Dominican inquisitors; and all citizens, from the noble to the peasant, were summoned to lend assistance, when called upon, under significant threats. In France some proceedings, in 1319 and 1320, at Béziers, Pamiers, and Montpellier show the episcopal courts in full activity, with the occasional appearance of an inquisitor in a subordinate capacity as assistant, or of an episcopal inquisitor as a colleague of equal rank with those who acted under papal authority. In fact we find one such, in 1322, representing the see of Ausch, contending with the great Bernard Gui himself over a prisoner whom they both claimed. When, also, in 1319, the great opponent of the Inquisition, Friar Bernard Délicieux, was to be tried for impeding it, John XXII. appointed a special commission for the work, consisting of the Archbishop of Toulouse and the Bishops of Pamiers and St. Papoul, while one of the most experienced inquisitors of the time, Jean de Beaune of Carcassonne, acted as prosecutor, and not as judge.*

In Germany, about the same time, there was a sudden development of episcopal activity in the prosecutions of the Beghards by the Bishop of Strassburg and the Archbishop of Cologne, leading to a fair trial of strength between the hierarchy and the Dominicans in the case of Master Eckhart, the teacher of Suso and Tauler and the founder of the German mystics. He was looked upon with pride by the whole Order as one of its most prominent members. He had taught theology with applause in the great University of Paris; in 1303, when Germany was divided into two provinces, he had been made the first provincial Prior of Saxony; in 1307 the general had appointed him Vicar of Bohemia. In 1326 we find him, as teacher of theology in the Dominican school of Cologne, falling under suspicion of complicity with the heresy of the Beghards, against whom a sharp persecution was raging. His

---

* Coll. Doat, XXVII. 7; XXXIV. 87.—Concil. Bergamens. ann. 1311, Rubr. 1. —MSS. Bib. Nat. Coll. Moreau. 1274, fol. 72.—Lib. Sententt. Inq. Tolosan, pp. 268, 282, 351-2.

lofty mysticism trenched dangerously on their pantheism, and possibly they may have sought to shelter themselves behind his great name. At the general chapter of 1325 complaints had been made that in Germany members of the Order preached to the people in the vulgar tongue doctrines that might lead to error, and Gervaise, Prior of Angers, was ordered to investigate them; while, about the same time, John XXII., in concurrence with the wishes of the Order, appointed Nicholas of Strassburg, lector or teacher of the Cologne Dominicans, as his inquisitor for the province of Germany, to inquire into the faith and life of the brethren. Thus far everything had been kept within the precincts of the Order, but the archbishop was growing hot in his pursuit of the Beghards. He evidently was dissatisfied with what was on foot, and he appointed two episcopal commissioners or inquisitors to look after Master Eckhart. Nicholas of Strassburg was himself inclined to mysticism; every motive conspired to lead him to deal tenderly with the accused, and Eckhart was accordingly acquitted, in July, 1326. The episcopal inquisitors were not content with this (one of them was a Franciscan), and proceeded to take evidence against Eckhart. After six months, on January 14, 1327, they summoned Nicholas, as was their right, to communicate to them his proceedings. He came, accompanied by ten friars, not to obey the command, but to enter a solemn protest against the whole business, demanding his "Apostoli," or letters of appeal to the pope, on the ground that Dominicans were not subject to the episcopal Inquisition, and that he in especial was an inquisitor appointed by the pope with full jurisdiction. As early as 1184 Lucius III. had abolished all immunities of monastic orders in cases of heresy, but the Dominicans were of later origin, they had been strengthened with special privileges, and they claimed this exemption although they could not prove it. The episcopal inquisitors promptly answered this by commencing the same day an action against Nicholas himself, who on the morrow interjected an appeal to the Holy See. They further summoned Master Eckhart to appear before them on January 31, but on the 24th he came with numerous supporters and filed an indignant protest, in which he complained bitterly of their protracting the proceedings for the purpose of ruining his reputation, in place of pushing them to an end, as they could readily have done six months before; besides, they were using for the same purpose certain vile Dominicans who were notorious for their crimes. He demanded his "Apostoli," and named May 4 as the term for prosecuting the appeal in the Roman court. To this the archiepiscopal inquisitors had by law thirty days to reply, and during the interval, on February 13, he took an extra-judicial step, which seems to show how greatly his reputation had suffered by these proceedings, and which has given rise to the assertion that he recanted his errors. After preaching in the Dominican church he caused a paper to be read in which he exculpated himself to the people from the erroneous doctrines attributed to him—denying that he had said that his little finger had created all things, or that there was in the soul something uncreated and uncreatable. At the expiration of the thirty days, on February 22, the archiepiscopal inquisitors rejected Eckhart's appeal as frivolous. Worn out with the controversy, he died soon after, but his Order had sufficient influence with John XXII. to obtain an evocation of the case to Avignon. There the regularity of the archbishop's action was recognized, and on March 27, 1329, judgment was rendered, defining in Eckhart's teachings seventeen heretical articles and eleven suspect of heresy. Although his assumed recantation saved his bones from exhumation and incremation, the result was none the less a full justification of the archbishop's proceedings. For once the old order had triumphed over the new. The episcopal jurisdiction was confirmed, for Eckhart's heresy was declared to have been proved both by the inquisition held by the archbishop under his ordinary authority, and by the investigation subsequently made in Avignon by papal command, and the decision was the more emphatic, since John XXII. had at the moment every motive to soothe the Dominicans, involved as he was in mortal struggle at once with Louis of Bavaria and with the whole puritanic section of the Franciscans.*

---

* W. Preger, Meister Eckart und die Inquisition, München, 1869.—Denifle, Archiv für Litteratur- und Kirchengeschichte, 1886, pp. 616, 640.—Raynald. ann. 1329, No. 70-2. — Gustav Schmidt, Päbstliche Urkunden und Regesten, Halle, 1886, p. 223.—Cf. Eymeric. Direct. Inquis. pp. 453 sqq.

The power of the Inquisition over the specially exempted orders of the Mendicants varied at times. Jurisdiction was conferred by Innocent IV., in 1254, by the bull *Ne comissum vobis* (Ripoll I. 252). About two hundred years later, Pius II. placed the Franciscans under the jurisdiction of their own minister-gen-

The episcopal Inquisition was thus fairly re-established as part of the recognized organization of the Church. The Council of Paris in 1350 treats of the persecution of heresy as part of the recognized duties of the bishop, and instructs the Ordinaries as to their powers of arrest and authority to call upon the secular officials for assistance in precisely the same terms as the Inquisition might do. A brief of Urban V. in 1363 refers to a knight and five gentlemen suspected of heresy, then in the custody of the Bishop of Carcassonne, and orders their trial by the bishop or inquisitor, or by both conjointly, the result to be referred to the papal court. When a bishop had spirit to resist the invasion of his rights by an inquisitor, he was able to make them respected. In 1423 the Inquisitor of Carcassonne had gone to Albi, where he swore in two notaries and some other officials to act for him; he had then taken certain evidence relating to a case before him, and had sworn the witnesses to secrecy in order that the accused might not receive warning. Of all this the Bishop of Albi complained as an invasion of his jurisdiction. The swearing in of the officials he claimed should only have been done in presence of his ordinary or of a deputy; the secrecy imposed on the witnesses was an impediment to his own inquisitorial procedure, as depriving him of evidence in the event of his prosecuting the case. The points were somewhat nice, and illustrate the friction and jealousy inseparable from the concurrent and competing jurisdictions; but in the present case, to avoid unseemly strife, the Bishop of Carcassonne was chosen as arbitrator, the inquisitor acknowledged himself in the wrong and annulled his acts, and a public instrument was drawn up in attesta-

---

eral. In 1479 Sixtus IV., by the golden bull *Sacri prædicatorum*, § 12, forbade all inquisitors from prosecuting members of the other Order (Mag. Bull. Roman. I. 420). Soon afterwards Innocent VIII. prohibited all inquisitors from trying Franciscan friars; but, with the rise of Lutheranism, this became inexpedient, and in 1530 Clement VII., in the bull *Cum sicut*, § 2, removed all exemptions, and again made all justiciable by the Inquisition (Mag. Bull. Rom. I. 681), which was repeated by Pius IV. in the bull *Pastoris æterni*, in 1562 (Eymeric. Direct. Inq. Append. p. 127; Pegnæ Comment. p. 557).

Whether a bishop could proceed against an inquisitor for heresy was a debatable question, and one probably never practically tested. Eymerich holds that he could not, but must refer the matter to the pope; but Pegna, in his commentaries, quotes good authorities to the contrary (Eymeric. op. cit. pp. 558-9).

tion of the settlement. Yet in spite of these inevitable quarrels a *modus vivendi* was practically established. Eymerich, writing about 1375, almost always represents the bishop and inquisitor as co-operating together, not only in the final sentence, but in the preliminary proceedings; he evidently seeks to represent the two powers as working harmoniously for a common end, and that the Inquisition in no way superseded the episcopal jurisdiction or relieved the bishop from the responsibility inherent in his office. A century later Sprenger, in discussing the jurisdiction of the Inquisition from the standpoint of an inquisitor, takes virtually the same position; and the commissions issued to inquisitors usually contained a clause to the effect that no prejudice was intended to the inquisitorial jurisdiction of the Ordinaries. In the habitual negligence of the episcopal officials, however, the inquisitors found little difficulty in trespassing upon their functions, and complaints of this interference continued until the eve of the Reformation.*

Technically there was no difference between the episcopal and papal Inquisitions. The equitable system of procedure borrowed from the Roman law by the courts of the Ordinaries was cast aside, and the bishops were permitted and even instructed to follow the inquisitorial system, which was a standing mockery of justice— perhaps the most iniquitous that the arbitrary cruelty of man has ever devised. In tracing the history of the institution, therefore, there is no distinction to be drawn between its two branches, and the exploits of both are to be recorded as springing from the same impulses, using the same methods, and leading to the same ends.†

Yet the papal Inquisition was an instrument of infinitely greater efficiency for the work in hand. However zealous an episcopal official might be, his efforts were necessarily isolated, temporary, and spasmodic. The papal Inquisition, on the other hand, constituted

---

* Concil. Parisiens. ann. 1350 c. 3, 4.—Arch. de l'Inq. de Carcassonne (Doat, XXXV. 132).—Archives de l'Évêché d'Albi (Doat, XXXV. 187).—Eymerici Direct. Inquis. p. 529.—Sprengeri Mall. Maleficar. P. III. Q. 1.—Ripoll II. 311, 324, 351.— Cornel. Agrippæ de Vanitate Scientiarum, cap. xcvi. Yet a bull of Nicholas V. to the inquisitor of France in 1451 seems to render him independent of episcopal co-operation (Ripoll III. 301).

† C. 17 Sexto v. 2.—See the "Modus examinandi hæreticos" printed by Gretser (Mag. Bib. Patrum XIII. 341) prepared for a German episcopal Inquisition.

a chain of tribunals throughout Continental Europe perpetually manned by those who had no other work to attend to. Not only, therefore, did persecution in their hands assume the aspect of part of the endless and inevitable operations of nature, which was necessary to accomplish its end, and which rendered the heretic hopeless that time would bring relief, but by constant interchange of documents and mutual co-operation they covered Christendom with a network rendering escape almost hopeless. This, combined with the most careful preservation and indexing of records, produced a system of police singularly perfect for a period when international communication was so imperfect. The Inquisition had a long arm, a sleepless memory, and we can well understand the mysterious terror inspired by the secrecy of its operations and its almost supernatural vigilance. If public proclamation was desired, it summoned all the faithful, with promises of eternal life and reasonable temporal reward, to seize some designated heresiarch, and every parish priest where he was suspected to be in hiding was bound to spread the call before the whole population. If secret information was required, there were spies and familiars trained to the work. The record of every heretical family for generations could be traced out from the papers of one tribunal or another. A single lucky capture and extorted confession would put the sleuth-hounds on the track of hundreds who deemed themselves secure, and each new victim added his circle of denunciations. The heretic lived over a volcano which might burst forth at any moment. During the fierce persecution of the Spiritual Franciscans in 1317 and 1318 a number of pitying souls had assisted fugitives, had stood by the pyres of their martyrs and had comforted them in various ways. Some had been suspected, had fled and changed their names: others had remained in favoring obscurity; all might well have fancied that the affair was forgotten. Suddenly, in 1325, some chance—probably the confession of a prisoner—placed the Inquisition on their track. Twenty or more were traced out and seized. Kept in prison for a year or two, their resolution broke down one by one; they successively confessed their half-forgotten guilt and were duly penanced. Even more significant was the case of Guillelma Maza of Castres, who lost her husband in 1302. In the first grief of her widowhood she was induced to listen to the teachings of two Waldensian missionaries whose exhortations brought her comfort. They visited her but twice, in the darkness of the night; she never saw their faces nor those of others. After twenty-five years of orthodox observance, in 1327, she is brought before the Inquisition of Carcassonne, confesses this single aberration from the faith, and repents. Unforgiving and unforgetting, no trifle was beneath the minute vigilance of the Holy Office. Thus in the case of Manenta Rosa, who, in 1325, was called before it at Carcassonne on the mortal charge of relapse, the prosecution was because, after having abjured the heresy of the Spirituals, she had been seen talking with a man who was under suspicion and had sent by him two sols to a sick woman likewise suspect.*

Flight was of little avail. Descriptions of heretics who disappeared were sent throughout Europe, to every spot where they could be supposed to seek refuge, putting the authorities on the alert to search for every stranger who wore the air of one differing in life and conversation from the ordinary run of the faithful. News of captures was transmitted from one tribunal to another, evidence of guilt was furnished, or the hapless victim was returned to the spot where his extorted evidence would be most effective in implicating others. In 1287 an arrest of heretics at Treviso included some from France. Immediately the French inquisitors request that they be sent to them, especially one who ranked as bishop among the Cathari, for they may be induced to reveal the names of many others; and Nicholas IV. forthwith sends instructions to Friar Philip of Treviso to deliver them, after extracting all he can from them, to the messenger of the French Inquisition. Well might the orthodox imagine that only the hand of God, the heretic that only the inspiration of Satan, could produce such results as would follow the return of these poor wretches. To human apprehension the papal Inquisition was well-nigh ubiquitous, omniscient, and omnipotent.†

Occasionally, it is true, the efficiency of the organization was marred with quarrels. Antagonisms could not always be avoided, and the jealousy and mutual dislike of the Dominican and Franciscan Orders would sometimes interfere with the harmony essential to mutual co-operation. I have already alluded to the troubles arising from this cause at Marseilles in 1266 and at Verona in 1291.

---

* Coll. Doat, XXXVII. 7; XXIX. 5.   † Coll. Doat, XXX. 132; XXXII. 155.

A further symptom of lack of unity is seen in 1327, when Pierre Trencavel, a noted Spiritual, who had escaped from the prison of Carcassonne, was captured in Provence with his daughter Andrée, likewise a fugitive. There could be no question as to their belonging to those from whom they had fled, yet Friar Michel, the Franciscan inquisitor of Provence, refused to surrender them, and the Carcassonne tribunal was obliged to appeal to John XXII., who intervened with a peremptory command to Friar Michel to lay aside all opposition and surrender the prisoners at once. Yet, considering the imperfections of human nature, these quarrels seem to have been few.*

Properly to govern and direct an engine of such infinite power, dealing with the life and happiness of countless thousands, would require more than human wisdom and virtue; and it may be worth a moment's attention to see what was the ideal of those to whom the practical working of the Holy Office was confided. Bernard Gui, the most experienced inquisitor of his day, concludes his elaborate instructions as to procedure with some general directions as to conduct and character. The inquisitor, he tells us, should be diligent and fervent in his zeal for the truth of religion, for the salvation of souls, and for the extirpation of heresy. Amid troubles and opposing accidents he should grow earnest, without allowing himself to be inflamed with the fury of wrath and indignation. He must not be sluggish of body, for sloth destroys the vigor of action. He must be intrepid, persisting through danger to death, laboring for religious truth, neither precipitating peril by audacity nor shrinking from it through timidity. He must be unmoved by the prayers and blandishments of those who seek to influence him, yet not be, through hardness of heart, so obstinate that he will yield nothing to entreaty, whether in granting delays or in mitigating punishment, according to place and circumstance, for this implies stubbornness; nor must he be weak and yielding through too great a desire to please, for this will destroy the vigor and value of his work—he who is weak in his work is brother to him who destroys his work. In doubtful matters he must be circumspect and not readily yield credence to what seems probable, for such is not always true; nor should he obstinately reject the opposite, for

---

* Coll. Doat, **XXXV.** 18.

that which seems improbable often turns out to be fact. He must listen, discuss, and examine with all zeal, that the truth may be reached at the end. Like a just judge let him so bear himself in passing sentence of corporal punishment that his face may show compassion, while his inward purpose remains unshaken, and thus will he avoid the appearance of indignation and wrath leading to the charge of cruelty. In imposing pecuniary penalties, let his face preserve the severity of justice as though he were compelled by necessity and not allured by cupidity. Let truth and mercy, which should never leave the heart of a judge, shine forth from his countenance, that his decisions may be free from all suspicion of covetousness or cruelty.*

To appreciate rightly the career and influence of the Inquisition will require a somewhat minute examination into its methods and procedure. In no other way can we fully understand its action; and the lessons to be drawn from such an investigation are perhaps the most important that it has to teach.

---

* Bern. Guidon. Practica P. IV. *ad finem* (Doat, XXX.). This sketch of the model inquisitor seems to have been a favorite. I find it in another MS. *Tractatus de Inquisitione* (Doat, XXXVI.).

CHAPTER II.

ORGANIZATION.

WE have seen how the Church had found persuasion powerless
to arrest the spread of heresy. St. Bernard, Foulques de Neuilly,
Durán de Huesca, St. Dominic, St. Francis, had successively tried
the rarest eloquence to convince, and the example of the sublimest
self-abnegation to convert. Only force remained, and it had been
pitilessly employed. It had subjected the populations, only to
render heresy hidden in place of public; and, in order to reap
the fruits of victory, it became apparent that organized, ceaseless
persecution continued to perpetuity was the only hope of preserving Catholic unity, and of preventing the garment of the Lord
from being permanently rent. To this end the Inquisition was
developed into a settled institution manned by the Mendicant Orders, which had been formed to persuade by argument and example, and which now were utilized to suppress by force.

The organization of the Inquisition was simple, yet effective.
It did not care to impress the minds of men with magnificence,
but rather to paralyze them with terror. To the secular prelacy
it left the gorgeous vestments and the imposing splendors of worship, the picturesque processions and the showy retinues of retainers. The inquisitor wore the simple habits of his Order.
When he appeared abroad he was at most accompanied by a few
armed familiars, partly as a guard, partly to execute his orders.
His principal scene of activity was in the recesses of the dreaded
Holy Office, whence he issued his commands and decided the fate
of whole populations in a silence and secrecy which impressed
upon the people a mysterious awe a thousand times more potent
than the external magnificence of the bishop. Every detail in the
Inquisition was intended for work and not for show. It was built
up by resolute, earnest men of one idea who knew what they

wanted, who rendered everything subservient to the one object, and who sternly rejected all that might embarrass with superfluities the unerring and ruthless justice which it was their mission to enforce.

The previous chapter has shown us the simplicity which marked the beginnings of the institution, consisting virtually of the individual friars selected to hunt up heretics and determine their guilt. Their districts were naturally coterminous with the provinces of the Mendicant Orders, whose provincials were charged with the duty of appointment, and these provinces each comprised many bishoprics. Though the chief town of each province came to be regarded as the seat of the Inquisition, with its building and prisons, yet it was the duty of the inquisitor to go in pursuit of the heretics, to visit all places where heresy might be suspected to exist, and to summon the people to assemble, exactly as the bishops formerly did in their visitations, with the added inducement of an indulgence of twenty or forty days for all who attended. It is true that at first the inquisitors of Toulouse established themselves in that city and cited before them all whom they wished to appear, but such complaints arose as to the intolerable hardship of this that, in 1237, the Legate Jean de Vienne ordered them to transport themselves to the places where they wished to make inquest. In obedience to this we see them going to Castelnaudari, where they were baffled by the people, who had entered into a common understanding not to betray each other, so they turned unexpectedly to Puy Laurens, where they took the population by surprise and gathered an ample harvest. The murders of Avignonet, in 1242, gave warning that these itinerant inquests were not without risk, yet they continued to be prescribed by the Cardinal of Albano, about 1244, and by the Council of Béziers, in 1246. Although, in 1247, Innocent IV. authorized inquisitors, when there was danger, to summon heretics and witnesses to some place of safety, yet the theory of personal visitation remained unchanged. In Italy we see it in the bulls *Ad extirpanda;* a contemporary German inquisitor describes it as the customary practice; in northern France we have the formulas used in 1278 by Friar Simon Duval for summoning the people on such occasions; about 1330 Bernard Gui alludes to it as one of the special privileges of the Inquisition; and, about 1375, Eymerich describes the method of conducting these inquests as part of the established routine.*

Nothing could well be devised more effective than these visitations, and though they may have become neglected when the machinery of spies and familiars was perfected, or when the heretics had been nearly weeded out, during the busy times of the Inquisition they must have formed an important portion of its functions. A few days in advance of his visit to a city, the inquisitor would send notice to the ecclesiastical authorities requiring them to summon the people to assemble at a specified time, with an announcement of the indulgence given to all who should attend. To the populace thus brought together he preached on the faith, urging them to its defence with such eloquence as he could command, summoning every one within a certain radius to come forward within six or twelve days and reveal to him whatever they may have known or heard of any one leading to the belief or suspicion that he might be a heretic, or defamed for heresy, or that he had spoken against any article of faith, or that he differed in life and morals from the common conversation of the faithful. Neglect to comply with this command incurred *ipso facto* excommunication, removable only by the inquisitor himself; compliance with it was rewarded with an indulgence of three years. At the same time he proclaimed a "time of grace," varying from fifteen to thirty days, during which any heretic coming forward spontaneously, confessing his guilt, abjuring, and giving full information about his fellow-sectaries, was promised mercy. This mercy varied at different times from complete immunity to exemption from the severer penalties of death, imprisonment, exile, or confiscation. The latter is the grace promised in the earliest allusion to the practice in

---

* Gregor. PP. IX. Bull. *Ille humani generis*, 20 Mai. 1236 (Eymeric. App. p. 3).—Vaissette, III. 410–11.—Guill. Pod. Laur. c. 43. — Concil. Biterrens. ann. 1246, Append. c. 1.—Arch. de l'Inq. de Carcassonne (Doat, XXXI. 5).—Raynald. ann. 1243, No. 31.—Innoc. PP. IV. Bull. *Quia sicut*, 19 Nov. 1247 (Potthast 12766.—Doat, XXXI. 112) —Ejusd. Bull. *Ad extirpanda* § 31.—Anon. Passaviens. (Mag. Bib. Pat. XIII. 308).—Doctrina de modo procedendi (Martene Thesaur. V. 1809–11).—Alex. PP. IV. Bull. *Cupientes*, 4 Mart. 1260 (Mag. Bull. Rom. I. 119). —Ripoll I. 128.—Guill. Pelisso Chron. Ed. Molinier, p. 27.—Bernardi Guidon. Practica P. IV. (Doat, XXX.).—Eymeric. Direct. Inquis. pp. 407–9.—MSS. Bib. Nat., fonds latin, No. 14930, fol. 220.

1235, and in a sentence of 1237 on such an occasion the offender escaped with a penance consisting of two of the shorter pilgrimages, the finding of a beggar daily during life, and a fine of ten livres Morlaas given "for the love of God" to the Inquisition. After the expiration of the term they were told that no mercy would be shown; while it lasted, the inquisitor was instructed to keep himself housed, so as to be ready at any moment to receive denunciations and confessions; and long series of interrogatories, most searching and suggestive, were drawn up to prompt him in the examination of those who should present themselves. Even as late as 1387 when Frà Antonio Secco attacked the heretics of the Waldensian valleys, he commenced by publishing in the church of Pignerol a summons giving a week of grace during which all who should confess as to themselves and others should escape public punishment except for perjury committed before the Inquisition, and all who did not come forward were denounced as excommunicates.*

Bernard Gui assures us that this device was exceedingly fruitful, not only in causing numerous happy conversions, but also in furnishing information of many heretics who would not otherwise have been thought of, as each penitent was forced to denounce all whom he knew or suspected; and he particularly dwells upon its utility in securing the capture of the "perfected" Catharans who habitually lay in hiding and who thus were betrayed by those in whom they trusted. It is easy, in fact, to imagine the terror into which a community would be thrown when an inquisitor suddenly descended upon it and made his proclamation. No one could know what stories might be circulating about himself which zealous fanaticism or personal enmity might exaggerate and carry to the inquisitor, and in this the orthodox and the heretic would suffer alike. All scandals passing from mouth to mouth would be brought to light. All confidence between man and man would disappear.

---

* Guill. Pod. Laur. c. 43.—Vaissette, III. 402, 403, 404; Pr. 386.—Raynald. ann. 1243, No. 31.—Concil. Narbonn. ann. 1244 c. 1.—Concil Biterrens. ann. 1246, Append. c. 2, 5.—Arch. de l'Inq. de Carc. circa 1245 (Doat, XXXI. 5).— Guid. Fulcod. Quæst. II.—Bern. Guidon. Practica P. IV. (Doat, XXX.).—Eymerici Direct. Inquis. pp. 407-9.—Practica super Inquisit. (MSS Bib. Nat., fonds latin, No. 14930, fol. 227-8).—Archivio Storico Italiano, 1865, No. 38, pp. 16-17.

Old grudges would be gratified in safety. To him who had been heretically inclined the terrible suspense would grow day by day more insupportable, with the thought that some careless word might have been treasured up to be now revealed by those who ought to be nearest and dearest to him, until at last he would yield and betray others rather than be betrayed himself. Gregory IX. boasted that, on at least one such occasion, parents were led to denounce their children, and children their parents, husbands their wives, and wives their husbands. We may well believe Bernard Gui when he says that each revelation led to others, until the invisible net extended far and wide, and that not the least of the benefits thence arising were the extensive confiscations which were sure to follow.*

These preliminary proceedings were commonly held in the convent of the Order to which the inquisitor belonged, if such there were, or in the episcopal palace if it were a cathedral town. In other cases the church or municipal buildings would afford the necessary accommodation, for the authorities, both lay and clerical, were bound to afford all assistance demanded. Each inquisitor, however, necessarily had his headquarters to which he would return after these forays, carrying with him the depositions of accusers and confessions of accused, and such prisoners as he deemed it important to secure, the secular authorities being bound to furnish him the necessary transportation and guards. Others he would cite to appear before him at a specified time, taking sufficient bail to secure their punctuality. In the earlier period, the seat of his tribunal was the Mendicant convent, while the episcopal or public prison was at his disposal for the detention of his captives; but in time special buildings were provided, amply furnished with the necessary appliances and dungeons—cells built along the walls and thence known as "*murus*," in contradistinction to the "*carcer*" or prison—where the unfortunates awaiting sentence were under the immediate supervision of their judge. It was here, for the most part, that the judicial proceedings were carried on, though we occasionally hear of the episcopal palace being used, especially when the bishop was zealous and co-operated with the Inquisition.

During the earlier period there was no limitation as to the age

---

* B. Guidon. loc. cit.—Ripoll I. 46.

of the inquisitor; the provincial who held the appointing power could select any member of his Order. That this frequently led to the nomination of young and inexperienced men is presumable from the language in which Clement V., when reforming the Holy Office, prescribed forty years as the minimum age in future. Bernard Gui remonstrated against this, not only because younger men were often thoroughly capable of the duties, but also because bishops and their ordinaries who exercised inquisitorial power were not required to be so old. The rule, however, held good. In 1422 the Provincial of Toulouse appointed an inquisitor of Carcassonne, Friar Raymond du Tille, who was only thirty-two years of age. Though he was confirmed by the general of the Order, it was held that the office was vacant until an appeal was made to Martin V., who ordered the Official of Alet to investigate his fitness, and, if found worthy, the Clementine canon might be suspended in his favor.*

The trials were usually conducted by a single inquisitor, though sometimes two would work together. One, however, sufficed, but he generally had subordinate assistants, who prepared the cases for him, and took the preliminary examinations. He had a right to call upon the provincial to assign to him as many of these assistants as he deemed necessary, but he could not select them for himself. Sometimes, when the bishop was eager for persecution and careless of the episcopal dignity, he would accept the position; and it was frequently filled by the Dominican prior of the local convent. When the state defrayed the expenses of the Inquisition, it seems to have exercised some control over the number of officials. Thus in Naples Charles of Anjou, in 1269, only provides for one assistant.†

These assistants represented the inquisitor during his absence, and thus were closely assimilated to the commissioners who came

---

* C. 2 Clement. v. iii.—Bern. Guidon Gravam. (Doat, XXX. 117, 128).—Ripoll II. 610.—In 1431 Eugenius IV. dispensed with the rule in the case of an inquisitor appointed in his thirty-sixth year (Ripoll III. 9).

† Concil. Biterrens. ann. 1246 c. 4.—Molinier, pp. 129, 131, 281-2.—Hauréau, Bernard Délicieux, p. 20.—Wadding. Annal. ann. 1261, No. 2.—Urbani PP. IV. Bull. *Ne catholicæ fidei*, 26 Oct. 1262.—Bernardi Guidonis Practica, P. IV. (Doat, XXX.).—Eymerici Direct. Inq. p. 557, 577.—Archivio di Napoli, MSS. Chioccarello T. VIII.; Ibid. Registro 6, Lett. D. f. 85.

to be a permanent feature of the Holy Office. Even in the twelfth
century it was determined that a judicial delegate of the Holy See
could delegate his powers ; and in 1246 the Council of Béziers authorized the inquisitor to appoint a deputy whenever he wished to
have an inquest made in any place to which he could not himself
proceed. Special commissions were sometimes issued, as when, in
1276, Pons de Pornac, Inquisitor of Toulouse, authorized the Dominican Prior of Montauban to take testimony against Bernard de
Solhac and forward it to him under seal. In the extensive districts of the Inquisition the work must necessarily have been divided in this manner, especially during the earlier period, when
the harvest of heresy was abundant and numerous laborers were
requisite. Yet the formal authority to appoint commissioners
with full powers does not seem to have been granted to inquisitors
until 1262 by Urban IV., and this had to be confirmed by Boniface VIII. towards the close of the century. These commissioners,
or vicars, differed from the assistants, inasmuch as they were appointed and discharged at the discretion of the inquisitor. They
became a permanent feature of the institution, and conducted its
business in places remote from the main tribunal ; or, in case of
the absence or incapacity of the inquisitor, one of them might be
summoned to replace him temporarily, or the inquisitor could appoint a vicar-general. Like their' principal, they had, after the
Clementine reforms in 1317, to be at least forty years of age, and
they wielded full inquisitorial powers, in the citation, arrest, and
examination of witnesses and prisoners, even to the infliction of
torture and condemnation to imprisonment. Whether they could
proceed to final sentence in capital cases was a disputed question,
and Eymerich recommends that such authority should always be
reserved to the inquisitor himself; but, as we shall see, the cases
of Joan of Arc and of the Vaudois of Arras show that this reservation was rarely observed. A further limitation on their powers
was the inability to appoint deputies.*

---

* C. 11, 19, 20 Extra ɪ. 29.—Concil. Biterrens. ann. 1246 c. 3.—Coll. Doat,
XXV. 230.—Urbani PP. IV. Bull. *Licet ex omnibus*, 20 Mart. 1262.—Guid. Fulcod.
Quæst. ɪv.— C. 11 Sexto v. 2.—C. 2 Clement. v. 3.—Bernardi Guidon. Practica
P. ɪv. (Doat, XXX.).—Eymerici Direct. pp. 403-6.—Zanchini Tract. de Hæret.
c. xxx.

It is not easy to understand why, in 1276, the Lombard Inquisitors Frà Niccolò

In the later period there seems to have been occasionally another official with the title of "counsellor." In 1370 the Inquisition of Carcassonne claimed the right to appoint three, who should be exempt from all local taxation. In a document of 1423 the person filling this position is not a Dominican, but is qualified as a licentiate in law; and doubtless such a functionary was a useful and usual member of the tribunal, though with no precise official status. Zanghino informs us that in general inquisitors were utterly ignorant of law. In most cases this made no difference, for, as we shall see, they enjoyed the widest latitude of arbitrary procedure, with little danger that any one would dare to complain, but occasionally they had to deal with victims not entirely unresisting, and then some adviser as to their legal duties and responsibilities was desirable. Eymerich, in fact, recommends that a commissioner should always associate with himself some discreet lawyer to save him from mistakes which may redound to the disadvantage of the Inquisition, call for papal interposition, and perhaps cost him his place.*

As absolute secrecy became a main feature of all the proceedings of the Inquisition after its earlier tentative period, it was a universal rule that testimony, whether of witnesses or of accused, should only be taken in the presence of two impartial men, not connected with the institution, but sworn to silence. The inquisitor was empowered to compel the attendance of any one whom he might summon to perform this duty. These representatives of the public were preferably clerics, and usually Dominicans, "discreet and religious men," who were expected to sign with the notary the written report of the testimony in attestation of its fidelity. Though not alluded to in the instructions of the Council of Béziers in 1246, a deposition taken in 1244 shows that already the practice had become customary; and the frequent repetitions of the rule by successive popes and its embodiment in the canon law show what importance was attached to it as a means of prevent-

---

da Cremona and Frà Daniele Giussano assembled experts in Piacenza to determine whether they had power to appoint delegates, when the question was decided in the negative (Campi, Dell' Historia Ecclesiastica di Piacenza, P. II. p. 308-9).

* Archives de l'Évêché d'Albi (Doat, XXXV. 136, 187).—Zanchini Tract. de Hæret. c. xv.—Eymerici Direct. p. 407.

ing injustice, and giving at least a color of impartiality to the proceedings. Yet in this, as in everything else, the inquisitors were a law unto themselves, and disregarded at pleasure the very slender restrictions imposed on them. One of the rare cases in which the Inquisition lost a victim turned upon the neglect of this rule. In 1325 a priest named Pierre de Tornamire, accused of Spiritual Franciscanism, was brought to the Inquisition of Carcassonne in a dying state. The inquisitor was absent. His deputy and notary took the deposition in the presence of three laymen who chanced to be present, and the priest died before it was well concluded. Two Dominicans came, after he was speechless, and, without making any inquiry as to its correctness, signed their names to the deposition in attestation. On this irregular evidence a prosecution against Pierre's memory was based, and was contested by his heirs to save his property from confiscation. Thirty-two years the struggle lasted, and when the inquisitor came, in 1357, to ask assent to his sentence of condemnation in the customary assembly of experts, twenty-five jurists unanimously voted against it on the ground of irregularity, and only two, both Dominicans, ventured to uphold it. It was not long after this that Eymerich instructed his brethren how the rule could be evaded, when it was inconvenient, by at least having two honest persons present at the close of the examination, when the testimony was read over to the deponent. No one else was allowed to be present at the trial, except at Avignon for a brief period, about the middle of the thirteenth century, when the magistrates temporarily secured the right of attendance for themselves and a certain number of seigneurs. With this exception, the unfortunates who were wrestling for their lives with their judges were wholly at the discretion of the inquisitor and his creatures.*

The *personnel* of the tribunal was completed by the notary— an official of considerable standing and dignity in the Middle Ages. All the proceedings of the Inquisition were taken down in writing—

---

* Coll. Doat, XXII. 237 sqq.—Innoc. PP. IV. Bull. *Licet ex omnibus*, 30 Mai. 1254.—Bernardi Guidon. Practica P. IV. (Doat, XXX.).—Clement PP. IV. Bull. *Præ cunctis*, 23 Feb. 1266.—C. 11, § 1 Sexto v. 2.—Concil. Biterrens. ann. 1246 c. 4.—Alex. PP. IV. Bull. *Præ cunctis*, 9 Nov. 1256.—Archives de l'Inq. de Carcassonne (Doat, XXXIV. 11).—Molinier, L'Inquis. dans le midi de la France, pp. 219, 287.—Eymeric. Direct. Inq. p. 426.

every question and every answer — each witness and each defendant being obliged to confirm his testimony when read over to him
at the close of the interrogatory, and judgment was finally rendered on an inspection of the evidence thus recorded. The function of the notary was no light one, and occasionally scriveners
were called in to his assistance, but he formally attested every
document. Not only was there the fearful multiplication of papers accumulating in the current business of the tribunal, and their
careful transcription for preservation, but the several Inquisitions
were continually furnishing each other with copies of their records,
so that a considerable force must have been necessarily employed.
As in everything else, the inquisitor was empowered to call for
gratuitous service on the part of any one whom he might summon,
but the continuous business of the office required undivided attention, and its proper despatch rendered desirable the peculiar training acquired by experience. In the earlier periods, the authorization to impress any notary to serve, and the advice to select if
possible Dominicans who had been notaries, with the power, if
none such could be had, to replace him with two discreet persons,
shows that the itinerant tribunals depended for the most part on
this chance conscription; but in the permanent seats of the Inquisition the notary was a regular official, in receipt of a salary. In
the attempted reform of Clement V. it was provided that he should
take his official oath before the bishop as well as before the inquisitor, and to this Bernard Gui objected on the ground that the
exigencies of business sometimes required the force to be suddenly increased to two or three or four, and that in places where no
public notaries were to be had, other competent persons were
necessarily employed on the spur of the moment, as it often happens that the guilty will confess when in the mood, and if their
confession is not promptly taken they draw back, and they are
always more given to concealment than to truth. Curiously
enough, the power to appoint notaries was regarded with so much
jealousy that it was denied to the inquisitor. He may if he choose,
says Eymerich, send three or four names to the pope, who will appoint them for him, but this leads to such bad feeling on the
part of the local authorities that he had better content himself
with the notaries of the bishops or of the secular rulers.*

* Bern. Guidon. Practica P. iv. (Doat, XXX.).—Urbani PP. IV. Bull. *Licet*

The enormous mass of documents produced by these innumerable busy hands was the object of well-deserved solicitude. At the very inception of the work its value was recognized. In 1235 we hear of the confessions of penitents being sedulously recorded in books kept for the purpose. This speedily became the universal custom, and the inquisitors were instructed to preserve careful records of all their proceedings, from the first summons to the final sentence in every case, together with lists of all who took the oath enforced on every one to defend the faith and persecute heresy. The importance attached to this is shown by the frequent iteration of the command, and by the further precaution that all the papers should be duplicated, and a copy lodged in a safe place or with the bishop. With what elaborate care they were rendered practically useful is shown by the Book of Sentences of the Inquisition of Toulouse, from 1308 to 1323, printed by Limborch, where at the end there is an index of the 636 culprits sentenced, grouped under their places of residence alphabetically arranged, with reference to the pages on which their names occur and brief mention of the several punishments inflicted on each, and of any subsequent modifications of the penalty, thus enabling the official who wished information as to the people of any hamlet to see at a glance who among them had been suspected and what had been done. One case in the same book will illustrate the completeness and the exactitude of the previous records. In 1316 an old woman was brought before the tribunal; on examination it was found that in 1268, nearly fifty years before, she had confessed and abjured heresy and had been reconciled, and as this aggravated her guilt the miserable wretch was condemned to perpetual imprisonment in chains. Thus in process of time the Inquisition accumu-

---

ex omnibus, ann. 1262, §§ 6, 7, 8 (Mag. Bull. Roman. I. 122).—C. 1 § 3 Clement v. 3.—Coll. Doat, XXX. 109-10.—Eymeric. Direct. Inq. p. 550.

The peculiar importance attached to the notariate and the limitations imposed on its membership are seen in the papal privileges issued for the appointment of notaries. Thus there is one of November 27, 1295, by Boniface VIII. to the Archbishop of Lyons authorizing him to create five; one of January 28, 1296, to the Bishop of Arras to create three, and one of January 22, 1296, to the Bishop of Amiens to create two. (Thomas, Registres de Boniface VIII., I. No. 640 *bis*, 660, 678 *bis*.)

In 1286 the Provincial of France complained to Honorius IV. of the scarcity of notaries in that kingdom, and was authorized to create two (Ripoll II. 16).

lated a store of information which not only increased greatly its efficiency, but which rendered it an object of terror to every man. The confiscations and disabilities which, as we shall see hereafter, were inflicted on descendants, rendered the secrets of family history so carefully preserved in its archives the means by which a crushing blow might at any moment fall on the head of any one; and the Inquisition had an awkward way of discovering disagreeable facts about the ancestry of those who provoked its ill-will, and possibly its cupidity. Thus, in 1306, during the troubles at Albi, when the royal *viguier*, or governor, supported the cause of the people, the inquisitor, Geoffroi d'Ablis, issued letters declaring that he had found among the records that the grandfather of the *viguier* had been a heretic, and his grandson consequently was incapable of holding office. The whole population was thus at the mercy of the Holy Office.*

The temptation to falsify the records when an enemy was to be struck down was exceedingly strong, and the opponents of the Inquisition had no hesitation in declaring that it was freely yielded to. Friar Bernard Délicieux, speaking for the whole Franciscan Order of Languedoc, in a formal document of the year 1300, not only declared that the records were unworthy of trust, but that they were generally believed to be so. We shall see hereafter facts which fully justified this assertion, and the popular mistrust was intensified by the jealous secrecy which rendered it an offence punishable with excommunication for any one to possess any papers relating to the proceedings of the Inquisition or to prosecutions against heretics. On the other hand, the temptation on the part of those who were endangered to destroy the archives was equally strong, and the attempts to effect this show the importance attached to their possession. As early as 1235 we find the citizens of Narbonne, in an insurrection against the Inquisition, carefully destroying all the books and records. The order of the Council of Albi in 1254, to make duplicates and lodge them in some safe place was doubtless caused by another successful

---

* Guill. Pelisso Chron. Ed. Molinier p. 28.—Concil. Narbonn. ann. 1244 c. 6. — Concil. Biterrens. ann. 1246 c. 31, 37. — Concil. Albiens. ann. 1254 c. 21.— Alex. PP. IV. Bull. *Licet vobis*, 7 Dec. 1255; Ejusd. Bull. *Præ cunctis*, 9 Nov. 1255, 13 Dec. 1255.—Lib. Sentt. Inq. Tolosan. pp. 198–9.—Coll. Doat, XXXIV. 104.

effort made in 1248 by the heretics of Narbonne. On the occasion of an assembly of bishops in that city a clerk and a messenger bearing records with the names of heretics were slain and the books burned, giving rise to a good many troublesome questions with regard to existing and future prosecutions. About 1285, at Carcassonne, a plot was entered into by the consuls of the town and several of its leading ecclesiastics to destroy the inquisitorial records. They bribed one of the familiars, Bernard Garric, to burn them, but the conspiracy was discovered and its authors punished. One of these, a lawyer named Guillem Garric, languished in prison for about thirty years before his final sentence in 1321.*

Not the least important among the functionaries of the Inquisition were the lowest class — the apparitors, messengers, spies, and bravos, known generally by the name of familiars, which came to have so ill-omened a significance in the popular ear. The service was not without risk, and it had few attractions for the honest and peaceable, but it was full of promise for the reckless and evil-minded. Not only did they enjoy the immunity from secular jurisdiction attaching to all in the service of the Church, but the special authority granted by Innocent IV., in 1245, to the inquisitors to absolve their familiars for acts of violence rendered them independent even of the ecclesiastical tribunals. Besides, as any molestation of the servants of the Inquisition was qualified as impeding its operations and thus savoring of heresy, any one who dared to resist aggression rendered himself liable to prosecution before the tribunal of the aggressor. Thus panoplied, they could tyrannize at will over the defenceless population, and it is easy to imagine the amount of extortion which they could practise with virtual impunity by threatening arrest or accusation at a time when falling into the hands of the Inquisition was about the heaviest misfortune which could befall any man, whether orthodox or heretic.†

---

* Arch. de l'Inq. de Carcass. (Doat, XXXIV. 123).—Ripoll I. 356, 396.—Vaissette, III. 406; Pr. 467.—Coll. Doat, XXXI. 105, 149.—Molinier, p. 35.—Bern. Guidon. Hist. Conv. Carcass. (D. Bouquet, XXI. 743).—Lib. Sententt. Inquis. Tolos. p. 282.

† Paramo de Orig. Offic. S. Inquis. p. 102.—Pegnæ Comment. in Eymeric. p. 584.—Arch. de l'Inq. de Carcassonne (Doat, XXXI. 70; XXXII. 143).

All that was needed to render this social scourge complete was devised when the familiars were authorized to carry arms. The murders at Avignonet, in 1242, with that of Peter Martyr, and other similar events, seemed to justify the inquisitors in desiring an armed guard; and the service of tracking and capturing heretics was frequently one of peril, yet the privilege was a dangerous one to bestow on such men as could be got for the work, while releasing them from the restraints of law. In the turbulence of the age the carrying of weapons was rigidly repressed in all peace-loving communities. As early as the eleventh century we find it prohibited in the city of Pistoja, and in 1228 in Verona. In Bologna knights and doctors only were allowed to bear arms, and to have one armed servant. In Milan, a statute of Gian-Galeazzo, in 1386, forbids the carrying of weapons, but allows the bishops to arm the retainers living under their roofs. In Paris an *ordonnance* of 1288 inhibits the citizens from carrying pointed knives, swords, bucklers, or other similar weapons. In Beaucaire, an edict of 1320 prescribes various penalties, including the loss of a hand, for bearing arms, except in the case of travellers, who are restricted simply to swords and knives. Such regulations were of inestimable value in the progress of civilization, but they amounted to little when the inquisitor could arm any one he pleased, and invest him with the privileges and immunities of the Holy Office.*

As early as 1249 the scandals and abuses arising from the unlimited employment of scriveners and familiars who oppressed the people with their extortions called forth the indignant rebuke of Innocent IV., who commanded that their numbers should be reduced to correspond with the bare exigencies of duty. In those countries in which the Inquisition was supported by the State there was not much opportunity for the development of overgrown abuses of this nature. Thus, in Naples, Charles of Anjou, in permitting the carrying of arms, specifies three as the number of familiars for each inquisitor; and when Bernard Gui protested

---

* Statuta Pistoriensia, c. 109 (Zachariæ Anect. Med. Ævi, p. 23).—Lib. Juris civilis Veronæ, ann. 1228, c. 104, 183 (Veronæ, 1728).—Statut. criminal. Communis Bononiæ, Ed. 1525, fol. 36 (cf. Barbarano de' Mironi, Hist. Eccles. di Vicenza, II. 69).—Antiqua Ducum Mediolan. Decreta (Ed. 1654, p. 95).—Statuta Criminalia Mediolani, Bergomi, 1594, cap. 127.—Actes du Parl. de Paris, I. 257. —Vaissette, Éd. Privat, X. Pr. 610.

against the reforms of Clement V. he pointed out the contrast between France, where the inquisitors relied upon the secular officials, and were forced to be content with few retainers, and Italy, where they had almost unlimited opportunities. There, in fact, as we shall see, the Inquisition was self-supporting and independent by reason of its share in the fines and confiscations, and restraint of any kind was difficult. Clement V. forbade the useless multiplication of officials and the abuse of the right to bear arms, but his well-meant efforts availed little. In 1321 we find John XXII. reproving the inquisitors of Lombardy for creating scandals and tumults in Bologna by their armed familiars of depraved character and perverse habits, who committed murders and other outrages. In 1337 the papal nuncio, Bertrand, Archbishop of Embrun, seeing by personal observation the troubles which existed in Florence, owing to the practice of the inquisitor issuing licenses to carry arms, which was abused to the frequent injury of defenceless citizens, restricted him to twelve armed familiars, informing him that the secular authorities would furnish whatever additional armed assistance might be necessary for the capture of heretics. Yet within nine years one of the accusations brought against a new inquisitor, Frà Piero di Aquila, was that he had sold licenses to carry arms to more than two hundred and fifty men, bringing him in an annual revenue of about one thousand gold florins, and proving sadly detrimental to the peace of the city. Accordingly a law was passed restricting the inquisitor to six familiars bearing arms, the Bishop of Florence to twelve, and the Bishop of Fiesole to six, all of whom were required to wear the insignia of their masters. Still, the profit arising from the sale of such licenses was too great a temptation, and in the Florentine code of 1355 we find general regulations intended to check it in another way. Any one caught bearing arms and pleading a license was deported beyond the territory of the republic, to a distance of at least fifty miles from the city, and had to give a bond to remain there for a year. Even the podestà was prohibited from issuing such licenses under the penalties of perjury and a fine of five hundred lire. All this was an infraction of the liberties of the Church, and formed the substance of one of the complaints of Gregory XI., when, in 1376, he excommunicated the republic; and when, in 1378, Florence was forced to submit, one of the conditions was that a papal commissioner should expunge from the statute-book all the obnoxious laws. Yet the excesses of these brawling ruffians were too great to be long submitted to, and in 1386 another device was tried. The two bishops and the inquisitor were forbidden to have armed familiars who were taxable or inscribed on the roll of citizens; those to whom they issued licenses had to be declared their familiars by the priors of the arts, and this declaration had to be renewed yearly by a public instrument delivered to them. Some restraint thus was exercised, and this provision was retained in the recension of the code in 1415. This same struggle was doubtless going on in all the Italian cities which had independence enough to seek a remedy for the daily outrages inflicted by these licensed bravos, though the record of the troubles may not be accessible to history. Even in Venice, which kept the Inquisition in so subordinate a position, and wisely maintained its rights by defraying the expenses of the institution—even Venice felt the necessity of restraining the multiplication of pretended armed retainers. In August, 1450, the Great Council, by a vote of fourteen to two, denounced the abuse by which the inquisitor had sold to twelve persons the license to bear arms; such a force, it is said, was wholly unnecessary, as he could always invoke the assistance of the secular power, and therefore he should, in accordance with ancient custom, be restricted to four armed familiars. Six months later, in February, 1451, at the earnest request of the Franciscan general minister, this regulation was rescinded; the inquisitor was allowed to increase the number to twelve, but the police were directed to observe and report whether they were really engaged in the duties of the Inquisition. Yet Eymerich assures us that all such interference is unlawful, and that any secular ruler who endeavors to prevent the familiars of the Holy Office from bearing arms is impeding the Inquisition and is a fautor of heresy, while Bernard Gui characterizes in similar terms any limitation of the number of officials below what the inquisitor may deem requisite, all of which, according to Zanghino, is punishable at the discretion of the inquisitor.*

---

* Arch. de l'Inq. de Carcass. (Doat, XXXI. 81). — Archivio di Napoli, MSS. Chioccarello T. VIII. ; Registro 3, Lett. A, fol. 64 ; Registro 6, Lett. D, fol. 35.— Coll. Doat, XXX. 119-20.—C. 2. Clement. v. 3.—Johann. PP. XXII. Bull. *Exegit ordinis*, 2 Mai. 1321.—Archivio di Firenze, Riformagioni, Archiv. Diplom. XXVII.,

In the preceding chapter I have alluded to the power claimed and often exercised of abrogating all local statutes obnoxious to the Holy Office, and of the duty of every secular official to lend aid whenever called upon. This duty was recognized and enforced so that the organization of the Inquisition may be said to have embraced that of the State, whose whole resources were placed at its disposition. The oath of obedience which the inquisitor was empowered and directed to exact of all holding official station was no mere form. Refusal to take it was visited with excommunication, leading to prosecution for heresy in case of obduracy, and humiliating penance on submission. At times it was neglected by careless inquisitors, but the earnest ones made a point of it. Bernard Gui, at all his *autos de fé*, solemnly administered it to all the royal officials and local magistrates, and when, in May, 1309, Jean de Maucochin, the royal seneschal of the Tolosain and Albigeois declined to take it, he was speedily brought to see his error, and submitted within a month. Bernard himself, as we have seen, admits that the help thus promised was efficiently rendered, and when, in 1329, Henri de Chamay, Inquisitor of Carcassonne, applied to Philippe de Valois for a reaffirmation of the privileges of the Inquisition, the monarch promptly responded in an edict in which he proclaimed that "each and all, dukes, counts, barons, seneschals, baillis, provosts, viguiers, castellans, sergeants, and other justiciaries of the kingdom of France are bound to obey the inquisitors and their commissioners in seizing, holding, guarding, and taking to prison all heretics and suspects of heresy, and to execute diligently the sentences of the inquisitors, and to give to the inquisitors, their commissioners and messengers, safe-conduct, prompt help and favor, through all the lands of their jurisdictions, in all that concerns the business of the Inquisition, whenever and how often soever they may be called upon." Any

---

LXXVIII.-IX.; Riform. Classe II. Distinz. 1, No. 14.—Villani, Cronica, Lib. XII. c. 58.—Archivio di Venezia, Misti, Cons. X. Vol. XIII. p. 192; Vol. XIV. p. 29.—Eymeric. Direct. Inq. pp. 374-5.—Bernard. Guidonis Practica P. IV. (Doat, XXX.).—Zanchini Tract. de Hæret. c. xxxi.—Urbani PP. IV. Bull. *Licet ex omnibus*, 1262 (Mag. Bull. Rom. I. 123).—Bernardi Comens. Lucerna Inquisit. s. v. *Inquisitores*, No. 14.

For further authorities on the subject, see Farinacii de Hæresi Quæst. 182, No. 89-94.

hesitation on the part of public officials to grant assistance when summoned was promptly punished. Thus, in 1303, when Bonrico di Busca, vicar of the podestà of Mandrisio, refused to furnish men to the representatives of the Milanese Inquisition, he was forthwith condemned to a fine of a hundred imperial solidi, to be paid within five days. Even the condition of an excommunicate, which rendered an official incapable of performing any other function, did not relieve him from this duty; he could be called upon to execute the commands of the inquisitor, but he was warned that he must not imagine himself competent therefore to do anything else.*

In addition to this the Inquisition had, to a greater or less extent, at its service the whole orthodox population, and especially the clergy. It was the duty of every man to give information as to all cases of heresy with which he might become acquainted under pain of incurring the guilt of fautorship. It was further his duty to arrest all heretics, as Bernard de St. Genais found in 1242, when he was tried by the Inquisition of Toulouse for the offence of not capturing certain heretics when it was in his power to do so, and was condemned to the penance of pilgrimages to the shrines of Puy, St. Gilles, and Compostella. The parish priests, moreover, were required, whenever called upon, to cite their parishioners for appearance, either publicly from the pulpit or secretly as the case might require, and to publish all sentences of excommunication. They were likewise held to the duty of surveillance over penitents to see that the penances enjoined were duly performed, and to report any cases of neglect. A very thorough system of local police, framed upon the model of the old synodal witnesses, was devised by the Council of Béziers in 1246, under which the inquisitor was

---

* Concil. Albiens. ann. 1254 c. 7.—Eymeric. Direct. Inquis. 392–402.—Gloss. Hostiens. super. Cap *Excommunicamus*, § *Moneamus.*—Gloss. Joan. Andreæ sup. eod. loc.—Lib. Sententt. Inq. Tolosan. pp. 1, 7, 36, 39, 292.—Archives de l'Inq. de Carcassonne (Doat, XXVII. 118).—Isambert, Anc. Loix Françaises, IV. 364–5. —Ogniben Andrea, I Guglielmiti del Secolo XIII., Perugia, 1867, p. 111.—Alex. PP. IV. Bull. *Quæsivistis*, 28 Mai. 1260.

As in France the office of bailli was a purchasable one, while the incumbent was forbidden to sell it, it is evident that he would be loath to endanger its tenure by risking disobedience to inquisitorial demands.—Statuta Ludov. IX. ann. 1254, c. xxv.–vii. (Vaissette, Éd. Privat, VIII. 1349).

empowered to appoint in every parish a priest and one or two lay-men, whose duty it should be to search for heretics, examining all houses, inside and out, and especially all secret hiding-places. In addition to this they were instructed to watch over penitents and enforce the faithful observance of the sentences of the Inquisi-tion, and a manual of practice of the period instructs inquisitors to see that this system is thoroughly carried out. In fact, the whole resources of the land, public and private, were freely placed at the disposal of the Holy Office, so that nothing should be want-ing in its sacred mission of extirpating heresy.*

An important feature in the organization of the Inquisition was the assembly in which the fate of the accused was finally de-termined. The inquisitor had technically no power to pass sen-tence by himself. We have seen how, after various fluctuations of policy, the co-operation of the bishops was established as indispensa-ble. As in everything else, the inquisitors contemptuously neglected this limitation on their powers, and when Clement V. endeavored to reform abuses he pronounced null and void any sentences ren-dered independently, yet to avert delays he permitted consent to be expressed in writing if after eight days a meeting could not be arranged. If, indeed, we may judge from some specimens of these written consultations which have reached us, they were perfunc-tory to the last degree and placed no real check upon the discre-tion of the inquisitor. Still Bernard Gui complained bitterly even of this restriction in terms which show how little respect had pre-viously been paid to the rule, and he adds, in justification, that one bishop kept the trials of some persons of his diocese from being finished for two years and more, while another delayed the cele-bration of an *auto de fé* for six months. He himself observed the regulation scrupulously, both before and after the publication of the Clementines, and in the reports of the *autos* held by him in Toulouse the participation of the bishops of the prisoners, or of episcopal delegates, is always carefully specified. Yet how easy was the evasion of this, as of all other regulations for the protec-

---

* Zanchini Tract. de Hæret. c. 5.—Coll. Doat, XXI. 226, 308.—Bern. Guidon. Practica P. IV. (Doat, XXX.).—Concil. Narbonn. ann. 1244 c. 8.—Concil. Biter-rens. ann. 1246 c. 34.—Practica super Inquisit. (MSS. Bib. Nat., fonds latin, No. 14930, fol. 223–4).

tion of the accused, is seen when even Bernard Gui accepted commissions from three bishops—those of Cahors, St. Papoul, and Montauban—to act for them in the *auto* of September 30, 1319. This device became frequent, and inquisitors constantly rendered sentence on their individual responsibility under power granted them by the bishops, as in the persecutions of the Waldenses of Piedmont in 1387, and that of the witches of Canavese in 1474. Sometimes, however, the bishops were not altogether free agents, as when, in the early persecution of the Spiritual Franciscans, about 1318, those of the province of Narbonne were coerced to consent to the burning of some unfortunates by the inquisitor threatening them with the pope, who was known to have the prosecutions much at heart.*

This episcopal concurrence in the sentence was reached in consultation with the assembly of experts. As the inquisitors from the beginning were chosen rather with regard to zeal than learning, and as they maintained a reputation for ignorance, it was soon found requisite to associate with them in the rendering of sentences men versed in the civil and canon law, which had by this time become an intricate study requiring the devotion of a lifetime. Accordingly they were empowered to call in experts to deliberate with them over the evidence and advise with them on the sentence to be rendered, and those who were thus summoned could not refuse to serve gratuitously, though it is intimated that the inquisitor can pay them if he feels so inclined. At first it would seem as though notables were assembled at the condemnation of prominent heretics rather to give solemnity to the occasion than for actual consultation, as when, in 1237, at the sentence passed on Alaman de Roaix in Toulouse, the presence is recorded of the Bishop of Toulouse, the Abbot of Moissac, the Dominican and Franciscan provincials, and a number of other notables. The amount of work, in fact, performed by the Inquisition of Languedoc in the early years of its existence would seem to preclude the idea of any serious deliberation by counsellors thus called in, who would have to consider the interminable reports of examinations and interro-

---

* C. 1, § 1, Clement v. 3.—Eymeric. Direct. Inq. p. 580.—Coll. Doat, XXXI. 57.—Bernardi Guidon. Practica P. IV. (Doat, XXX.).—Coll. Doat, XXX. 104.— Lib. Sententt. Inq. Tolosan. passim, especially pp. 208-10.—Ibid. p. 300.—Archivio Storico Italiano, No. 38, p. 26 sqq.—Curiosità di Storia Subalpina, 1874, p. 215.

gations; especially as, at a comparatively early date, the practice was adopted of allowing a number of culprits to accumulate whose fate was determined and announced in a solemn " *Sermo* " or *auto de fé*. Still, the form was kept up, and in 1247 a sentence rendered by Bernard de Caux and Jean de St. Pierre on seven relapsed heretics is specified as being " with the counsel of many prelates and other good men." In the final shape which the assembly of counsellors assumed, we find it summoned to meet on Fridays, the " *Sermo* " always taking place on Sundays. When the number of criminals was large there was thus not much time for deliberation on special cases. The assessors were always to be jurists and Mendicant friars, selected by the inquisitor in such numbers as he saw fit. They were severally sworn on the Gospels to secrecy, and to give good and wise counsel, each one according to his conscience and the knowledge vouchsafed him by God. The inquisitor then read over to them his summary of each case, sometimes withholding the name of the accused, and they voted the sentence—" Penance at the discretion of the inquisitor"—" That person is to be imprisoned, or abandoned to the secular arm," while the Gospels lay on the table in their midst, " so that our judgment may come from the face of God and our eyes may see justice." *

As a rule it is safe to assume that these proceedings were scarcely more than formal. Not only was the inquisitor at liberty to present each case in such aspect as he saw fit, but it became the custom to call in such numbers of experts that in the press of business deliberation was scarce possible. Thus the Inquisitor of Carcassonne, Henri de Chamay, assembled at Narbonne, December 10, 1328, besides himself and the episcopal Ordinary, forty-two counsellors, consisting of canons, jurisconsults, and lay experts. In the two days allotted to them this unwieldly assemblage despatched thirty-four cases, which would show that little consideration could have been given to each. In only two cases, indeed, was there any dif-

---

* Alex. PP. IV. Bull. *Cupientes*, 15 Apr. 1255.—Ejusd. Bull. *Præ cunctis*, 9 Nov. 1256.—Urbani PP. IV. Bull. *Licet ex omnibus*, § 10, 1262 (Mag. Bull. Rom. I. 122). —Bern. Guidon. Practica P. IV. (Doat, XXX.). — Zanchini de Hæret. c. xv.— Bernardi Comens. Lucerna Inquisitor. s. v. *Advocatus.* — Coll. Doat, XXI. 143; XXVII. 156–62, 232; XXXI. 139. — Doctrina de modo procedendi (Martene Thesaur. V. 1795).—Tractatus de Inquis. (Doat, XXXVI.).—MSS. Bib. Nat., fonds latin, No. 14930, fol. 205.

ference of opinion expressed, and these were of no special importance. On September 8, 1329, he held another assembly at Carcassonne, attended by forty-seven experts, which in its two days'
session acted upon forty cases. Yet these assemblies were not always so expeditious and self-effacing. From Narbonne Henri de
Chamay passed to Pamiers, where, January 7, 1329, he called together thirty-five experts besides the Bishop of Toulouse. On the
first day several cases were postponed for greater deliberation, and
of these some were acted upon and others were not. Considerable
debate took place, each individual expressing his opinion, and the
result was apparently settled by the majority vote. They evidently felt and assumed the responsibility of the decision; and yet
the impossibility of deliberate action by so cumbrous a body is
seen in their bunching together all the cases of "believing" heretics, condemning them *en masse* to prison, and leaving it with the
inquisitor to determine the character of the imprisonment for each
individual. Curiously enough, this assembly also assumed legisla-
tive functions in laying down general rules of punishment for false-
witness. A still more notable instance of deliberation occurred at
an assembly convoked by Henri de Chamay at Béziers, May 19,
1329, where there were thirty-five experts present. In the case of
a Franciscan friar, Pierre Julien, all agreed that, strictly speaking,
he was a "relapsed," but many were anxious to show him mercy.
After long debate, the inquisitor told them to meet again in the
evening, and in the meanwhile consider whether they could devise
some means of grace. At the evening session there was again
earnest discussion, and postponement was agreed to on the excuse
that no bishop could be had in time for his degradation. The experts were finally summoned, under pain of excommunication, to
give their opinions, which were taken down in writing and ranged
from simple purgation to abandonment to the secular arm. The
assembly then was dismissed and consultation was held with some
of the more prominent members, when it was agreed either to send
to Avignon, Toulouse, or Montpellier for advice or to await an *auto
de fé* at Carcassonne for further counsel.*

Yet, while the forms were thus preserved, the inquisitors, with
their customary arbitrary disregard of all that limited their dis-

---

* Coll. Doat, XXVII. 118, 140, 156, 162.

cretion, paid attention or not to the decisions of the experts, as best
suited them. In the sentences which follow the reports of these
assemblies it is by no means unusual to find names which had
never been laid before them. After the assembly of Pamiers, for
instance, which showed so much disposition to act for itself, there
is a sentence condemning five defuncts, only two of whom are
named in the proceedings. On the same occasion, another culprit,
Ermessende, daughter of Raymond Monier, was condemned by the
assembly for false-witness to the "*murus largus*," or simple prison,
and was sentenced by the inquisitor to "*murus strictus*," or imprisonment in chains, which was a very different penalty. In fact,
it was a disputed point whether the inquisitor was bound to obey
the counsel of the assembly, and though Eymerich decides in the
affirmative, Bernardo di Como positively asserts the negative.*

From the necessity of these consultations with bishops and experts it is easy to understand the origin of the "*Sermo generalis*,"
or *auto de fé*. It was evidently impossible to bring all parties together to consult over each individual case, and convenience was
not only served by allowing the cases to accumulate, but opportunity was also afforded of arranging an impressive solemnity
which should strike terror on the heretic and comfort the hearts
of the faithful. In the rudimentary Inquisition of Florence, in
1245, where the inquisitor Ruggieri Calcagni and Bishop Ardingho
were zealously co-operating, and no assembly of experts was required, we find the heretics sentenced and executed day by day,
singly or in twos or threes, but the form was already adopted of
assembling the people in the cathedral and reading the sentence
to them, when doubtless the occasion was improved of delivering
a discourse upon the wickedness of dissent and the duty of all citizens to persecute the children of Satan. In Toulouse the fragment of the register of sentences of Bernard de Caux and Jean de
Saint-Pierre, from March, 1246, to June, 1248, shows a similar disregard of form. The *autos* or *Sermones* are sometimes held every
few days—there are five in May, 1246—and often there are only
one or two heretics to be sentenced, rendering it exceedingly proba-

---

* Coll. Doat, XXVII. 118, 131, 133.—Eymerici Direct. Inq. p. 630.—Bernard.
Comens. Lucerna Inquisitor. s. v. *Advocatus*.

ble that the co-operation of the bishop was not asked for, especially as he is never mentioned as joining in the condemnation. There are always present, however, a certain number of local magistrates, civil and ecclesiastical, and the ceremony is usually performed in the cloister of the church of St. Sernin, though other places are sometimes mentioned, and among them the Hotel-de-Ville twice, showing that divine service as yet formed no part of the solemnity.*

With time the ceremony grew in stateliness and impressiveness. Sunday became prescribed for it, and as no other sermons were allowed on that day in the city, it was forbidden to be held on Quadragesima or Advent Sunday, or any other of the principal feast-days. Notice was given in advance from all the pulpits summoning all the people to be present and obtain the indulgence of forty days. A staging was erected in the centre of the church, on which the "penitents" were placed, surrounded by the secular and clerical officials. The sermon was delivered by the inquisitor, after which the oath of obedience was administered to the representatives of the civil power, and a solemn decree of excommunication was fulminated against all who should in any manner impede the operations of the Holy Office. Then the notary commenced reading the confessions one by one in the vulgar tongue, and as each was finished the culprit was asked if he acknowledged it to be true—care being taken, however, only to do this when he was known to be truly penitent and not likely to create scandal by a denial. On his replying in the affirmative he was asked whether he would repent, or lose body and soul by persevering in heresy; and on his expressing a desire to abjure, the form of abjuration was read and he repeated it, sentence by sentence. Then the inquisitor absolved him from the *ipso facto* excommunication which he had incurred by heresy, and promised him mercy if he behaved well under the sentence about to be imposed. The sentence followed, and thus the penitents were brought foward successively, commencing with the least guilty and proceeding with those incurring severer penalties. Those who were to be "relaxed," or abandoned to the secular arm, were reserved to the last, and for them the ceremony was adjourned to the pub

---

* Lami, Antichità Toscane, pp. 557-9.—Coll. Doat, XXXI. 139.—MSS. Bib. Nat., fonds latin, No. 9992.—Alex. PP. IV. Bull. *Præ cunctis,* § 15, 9 Nov. 1256.

lic square, where a platform had been constructed for the purpose, in order that the holy precincts of the church might not be polluted by a sentence leading to blood. For the same reason it was not to be performed on a holy day. The execution, however, was not to take place on the same day, but on the following, so as to afford the convicts time for conversion, that their souls might not pass from temporal to eternal flame, and care was enjoined not to permit them to address the people, lest sympathy should be aroused by their assertions of innocence.*

We can readily picture to ourselves the effect produced on the popular mind by these awful celebrations, when, at the bidding of the Inquisition, all that was great and powerful in the land was called together humbly to take the oath of obedience and witness its exercise of the highest expression of human authority, regulating the destinies of fellow-creatures here and hereafter. In the great *auto de fé* held by Bernard Gui at Toulouse, in April, 1310, the solemnities lasted from Sunday the 5th until Thursday the 9th. After the preliminary work of mitigating the penances of some deserving penitents, twenty persons were condemned to wear crosses and perform pilgrimages, sixty-five were consigned to perpetual imprisonment, three of them in chains, and eighteen were delivered to the secular justice and were duly burned. In that of April, 1312, fifty-one were sentenced to crosses, eighty-six to imprisonment, ten defunct persons were pronounced worthy of prison and their estates confiscated, the bones of thirty-six were ordered to be exhumed and burned, five living ones were handed over to the secular court to be burned, and five more condemned for contumacy in absenting themselves. The faith which could thus vindicate itself might certainly inspire the respect of fear if not the attraction of love. Sometimes, however, a godless heretic would interfere with the prescribed order of solemnities, as when, in October, 1309, Amiel de Perles, a noted Catharan teacher, who defiantly avowed his heterodoxy, immediately on his capture commenced the *endura* and refused all food and drink. Unwilling thus to be robbed of his victim, Bernard hastened the usual dila-

---

* Eymeric. Direct. Inquis. pp. 503–12.—Doctrina de modo Procedendi (Martene Thesaur. V. 1795–6).—Tract. de Paup. de Lugduno (Ib. 1792).—Lib. Sententt. Inquis. Tolosan. pp. 1, 6, 39, 98.

tory proceedings, and gave to Amiel the honor of a special *auto* in which he was the only victim. A similar case occurred in 1313, when a certain Pierre Raymond, who as a Catharan "*credens*" had been led to abjure and seek reconciliation in the *auto* of 1310, and had been condemned to imprisonment, repented of his weakness in his solitary cell. The mental tortures of the poor wretch grew so strong that at last he defiantly proclaimed his relapse into heresy, in which he declared he would live and die, only regretting that he could not have access to some minister of his faith in order to be "perfected" or "hereticated." He likewise placed himself in *endura*, and after six days of starvation, as he was evidently nearing the end which he so resolutely sought, he was hurriedly sentenced, and a small *auto* was arranged with a few other culprits in order that the stake might not be cheated of its prey.*

With such an organization as this, in the hands of able, vigorous, and earnest men, it shows the marvellous constancy of the heretics that the Cathari for a hundred years opposed to it the simple resistance of inertia, and that the Waldenses were never trampled out. The effectiveness of the organization was unhampered by any limits of jurisdiction, and was multiplied by the cooperation of the tribunals everywhere, so that there was no resting-place, no harbor of refuge for the heretic in any land where the Inquisition existed. Vainly might he change his abode, it was ever on his track. A suspicious stranger would be observed and arrested; his birthplace would be ascertained, and as soon as swift messengers could traverse the intervening distance, full official documents as to his antecedents would be received from the Holy Office of his former home. It was a mere matter of convenience whether he should be tried where he was caught or sent back, for every tribunal had full jurisdiction over all offences committed within its district, and over all such offenders wherever they should stray. When Jacopo della Chiusa, one of the assassins of St. Peter Martyr, discreetly absented himself, notices commanding his capture were sent as far as the Inquisition of Carcassonne. Of course, questions sometimes arose which seemed likely to give trouble. Before the Inquisition was thoroughly organized, Jayme I. of Ara-

---

* Lib. Sententt. Inquis. Tolosan. pp. 37, 39–93, 99–175, 178–9.

gon, in 1248, complained of the Tolosan inquisitor, Bernard de Caux, for citing his subjects to appear, and Innocent IV. commanded that the abuse should cease, an order which received but slack obedience; and with the growth of the Holy Office such reclamations were not likely to be repeated. Cases, of course, occurred, in which two tribunals would claim the same culprit, and in this the rule of the Council of Narbonne, in 1244, was generally observed, that he should be tried by the inquisitor who had first commenced prosecution. Considering, indeed. the abundant causes of jealousy, and especially the bitter rivalry between the Dominican and Franciscan Orders, the cases of quarrel seem to have been singularly few. Whatever there were, they were hushed up with prudent reserve, and with occasional exceptions we find a hearty and zealous co-operation in the holy work to which all were alike devoted.*

The implacable energy with which the resources of this organization were employed may be understood from one or two instances. Under the Hohenstaufens the two Sicilies had served as a refuge for many heretics self-exiled by the rigor of the Inquisition of Languedoc, and merciless as was Frederic when it suited him, his system was by no means so searching and unintermittent as that of the Holy Office. After his death, the active warfare between Manfred and the papacy doubtless left the heretics in comparative peace, but when Charles of Anjou conquered the kingdom as the vassal of Rome, it was at once thrown open and the French inquisitors made haste to pursue those who had eluded them. But seven months after the execution of Conradin, Charles issued his letters-patent, May 31, 1269, to all the nobles and magistrates of the realm, setting forth that the inquisitors of France were about coming or sending agents to track and seize the fugitive heretics who had sought refuge in Italy, and ordering his subjects to give them safe-conduct and assistance whenever they might require it. In

---

* Lib. Sententt. Inq. Tolosan. pp. 252–4.—MSS. Bib. Nat., fonds latin, 11847 *ad finem.*—Arch. de l'Inquis. de Carcassonne (Doat, XXXI. 83, 94–5).—Guid. Fulcod. Quæst. v.—Alex. PP. IV. Bull. *Cupientes,* 4 Mart. 1260.—Urbani PP. IV. Bull. *Licet ex omnibus,* § 11, 1262.—Ejusd. Bull. *Præ cunctis,* 2 Aug. 1264.—C. 2 Sexto v. 2.—Bern. Guidon Practica P. IV. (Doat, XXX.).—Zanchini Tract. de Hæret. c. viii.—Concil. Narbonn. ann. 1244 c. 20.—Eymeric. Direct. Inquis. pp. 461–5.

fact, the inquisitor's jurisdiction was personal as well as local, and it accompanied him. When, in 1359, some renegade converted Jews escaped from Provence to Spain, Innocent VI. authorized the Provençal inquisitor, Bernard du Puy, to follow them, arrest, try, condemn, and punish them wherever he might find them, with power to coerce the aid of the secular authorities everywhere; and he wrote at the same time to the kings of Aragon and Castile, instructing them to give to Bernard all necessary assistance.*

How the same tireless and unforgiving zeal was habitually brought to bear upon the humblest objects is seen in the case of Arnaud Ysarn, who, when a youth of fifteen, was condemned at Toulouse in 1309, after an imprisonment of two years, to wear crosses and perform certain pilgrimages, his sole offence being that he had once "adored" a heretic at the command of his father. He wore the insignia of his shame for more than a year, when, finding that they prevented him from earning a livelihood, he threw them off and obtained employment as a boatman on the Garonne between Moissac and Bordeaux. In his obscurity he might well fancy himself safe; but the inquisitorial police was too well organized, and he was discovered. Cited in 1312 to appear, he was afraid to do so, though urged by his father to take the chance of mercy. In 1315 he was excommunicated for contumacy, and, remaining under the censure for a year, he was finally declared a heretic, and was condemned as such in the *auto de fé* of 1319. In June, 1321, by command of Bernard Gui, he was captured at Moissac, but escaped on the road to be recaptured and taken to Toulouse. He had been guilty of no act of heresy during the interval, but his contumacious rejection of the parental chastisement of the Inquisition was an offence worthy of death, and he was mercifully treated in being condemned, in 1322, to imprisonment for life on bread and water. The net of the Inquisition extended everywhere, and no prey was too small to elude its meshes.†

The whole organization of the Church was at its service. In 1255 a Dominican of Alessandria, Frà Niccolò da Vercelli, confessed voluntarily some heretical beliefs to his sub-prior, who thereupon

---

* Archivio di Napoli, Registro 3, Lett. A, fol. 64. — Wadding. ann. 1359, No. 1–3.

† Lib. Sententt. Inq. Tolosan. pp. 350–1.

promptly ejected him. He entered a neighboring Cistercian convent, and then, fearing the pursuit of the Inquisition, quietly disappeared to some other convent beyond the Alps. There would not seem much to be feared from a heretic who would bury himself in the rigid Cistercian Order, and yet at once Alexander IV. issued letters to all Cistercian abbots and to all archbishops and bishops everywhere, commanding them to seize him and send him to Rainerio Saccone, the Lombard inquisitor.*

To render it an instrumentality perfect for the work assigned to it, all that was wanting to the Inquisition was its subjection to a chief who should command the implicit obedience of its members and weld the organization into an organic whole. This function the pope could perform but imperfectly amid the overwhelming diversity of his cares, and he needed a minister who, as inquisitor-general, could devote his undivided attention to the innumerable questions arising from the conflict between orthodoxy and heresy, and between papal supremacy and local episcopal independence. The importance of such a measure seems to have made itself felt at a comparatively early period, and in 1262 Urban IV. created a virtual inquisitor-general when he ordered all inquisitors to report, either in person or by letter, to Caietano Orsini, Cardinal of S. Niccolò in carcere Tulliano, all impediments to the due performance of their functions, and to obey the instructions which he might give. Cardinal Orsini speaks of himself as inquisitor-general, and he labored to bring the several tribunals into the closest relations with each other and subjection to himself. May 19, 1273, we find him ordering the Italian inquisitors to furnish to the inquisitors of France facilities for the transcription of all the depositions of witnesses already on record in their archives, as well as of all future ones. The perpetual migration of Catharans and Waldenses between France and Italy rendered this information most valuable, and the French inquisitors had requested it of him, but the excessive diffuseness of the inquisitorial documents made the task appalling in magnitude and cost, and the terms of the cardinal's missive show that it was not expected to be welcome. Whether any further attempt was made to carry out this gigantic

---

* Ripoll I. 285.

plan, which would have so greatly multiplied the effectiveness of the Inquisition, does not appear, but its conception shows the view entertained by Orsini of the powers of his office and of the possibilities of what the Inquisition might become under energetic supervision. Another letter of his, dated May 24, 1273, to the inquisitors of France, indicates that for a time at least the general instructions to the functionaries of the Holy Office were issued through him.*

We have no further evidence of his activity, but his elevation to the papacy in 1277, as Nicholas III., may possibly indicate that the position was one which afforded abundant opportunities of influence, perhaps rendering its possessor disagreeably, if not dangerously powerful, and when Nicholas appointed his nephew, Cardinal Latino Malebranca, as his successor in the office vacated by his elevation, he may have felt it necessary to secure himself by keeping the position in his family. Malebranca was Dean of the Sacred College, and his influence was shown when, in 1294, he ended the weary conflict of the conclave by procuring the election of the hermit, Pietro Morrone, as pope, under the name of Celestin V. He did not survive the short pontificate of Celestin, and the proud and vigorous Boniface VIII. regarded it as impolitic or unnecessary to continue the office. It remained in abeyance under the Avignonese popes, until Clement VI. revived it for William, Cardinal of S. Stefano in Monte Celio, who signalized his zeal by burning several heretics, and in other ways. After his death the post remained vacant, and at no time does it appear to have exercised any special influence over the development and activity of the Inquisition.†

---

* Ripoll I. 434.—Pegnæ Comment. in Eymeric. pp. 406–7.—Wadding. Annal. Regest. Nich. PP. III. No. 10.—Arch. de l'Inq. de Carcassonne (Doat, XXXII. 101).—Raynald. ann. 1278, No. 78.—MSS. Bib. Nat., fonds latin, No. 14930, fol. 218.

† Paramo de Orig. Offic. S. Inquis. pp. 124–5.—Wadding. Annal. ann. 1294, No. 1.—Milman, Latin Christianity, IV. 487.

CHAPTER III.

THE procedure of the episcopal courts, as described in a former chapter, was based on the principles of the Roman law, and whatever may have been its abuses in practice, it was equitable in theory, and its processes were limited by strictly defined rules. In the Inquisition all this was changed, and if we would rightly appreciate its methods we must understand the relations which the inquisitor conceived to exist between himself and the offenders brought before his tribunal. As a judge, he was vindicating the faith and avenging God for the wrongs inflicted on him by misbelief. He was more than a judge, however, he was a father-confessor striving for the salvation of the wretched souls perversely bent on perdition. In both capacities he acted with an authority far higher than that of an earthly judge. If his sacred mission was accomplished, it mattered little what methods were used. If the offender asked mercy for his unpardonable crime it must be through the most unreserved submission to the spiritual father who was seeking to save him from the endless torment of hell. The first thing demanded of him when he appeared before the tribunal was an oath to stand to the mandates of the Church, to answer truly all questions asked of him, to betray all heretics known to him, and to perform whatever penance might be imposed on him; and refusal to take this oath was to proclaim himself at once a defiant and obstinate heretic.*

---

* Arch. de l'Inquis. de Carcassonne (Doat, XXXI. 5, 103).—Zanchini Tract. de Hæret. c. ix.

In the Cismontane Inquisition the preliminary oath seems only to pledge the accused to tell the truth as to himself and others (Eymeric. p. 421). In Italy, however, it was the more elaborate affair described in the text. In the trials of the Guglielmites at Milan, in 1300, the accused were, in addition, made to impose

The duty of the inquisitor, moreover, was distinguished from
that of the ordinary judge by the fact that the task assigned to
him was the impossible one of ascertaining the secret thoughts
and opinions of the prisoner. External acts were to him only of
value as indications of belief, to be accepted or rejected as he
might deem them conclusive or illusory. The crime he sought to
suppress by punishment was purely a mental one—acts, however
criminal, were beyond his jurisdiction. The murderers of St. Peter
Martyr were prosecuted, not as assassins, but as fautors of heresy
and impeders of the Inquisition. The usurer only came within his
purview when he asserted or showed by his acts that he considered usury no sin; the sorcerer when his incantations proved that
he preferred to rely on the powers of demons rather than those of
God, or that he entertained wrongful notions upon the sacraments.
Zanghino tells us that he witnessed the condemnation of a concu-
binary priest by the Inquisition, who was punished not for his
licentiousness, but because while thus polluted he celebrated daily
mass and urged in excuse that he considered himself purified by
putting on the sacred vestments. Then, too, even doubt was heresy; the believer must have fixed and unwavering faith, and it
was the inquisitor's business to ascertain this condition of his
mind. * External acts and verbal professions were as naught.
The accused might be regular in his attendance at mass; he might
be liberal in his oblations, punctual in confession and communion,
and yet be a heretic at heart. When brought before the tribunal
he might profess the most unbounded submission to the decisions
of the Holy See, the strictest adherence to orthodox doctrine, the
freest readiness to subscribe to whatever was demanded of him,

---

on themselves, in case of violating its pledges, a forfeit varying from ten to fifty
imperial lire, to secure which they pledged to the inquisitor all their property,
real and personal, and renounced all legal defence. Moreover, this pecuniary
penalty was not to relieve them from the canonical punishment attendant upon
the non-fulfilment of the obligations assumed. This, I presume, was the official
formula customary in the Lombard Inquisition.—Ogniben Andrea, I Guglielmiti del Secolo XIII., Perugia, 1867, pp. 5–6, 13, 27, 35, 37, etc.

In some witch trials of 1474 in Piedmont the oath to tell the truth was enforced with excommunication and " *tratti di corde*," or infliction of the torture
known as the strappado, varying from ten to twenty-five times—and also with
pecuniary forfeits.—P. Vayra (Curiosità di Storia Subalpina, 1875, pp. 682, 693).

* Zanchini Tract. de Hæret. c. ii.

and yet be secretly a Catharan or a Vaudois, fit only for the stake. Few, indeed, were there who courageously admitted their heresy when brought before the tribunal, and to the conscientious judge, eager to destroy the foxes which ravaged the vineyard of the Lord, the task of exploring the secret heart of man was no easy one. We cannot wonder that he speedily emancipated himself from the trammels of recognized judicial procedure which, in preventing him from committing injustice, would have rendered his labors futile. Still less can we be surprised that fanatic zeal, arbitrary cruelty, and insatiable cupidity rivalled each other in building up a system unspeakably atrocious. Omniscience alone was capable of solving with justice the problems which were the daily routine of the inquisitor; human frailty, resolved to accomplish a predetermined end, inevitably reached the practical conclusion that the sacrifice of a hundred innocent men were better than the escape of one guilty.

Thus of the three forms of criminal actions, accusation, denunciation, and inquisition, the latter necessarily became, in place of an exception, the invariable rule, and at the same time it was stripped of the safeguards by which its dangerous tendencies had been in some degree neutralized. If a formal accuser presented himself, the inquisitor was instructed to discourage him by pointing out the danger of the *talio* to which he was exposed by inscribing himself; and by general consent this form of action was rejected in consequence of its being "litigious"—that is, because it afforded the accused some opportunities of defence. That there was danger to the accuser, and that the Inquisition practically discouraged the process, was shown in 1304, when an inquisitor, Frà Landulfo, imposed a fine of one hundred and fifty ounces of gold on the town of Theate because it had officially accused a man of heresy and had failed in the proof. The action by denunciation was less objectionable, because in it the inquisitor acted *ex officio;* but it was unusual, and the inquisitorial process at an early period became substantially the only one followed.*

---

* Eymeric. Direct. Inquis. pp. 413–17.—Archivio di Napoli, Reg. 138, Lett. F, fol. 105.

To appreciate the contrast between the processes of the Inquisition and of the secular courts, it will suffice to allude to the practice of the latter in Milan in the first half of the fourteenth century. An accuser bringing a criminal action was

Not only, as we shall see, were its safeguards withdrawn, but virtually the presumption of guilt was assumed in advance. About 1278 an experienced inquisitor lays down the rule as one generally received, that in places much suspected of heresy every inhabitant must be cited to appear, must be forced to abjure heresy and to tell the truth, and be subjected to a detailed interrogatory about himself and others, in which any lack of frankness will subject him hereafter to the dreadful penalties of relapse. That this was not a mere theoretical proposition appears from the great inquests held by Bernard de Caux and Jean de Saint-Pierre in 1245 and 1246, when there are recorded two hundred and thirty interrogatories of inhabitants of the little town of Avignonet, one hundred of those of Fanjeaux, and four hundred and twenty of Mas-Saintes-Puelles.*

From this responsibility there was no escape for any one who had reached the age at which the Church held him able to answer for his own acts. What this age was, however, was a subject of dispute. The Councils of Toulouse, Béziers, and Albi assumed it to be fourteen for males and twelve for females, when they prescribed the oath of abjuration to be taken by the whole population, and

---

obliged to inscribe himself and to furnish ample security that in case of failure he would undergo the fitting penalty and indemnify the accused for all expenses ; in default of security he was to remain in jail until the end of the trial. The judge was, moreover, bound to render his decision within three months.

If the judge proceeded by inquisition he was obliged to give the accused notice in advance. The latter was entitled to counsel and to have the names and testimony of the witnesses communicated to him, and the judge was required, under a penalty of fifty lire, to complete the matter within thirty days.—Statuta Criminalia Mediolani, e tenebris in lucem edita, Bergami, 1594, c. 1-3, 153.

It is true that, under the influence of the Inquisition, the lay courts outgrew these wholesome provisions against injustice, but meanwhile it is important to bear them in mind when considering the secrecy, the delays, and the practical denial of justice in every way which characterized the proceedings against heretics. The gradual demoralization of the secular courts under these influences was a subject of complaint. In 1329 the consuls of Béziers represented to Philippe de Valois that his judges were neglecting to take from accusers proper security to indemnify the accused in case of the failure of the prosecution, and the king promptly ordered the abuse to be corrected.—Vaissette, Éd. Privat, X. Pr. 687.

* Doctrina de modo procedendi (Martene Thesaur. V. 1805).—Molinier, L' Inquisition dans le midi de la France, pp. 186-7.

this rule was adopted by some authorities. Others contented themselves with the definition that the child must be old enough to understand the purport of an oath, while there were not wanting high authorities who reduced the age of responsibility to seven years, and those who more charitably fixed it at nine and a half for girls and ten and a half for boys. It is true that in Latin countries, where minority did not cease until the age of twenty-five, no one beneath that age had a standing in court, but this was readily evaded by appointing for him a "curator," under whose shadow he could be tortured and condemned; and when we are told that no one below the age of fourteen should be tortured, we are left to conjecture the minimum age of responsibility for heresy.*

Nor could the offender escape by absenting himself. Absence was contumacy and only increased his guilt, by adding a fresh and unpardonable offence, besides being technically tantamount to confession. In fact, before the Inquisition was thought of, the inquisitorial process was rendered absolute in ecclesiastical jurisprudence precisely to meet such cases, as when Innocent III. degraded the Bishop of Coire on evidence taken *ex parte* by his commissioners, after the bishop had repeatedly refused to appear before them; and the importance of this decision is shown by the fact that Raymond of Pennaforte embodied it in the canon law to prove that in cases of contumacy the testimony taken in an *inquisitio* was valid ground for condemnation without a *litis contestatio* or contest between the prosecution and the defence. Accordingly, when a party failed to appear, after due citation published in his parish church and proper delay, there was no hesitation in proceeding against him to conviction *in absentia*—the absence of the culprit being piously supplied by "the presence of God and the Gospels" when the sentence was rendered. Contumacious absence, in fact, was in itself enough. Frederic II. in his earliest edict, in 1220, following the Lateran Council of 1215, had declared that the suspect who

---

* Concil. Tolosan. ann. 1229 c. 10.—Concil. Biterrens. ann. 1244 c. 31.—Concil. Albiens. ann. 1254 c. 5.—Modus examinandi hæreticos (Mag. Bib. Patrum XIII. 341).—Joan. Andreæ Gloss. sup. c. 13 Sexto v. 2.— Pegnæ Comment. in Eymeric. p. 490. — Bernardi Comens. Lucerna Inquis. s. vv. *Minor*, *Torturæ* No. 33.

did not clear himself within twelve months was to be condemned
as a heretic, and this was applied to the absent, who were ordered
to be sentenced after a year's excommunication, whether anything
was proved against them or not. Enduring excommunication for
a year without seeking its removal was evidence of heresy as to
the sacraments and the power of the keys, if as to nothing else;
and some authorities were so rigid with regard to this that the
Council of Béziers denounced the punishment of heresy for all
who remained excommunicate for forty days. Even the delay of
a twelvemonth, however, was evaded, for inquisitors were instructed when citing the absent to summon them, not only to appear, but to purge themselves within a given time, and then as soon
as it had elapsed the accused was held to be convicted. Yet the
extreme penalty of relaxation was rarely enforced in such cases,
and the Inquisition contented itself generally with imprisoning for
life those against whom no offence was proved save contumacy,
unless, indeed, when caught they refused to submit and abjure.*
    As little was there any escape by death. It mattered not that
the sinner had been called to the judgment-seat of God, the faith
must be vindicated by his condemnation and the faithful be edified
by his punishment. If he had incurred only imprisonment or the
lighter penalties, his bones were simply dug up and cast out. If
his heresy had deserved the stake, they were solemnly burned. A
simulacrum of defence was allowed to heirs and descendants, on
whom were visited the heavy penalties of confiscation and personal disabilities. How unflagging was the zeal with which these
mortuary prosecutions were sometimes carried on is visible in the
case of Armanno Pongilupo of Ferrara, over whose remains war
was waged between the Bishop and the Inquisitor of Ferrara for

---

* C. 8 Extra II. 14.—Concil. Narbonn. ann. 1244 c. 19.—Concil. Biterrens.
ann. 1246 c. 8; Append. c. 14.—Guid. Fulcod. Quæst. VI.—Coll. Doat, XXI. 143.
—Eymeric. Direct. Inq. pp. 382, 495, 528-31.—Lib. Sententt. Inq. Tolosan. pp. 175,
367-74.—Zanchini Tract. de Hæret. c. ii., viii., ix.—MSS. Bib. Nat., fonds latin,
No. 14930, fol. 221.—Bernardi Comens. Lucerna Inquisit. s. vv. *Contumax, Con-
vincitur.*—Concil. Lateran. IV. ann. 1215 c. 28.—Hist. Diplom. Frid. II. T. II.
p. 4.—Concil. Albiens. ann. 1254 c. 28.—Alex. PP. IV. Bull. *Consultationi vestræ,*
28 Mai. 1260.—C. 13 Extra. v. 38 (cf. Concil. Trident. Sess. 25 de Reform. c. 3).
—Arch. de l'Inq. de Carcass. (Doat, XXXI. 83).—Bernardi Comens. Lucerna
Inquisit. s. v. *Procedere,* No. 10.

thirty-two years after his death, in 1269, ending with the triumph of the Inquisition in 1301. No prescription of time barred the Church in these matters, as the heirs and descendants of Gherardo of Florence found when, in 1313, Frà Grimaldo the inquisitor commenced a successful prosecution against their ancestor who had died prior to 1250.*

At best the inquisitorial process was a dangerous one in its conjunction of prosecutor with judge, and when it was first introduced in ecclesiastical jurisprudence careful limitations to prevent abuse were felt to be absolutely essential. The danger was doubled when the prosecuting judge was an earnest zealot bent on upholding the faith and predetermined on seeing in every prisoner before him a heretic to be convicted at any cost; nor was the danger lessened when he was merely rapacious and eager for fines and confiscations. Yet the theory of the Church was that the inquisitor was an impartial spiritual father whose functions in the salvation of souls should be fettered by no rules. All the safeguards which human experience had shown to be necessary in judicial proceedings of the most trivial character were deliberately cast aside in these cases, where life and reputation and property through three generations were involved. Every doubtful point was decided "in favor of the faith." The inquisitor, with endless iteration, was empowered and instructed to proceed summarily, to disregard forms, to permit no impediments arising from judicial rules or the wrangling of advocates, to shorten the proceedings as much as possible by depriving the accused of the ordinary facilities of defence, and by rejecting all appeals and dilatory exceptions. The validity of the result was not to be vitiated by the omission at any stage of the trial of the forms which had been devised to prevent injustice and subject the judge to responsibility.†

---

* Muratori, Antiquitat. Ital. Dissert. 60.—Zanchini Tract. de Hæret. c. xxiv., xl.—Lami, Antichità Toscane, p. 497.

† Alex. PP. IV. Bull. *Præ cunctis*, § 11, 9 Nov. 1256.—Ejusd. Bull. *Cupientes*, 10 Dec. 1257; 4 Mart. 1264.—Urbani PP. IV. Bull. *Licet ex omnibus*, 1262 (Mag. Bull. Rom. I. 122).—Ejusd. Bull. *Præ cunctis*, 2 Aug. 1264.—Clement. PP. IV. Bull. *Præ cunctis*, 23 Feb. 1266.—C. 20 Sexto v. 2.—Joan. Andreæ Gloss. sup. eod.—C. 2 Clement. v. 11.—Bernardi Guidonis Practica P. IV. (Doat, XXX.).—Eymeric. Direct. Inq. p. 583.

Had the proceedings been public, there might have been some check upon this hideous system, but the Inquisition shrouded itself in the awful mystery of secrecy until after sentence had been awarded and it was ready to impress the multitude with the fearful solemnities of the *auto de fé*. Unless proclamation were to be made for an absentee, the citation of a suspected heretic was made in secret. All knowledge of what took place after he presented himself was confined to the few discreet men selected by his judge, who were sworn to inviolable silence, and even the experts assembled to consult over his fate were subjected to similar oaths. The secrets of that dismal tribunal were guarded with the same caution, and we are told by Bernard Gui that extracts from the records were to be furnished rarely and only with the most careful discretion. Paramo, in the quaint pedantry with which he ingeniously proves that God was the first inquisitor and the condemnation of Adam and Eve the first model of the inquisitorial process, triumphantly points out that he judged them in secret, thus setting the example which the Inquisition is bound to follow, and avoiding the subtleties which the criminals would have raised in their defence, especially at the suggestion of the crafty serpent. That he called no witnesses is explained by the confession of the accused, and ample legal authority is cited to show that these confessions were sufficient to justify the conviction and punishment. If this blasphemous absurdity raises a smile, it has also its melancholy side, for it reveals to us the view which the inquisitors themselves took of their functions, assimilating themselves to God and wielding an irresponsible power which nothing short of divine wisdom could prevent from being turned by human passions into an engine of the most deadly injustice. Released from all the restraint of publicity and unrestricted by the formalities of law, the procedure of the Inquisition, as Zanghino tells us, was purely arbitrary. How the inquisitors construed their powers and what use they made of their discretion we shall have abundant opportunity of seeing hereafter.*

---

* Doctrina de modo procedendi (Martene Thesaur. V. 1811–12).—Concil. Biterrens. ann. 1246, Append. c. 16.—Arch. de l'Inq. de Carcassonne (Doat, XXVII. 156, 162, 178).—Bern. Guidon. Gravamina (Doat, XXX. 102).—Ejusd. Practica (Doat, XXIX. 94). — Eymeric. Direct. Inquis. pp. 631–33. — Jacob. Laudens. Orat. ad

The ordinary course of a trial by the Inquisition was this. A man would be reported to the inquisitor as of ill-repute for heresy, or his name would occur in the confessions of other prisoners. A secret inquisition would be made and all accessible evidence against him would be collected. He would then be secretly cited to appear at a given time, and bail taken to secure his obedience, or if he were suspected of flight, he would be suddenly arrested and confined until the tribunal was ready to give him a hearing. Legally there required to be three citations, but this was eluded by making the summons "one for three;" when the prosecution was based on common report the witnesses were called apparently at random, making a sort of drag-net, and when the mass of surmises and gossip, exaggerated and distorted by the natural fear of the witnesses, eager to save themselves from suspicion of favoring heretics, grew sufficient for action, the blow would fall. The accused was thus prejudged. He was assumed to be guilty, or he would not have been put on trial, and virtually his only mode of escape was by confessing the charges made against him, abjuring heresy, and accepting whatever punishment might be imposed on him in the shape of penance. Persistent denial of guilt and assertion of orthodoxy, when there was evidence against him, rendered him an impenitent, obstinate heretic, to be abandoned to the secular arm and consigned to the stake. The process thus was an exceedingly simple one, and is aptly summarized by an inquisitor of the fifteenth century in an argument against admitting the accused to bail. If one is caught in heresy, by his own confession, and is impenitent, he is to be delivered to the secular arm to be put to death; if penitent, he is to be thrust in prison for life, and therefore is not to be let loose on bail; if he denies, and is legitimately convicted by witnesses, he is, as an impenitent, to be delivered to the secular court to be executed.*

Concil. Constant. (Von der Hardt. III. 60).—Paramo de Orig. Offic. S. Inquis. pp. 32-33.—Zanchini Tract. de Hæret. c. ix.

* Eymeric. Direct. Inq. pp. 413, 418, 423-4, 461-5, 521-4.—Zanchini Tract. de Hæret. c. ix.—Bernardi Comens. Lucerna Inquisit. s. v. *Impœnitens.*—Albertin. Repert. Inquis. s. v. *Cautio.*

The contrast between this and the secular jurisprudence of the thirteenth century is illustrated in the charter granted by Alphonse of Poitiers to the town of Auzon (Auvergne), about 1260. Any one accused of crime by common report

Yet many reasons led the inquisitor earnestly to desire to secure confession. In numerous cases—indeed, no doubt in a majority—the evidence, while possibly justifying suspicion, was of too loose and undefined a character to justify condemnation, for every idle rumor was taken up, and any flimsy pretext which led to prosecution assumed importance when the inquisitor found himself bound to show that he had not acted unadvisedly, or when he had in prospect fines and confiscations for the benefit of the faith. Even when the evidence was sufficient, there were motives equally strong to induce the inquisitor to labor with his prisoner in the hope of leading him to withdraw his denial and throw himself upon the mercy of the tribunal. Except in the somewhat rare cases of defiant heretics, confession was always accompanied with professions of conversion and repentance. Not only thus was a soul snatched from Satan, but the new convert was bound to prove his sincerity by denouncing all whom he knew or might suspect to be heretic, thus opening fresh avenues for the extirpation of heresy.

Bernard Gui, copying an earlier inquisitor, tells us eloquently that when the external evidence was insufficient for conviction, the mind of the inquisitor was torn with anxious cares. On the one side, his conscience pained him if he punished one who was neither confessed nor convicted; but he suffered still more, knowing by constant experience the falsity and cunning and malice of these men, if he allowed them to escape through their vulpine astuteness, to the damage of the faith. In such case they were strengthened and multiplied, and rendered keener than ever, while the laity were scandalized at seeing the inefficiency of the Inquisition, baffled in its undertakings, and its most learned men played with and defied by rude and illiterate persons, for they believed the inquisitors to have all the proofs and arguments of the faith so ready at hand that no heretic could elude them or prevent their converting him. From this it is easy to see how the self-conceit of the inquisitor led him inevitably to conviction. In another passage he points out

---

could clear himself by his own oath and that of a single legal conjurator, unless there was a legitimate plaintiff or accuser; and no one could be tried by the inquisitorial process without his own consent. — Chassaing, Spicilegium Brivatense, Paris, 1886, p. 92.

how greatly profitable to the faith was the conversion of such persons, because not only were they obliged to betray their fellows and the hiding-places and conventicles of darkness, but those whom they had influenced were more ready to acknowledge their errors and seek in turn to be converted. As early as 1246 the Council of Béziers had pointed out the utility of such conversions, and had instructed the inquisitors to spare no pains in procuring them, and all subsequent authorities evidently regarded this as the first of their duties. They all agree, moreover, in holding delation of accomplices as the indispensable evidence of true conversion. Without this the repentant heretic in vain might ask for reconciliation and mercy; his refusal to betray his friends and kindred was proof that he was unrepentant, and he was forthwith handed over to the secular arm, exactly as in the Roman law a converted Manichæan who consorted with Manichæans without denouncing them to the authorities was punishable with death. How useful this was is seen in the case of Saurine Rigaud, whose confession is recorded at Toulouse in 1254, where it is followed by a list of one hundred and sixty-nine persons incriminated by her, their names being carefully tabulated with their places of residence for immediate action. How strictly, moreover, the duty of the reconciled heretic was construed is seen in the fate of Guillem Sicrède at Toulouse in 1312. He had abjured and been reconciled in 1262. Fifty years afterwards, in 1311, he had been present at the death-bed of his brother, where heretication had been performed, and he had failed to betray it, though he had vainly objected to it. When asked for his reasons, he simply said that he had not wished to injure his nephews, and for this, in 1312, he was imprisoned for life. Delation was so indispensable to the Inquisition that it was to be secured by rewards as well as by punishments. Bernard Gui tells us that those who voluntarily come forward and prove their zeal by confession and by betraying all their associates are not only to be pardoned, but their livelihood must be secured at the hands of princes and prelates; while betraying a single "perfected" heretic insured immunity and perhaps additional reward.*

---

* Bernard. Guidon. Practica P. IV., v. (Doat, XXX.).—Concil. Biterrens. ann. 1246, Append. c. 16.—Tractat. de Paup. de Lugdun. (Martene Thesaur. V. 1791-4). —Anon. Passaviens. (Mag. Bib. Pat. XIII. 308).—Const. xvi. Cod. I., v.—Molinier,

The inquisitor's anxiety to secure confession was well grounded, not only through the advantages thus secured, but to satisfy his own conscience. In ordinary crimes, a judge was usually certain that an offence had been committed before he undertook to prosecute a prisoner accused of murder or theft. In many cases, however, the inquisitor could have no assurance that there had been any crime. A man might be reasonably suspected, he might have been seen conversing with those subsequently proved to be heretics, he might have given them alms or other assistance, he might even have attended a meeting of heretics, and yet be thoroughly orthodox at heart; or he might be a bitter heretic and yet have given no outward sign. His own assertion of orthodoxy, his willingness to subscribe to the faith of Rome, went for nothing, for experience had proved that most heretics were willing to subscribe to anything, and that they had been trained by persecution to conceal their beliefs under the mask of rigid orthodoxy. Confession of heresy thus became a matter of vital importance, and no effort was deemed too great, no means too repulsive, to secure it. This became the centre of the inquisitorial process, and it is deserving of detailed consideration, not only because it formed the basis of procedure in the Holy Office, but also because of the vast and deplorable influence which it exercised for five centuries on the whole judicial system of Continental Europe.

The first and readiest means was, of course, the examination of the accused. For this the inquisitor prepared himself by collecting and studying all the adverse evidence that could be procured, while the prisoner was kept in sedulous ignorance of the charges against him. Skill in interrogation was the one pre-eminent requisite of the inquisitor, and manuals prepared by experienced brethren for the benefit of the younger officials are full of details with regard to it and of carefully prepared forms of interrogations suited for every heretical sect. Constant training developed a class of acute and subtle minds, practised to read the thoughts of the accused, skilled to lay pitfalls for the incautious, versed in every art to confuse, prompt to detect ambiguities, and quick to take advan-

---

L'Inquisition dans le midi de la France, p. 240.—Lib. Sententt. Inq. Tolosan. p. 147.—Epist. Petri Card. Alban. (Doat, XXXI. 5).—Bernard. Guidon. Gravamina (Doat, XXX. 114).

tage of hesitation or contradiction. Even in the infancy of the institution the consuls of Narbonne complained to those of Nîmes that the inquisitors, in their efforts to entrap the unwary, did not hesitate to make use of dialectics as sophistical as those with which students encountered each other in scholastic diversion. Nothing more ludicrous can well be imagined than the complaints of these veteran examiners, restricted by no rules, of the shrewd duplicity of their victims, who struggled, occasionally with success, to avoid criminating themselves, and they sought to explain it by asserting that wicked and shameless priests instructed them how to equivocate on points of faith.*

An experienced inquisitor drew up for the guidance of his successors a specimen examination of a heretic, to show them the quibbles and tergiversations for which they must be prepared when dealing with those who shrank from boldly denying their faith. Its fidelity is attested by Bernard Gui reproducing it fifty years later in his "Practica," and it is too characteristic an illustration of the encounter between the trained intellect of the inquisitor and the untutored shrewdness of the peasant struggling to save his life and his conscience, to be omitted.

"When a heretic is first brought up for examination, he assumes a confident air, as though secure in his innocence. I ask him why he has been brought before me. He replies, smiling and courteous, 'Sir, I would be glad to learn the cause from you.'

"I. 'You are accused as a heretic, and that you believe and teach otherwise than Holy Church believes.'

"A. (Raising his eyes to heaven, with an air of the greatest faith) 'Lord, thou knowest that I am innocent of this, and that I never held any faith other than that of true Christianity.'

"I. 'You call your faith Christian, for you consider ours as false and heretical. But I ask whether you have ever believed as true another faith than that which the Roman Church holds to be true?'

_____

* Bernard. Guidon. Practica P. v. (Doat, XXX.).—Modus examinandi Hæreticos (Mag. Bib. Pat. XIII. 342).—Tractat. de Paup. de Lugd. (Martene Thesaur. V. 1793-4).—MS. Vatican, No. 8668 (Ricchini, Prolog. ad Monetam, p. xxiii.).—Anon. Passav. (Mag. Bib. Pat. XIII. 301).—Molinier, L'Inq. dans le midi de la France, p. 234.—Alex. PP. IV. Bull. *Quod super nonnullis*, § 10, 15 Dec. 1258.

"A. 'I believe the true faith which the Roman Church believes, and which you openly preach to us.'

"I. 'Perhaps you have some of your sect at Rome whom you call the Roman Church. I, when I preach, say many things, some of which are common to us both, as that God liveth, and you believe some of what I preach. Nevertheless you may be a heretic in not believing other matters which are to be believed.'

"A. 'I believe all things that a Christian should believe.'

"I. 'I know your tricks. What the members of your sect believe you hold to be that which a Christian should believe. But we waste time in this fencing. Say simply, Do you believe in one God the Father, and the Son, and the Holy Ghost?'

"A. 'I believe.'

"I. 'Do you believe in Christ born of the Virgin, suffered, risen, and ascended to heaven?'

"A. (Briskly) 'I believe.'

"I. 'Do you believe the bread and wine in the mass performed by the priests to be changed into the body and blood of Christ by divine virtue?'

"A. 'Ought I not to believe this?'

"I. 'I don't ask if you ought to believe, but if you do believe.'

"A. 'I believe whatever you and other good doctors order me to believe.'

"I. 'Those good doctors are the masters of your sect; if I accord with them you believe with me; if not, not.'

"A. 'I willingly believe with you if you teach what is good to me.'

"I. 'You consider it good to you if I teach what your other masters teach. Say, then, do you believe the body of our Lord Jesus Christ to be in the altar?'

"A. (Promptly) 'I believe.'

"I. 'You know that a body is there, and that all bodies are of our Lord. I ask whether the body there is of the Lord who was born of the Virgin, hung on the cross, arose from .the dead, ascended, etc. ?'

"A. 'And you, sir, do you not believe it?'

"I. 'I believe it wholly.'

"A. 'I believe likewise.'

"I. 'You believe that I believe it, which is not what I ask, but whether you believe it.'

"A. 'If you wish to interpret all that I say otherwise than simply and plainly, then I don't know what to say. I am a simple and ignorant man. Pray don't catch me in my words.'

"I. 'If you are simple, answer simply, without evasions.'

"A. 'Willingly.'

"I. 'Will you then swear that you have never learned anything contrary to the faith which we hold to be true?'

"A. (Growing pale) 'If I ought to swear, I will willingly swear.'

"I. 'I don't ask whether you ought, but whether you will swear.'

"A. 'If you order me to swear, I will swear.'

"I. 'I don't force you to swear, because as you believe oaths to be unlawful, you will transfer the sin to me who forced you; but if you will swear, I will hear it.'

"A. 'Why should I swear if you do not order me to?'

"I. 'So that you may remove the suspicion of being a heretic.'

"A. 'Sir, I do not know how unless you teach me.'

"I. 'If I had to swear, I would raise my hand and spread my fingers and say, "So help me God, I have never learned heresy or believed what is contrary to the true faith."'

"Then trembling as if he cannot repeat the form, he will stumble along as though speaking for himself or for another, so that there is not an absolute form of oath and yet he may be thought to have sworn. If the words are there, they are so turned around that he does not swear and yet appears to have sworn. Or he converts the oath into a form of prayer, as 'God help me that I am not a heretic or the like;' and when asked whether he had sworn, he will say: 'Did you not hear me swear?' And when further hard pressed he will appeal, saying 'Sir, if I have done amiss in aught, I will willingly bear the penance, only help me to avoid the infamy of which I am accused through malice and without fault of mine.' But a vigorous inquisitor must not allow himself to be worked upon in this way, but proceed firmly till he makes these people confess their error, or at least publicly abjure heresy, so that if they are subsequently found to have sworn falsely, he can, without further hearing, abandon them to the secular arm.   If one consents to swear that he is not a heretic, I say to him, ' If you wish to swear so as to escape the stake, one oath will not suffice for me, nor ten, nor a hundred, nor a thousand, because you dispense each other for a certain number of oaths taken under necessity, but I will require a countless number.   Moreover, if I have, as I presume, adverse witnesses against you, your oaths will not save you from being burned.   You will only stain your conscience without escaping death.   But if you will simply confess your error, you may find mercy.'   Under this anxiety, I have seen some confess." *

The same inquisitor illustrates the ease with which the cunning of these simple folk fenced and played with the best-trained men of the Holy Office by a case in which he saw a serving-wench elude the questions of picked examiners for several days together, and she would have escaped had there not by chance been found in her chest the fragment of a bone of a heretic recently burned, which she had preserved as a relic, according to one of her companions who had collected the bones with her.   But the inquisitor does not tell us how many thousand good Catholics, confused by the awful game which they were playing, mystified with the intricacies of scholastic theology, ignorant how to answer the dangerous questions put to them so searchingly, and terrified with the threats of burning for persistent denial, despairingly confessed the crime of which they were so confidently assumed to be guilty, and ratified their conversion by inventing tales about their neighbors, while expiating the wrong by suffering confiscation and lifelong imprisonment.

Yet the inquisitor was frequently baffled in this intellectual digladiation by the innocence or astuteness of the accused.   His resources, however, were by no means exhausted, and here we approach one of the darkest and most repulsive aspects of our theme. Human inconsistency, in its manifold development, has never exhibited itself in more deplorable fashion than in the instructions on this subject transmitted to their younger brethren by the veterans of the Holy Office—instructions intended for none but official eyes, and therefore framed with the utmost unreserve.   Trained through long experience in an accurate knowledge of all that can move

---

* Tract. de Paup. de Lugduno (Martene Thes. V. 1792).—Cf. Bernard. Guidon. Practica P. v. (Doat, XXX.).

the human breast; skilled not only to detect the subtle evasions of the intellect, but to seek and find the tenderest point through which to assail the conscience and the heart; relentless in inflicting agony on body and brain, whether through the mouldering wretchedness of the hopeless dungeon protracted through uncounted years, the sharper pain of the torture-chamber, or by coldly playing on the affections; using without scruple the most violent alternatives of hope and fear; employing with cynical openness every resource of guile and fraud on wretches purposely starved to render them incapable of self-defence, the counsels which these men utter might well seem the promptings of fiends exulting in the unlimited power to wreak their evil passions on helpless mortals. Yet through all this there shines the evident conviction that they are doing the work of God. No labor is too great if they can win a soul from perdition; no toil too repulsive if they can bring a fellow-creature to an acknowledgment of his wrongdoing and a genuine repentance that will wipe out his sins; no patience too prolonged if it will avoid the unjust conviction of the innocent. All the cunning fence between judge and culprit, all the fraud, all the torture of body and mind so ruthlessly employed to extort unwilling confessions, were not necessarily used for the mere purpose of securing a victim, for the inquisitor was taught to be as earnest with the recalcitrants against whom he had sufficient testimony as with the cases in which evidence was deficient. With the former he was seeking to save a soul from immolating itself in the pride of obstinacy; with the latter he was laboring to preserve the sheep by not liberating an infected one to spread pestilence among the flock. It mattered little to the victim what were the motives actuating his persecutor, for conscientious cruelty is apt to be more cold-blooded and calculating, more relentless and effective, than passionate wrath, but the impartial student must needs recognize that while many inquisitors were doubtless dullards who followed unthinkingly a prescribed routine as a vocation, and others were covetous or sanguinary tyrants actuated only by self-interest or ambition, yet among them were not a few who believed themselves to be discharging a high and holy duty, whether they abandoned the impenitent to the flames, or by methods of unspeakable baseness rescued from Satan a soul which he had reckoned as his own. They were instructed that

it was better to let the guilty escape than to condemn the innocent, and, therefore, that they must have either clear proofs or
confession. In the absence of absolute evidence, therefore, the
very conscientiousness of the judge, under such a system, led him
to resort to any means to satisfy himself by wringing an acknowledgment from his victim.* The resources for procuring unwilling confession, at command
of the inquisitor, may be roughly divided into two classes—deceit
and torture, the latter comprehending both mental and physical
pain, however administered. Both classes were resorted to freely
and without scruple, and there was ample variety to suit the idio-
syncrasies of all judges and prisoners.

Perhaps the mildest form of the devices to entrap an unwary
prisoner was the recommendation that the examiner should always assume the fact of which he was in quest and ask about the
details, as, for instance, "How often have you confessed as a
heretic?" "In what chamber of yours did they lie?" Going a
step further, the inquisitor is advised during the examination to
turn over the pages of evidence as though referring to it, and then
boldly inform the prisoner that he is not telling the truth, for
it is thus and thus; or to pick up a paper and pretend to read
from it whatever is necessary to deceive him; or he can be told
circumstantially that some of the masters of the sect have incriminated him in their revelations. To render these devices
more effective, the jailer was instructed to worm himself into the
confidence of the prisoners, with feigned interest and compassion,
and urge them to confess at once, because the inquisitor is a merciful man who will take pity on them. Then the inquisitor was to
pretend that he had conclusive evidence, and that if the accused
would confess and point out those who had led him astray, he
should be allowed to go home forthwith, with any other blandishments likely to prove effective. A more elaborate trap was that
of treating the prisoner with kindness in place of rigor; sending
trusty agents to his cell to gain his confidence, and then urge him
to confess, with promises of mercy and that they would intercede
for him. When everything was ripe, the inquisitor himself would
appear and confirm these promises, with the mental reservation

---

* Practica super Inquisitione (MSS. Bib. Nat., fonds latin, No. 14930, fol. 221).

that all which is done for the conversion of heretics is merciful, that penances are mercies and spiritual remedies, so that when the unlucky wretch was prevailed upon to ask for mercy in return for his revelations, he was to be led on with the general expression that more would be done for him than he asked.*

That spies should play a prominent part in such a system was inevitable. The trusty agents who were admitted to the prisoner's cell were instructed to lead him gradually on from one confession to another until they should gain sufficient evidence to incriminate him, without his realizing it. Converted heretics, we are told, were very useful in this business. One would be sent to visit him and say that he had only pretended conversion through fear, and after repeated visits overstay his time and be locked up. Confidential talk would follow in the darkness, while witnesses with a notary were crouching within earshot to take down all that might fall from the lips of the unconscious victim. Fellow-prisoners were utilized whenever possible, and were duly rewarded for treachery. In the sentence of a Carmelite monk, January 17, 1329, guilty of the most infamous sorceries, it is recorded in extenuation of his black catalogue of guilt, that while in prison with sundry heretics he had aided greatly in making them confess and had revealed many important matters which they had confided to him, from which the Inquisition had derived great advantage and hoped to gain more. †

These artifices were diversified with appeals to force. The heretic, whether acknowledged or suspected, had no rights. His body was at the mercy of the Church, and if through tribulation of the flesh he could be led to see the error of his ways, there was no hesitation in employing whatever means were readiest to save his soul and advance the faith. Among the miracles for which St. Francis was canonized it is related that a certain Pietro of Assisi was captured in Rome on an accusation of heresy, and confided for conversion to the Bishop of Todi, who loaded him with chains and fed him on measured quantities of bread and water in a dark dungeon. Thus brought through suffering to repentance, on the

---

* Tract. de Paup. de Lugduno (Martene Thesaur. V. 1793).—Eymeric. Direct. Inq. pp. 433–4.—Modus examinandi Hæreticos (Mag. Bib. Pat. XIII. 341).

† Tract. de Paup. de Lugduno (Martene Thesaur. V. 1787–88).—Eymeric. p. 434.—Archives de l'Inq. de Carcass. (Doat, XXVII. 150).

vigil of St. Francis he invoked the saint for help with passionate tears. Moved by his zeal, St. Francis appeared to him and ordered him forth. His chains fell off and the doors flew open, but the poor wretch was so crazed by the sudden answer to his prayer that he clung to the doorpost with cries which brought the jailers running to him. The pious bishop hastened to the prison, and reverently acknowledging the power of God, sent the shivered fetters to the pope in token of the miracle. Even more illustrative and better authenticated is a case related with much gratulation by Nider as occurring when he was teaching in the University of Vienna. A heretic priest, thrown into prison by his bishop, proved obstinate, and the most eminent theologians who labored for his conversion found him their match in disputation. Believing that vexation brings understanding, they at length ordered him to be bound tightly to a pillar. The cords eating into the swelling flesh caused such exquisite torture that when they visited him the next day he begged piteously to be taken out and burned. Coldly refusing, they left him for another twenty-four hours, by which time physical pain and exhaustion had broken his spirit. He humbly recanted, retired to a Paulite monastery, and lived an exemplary life.*

It will readily be believed that there was scant hesitation in employing any methods likely to crush the obduracy of the prisoner who refused the confession and recantation demanded of him. If he were likely to be reached through the affections, his wife and children were admitted to his cell in hopes that their tears and pleadings might work on his feelings and overcome his convictions. Alternate threats and blandishments were tried; he would be removed from his foul and dismal dungeon to commodious quarters, with liberal diet and a show of kindness, to see if his resolution would be weakened by alternations of hope and despair. Master of the art of playing upon the human heart, the trained inquisitor left no method untried which promised victory in the struggle between him and the helpless wretch abandoned to his experiments. Among these, one of the most efficient was the slow torture of delay. The prisoner who refused to confess, or whose confession was deemed imperfect, was remanded to his cell, and left to pon-

---

* Wadding. Annal. ann. 1228, No. 45.—Nideri Formicar. Lib. III. c. 10.

der in solitude and darkness. Except in rare cases time was no object with the Inquisition, and it could afford to wait. Perhaps in a few weeks his resolution might break down, and he might ask to be heard. If not, six months might elapse before he was again called up for hearing. If still obstinate he would be again sent back. Months would lengthen into years, perhaps years into decades, and find him still unconvicted and still a prisoner, hopeless and despairing. Should friendly death not intervene, the terrible patience of the Inquisition was nearly certain to triumph in the end, and the authorities all agree upon the effectiveness of delay. This explains what otherwise would be hard to understand—the immense protraction of so many of the inquisitorial trials whose records have reached us. Three, five, or ten years are common enough as intervals between the first audience of a prisoner and his final conviction, nor are instances wanting of even greater delays. Bernalde, wife of Guillem de Montaigu, was imprisoned at Toulouse in 1297, and made a confession the same year, yet she was not formally sentenced to imprisonment until the *auto* of 1310. I have already alluded to the case of Guillem Garric, brought to confess at Carcassonne in 1321 after a detention of nearly thirty years. In the *auto de fé* of 1319, at Toulouse, Guillem Salavert was sentenced, who had made an unsatisfactory confession in 1299 and another in 1316; to the latter he had unwaveringly adhered, and at last Bernard Gui, overcome by his obstinacy, let him off with the penance of wearing crosses, in consideration of his twenty years' imprisonment without conviction. At the same *auto* were sentenced six wretches who had recently died in prison, two of whom had made their first confession in 1305, one in 1306, two in 1311, and one in 1315. Nor was this hideous torture of suspense peculiar to any special tribunal. Guillem Salavert was one of those implicated in the troubles of Albi in 1299, when many of the accused were speedily tried and sentenced by the bishop, Bernard de Castenet, and Nicholas d'Abbeville, inquisitor of Carcassonne, but some were reserved for the harder fate of detention without trial. The intervention of the pope was sought, and in 1310 Clement V. wrote to the bishop and the inquisitor, giving the names of ten of them, including some of the most respectable citizens of Albi, who had lain for eight years or more in jail awaiting judgment, many of them in

chains and all in narrow, dark cells. His order for their immediate trial was disobeyed, and in a subsequent letter he speaks of
several of them having died before his previous epistle, and reiterated his command for the prompt disposal of the survivors. The
Inquisition was a law unto itself, however, and again his mandate
was disregarded. In 1319, besides Guillem Salavert, two others,
Guillem Calverie and Isarn Colli, were brought from their dungeon
and retracted their confessions which had been extorted from
them by torture. Calverie figured with Salavert in the *auto* of
Toulouse in the same year. When Colli was sentenced we do not
know, but in the accounts of Arnaud Assalit, royal steward of
confiscations, for 1322–3, there appears the property of " Isarnus
Colli condemnatus," showing his ultimate fate. In the *auto* of
1319, moreover, occur the names of two citizens of Cordes, Durand
Boissa and Bernard Ouvrier (then deceased), whose confessions
date respectively from 1301 and 1300, doubtless belonging to the
same unfortunate group, who had eaten their hearts in despair
and misery for a score of years.*

When it was desired to hasten this slow torture, the object was
easily accomplished by rendering the imprisonment unendurably
harsh. As we shall see hereafter, the dungeons of the Inquisition
at best were abodes of fearful misery, but when there was reason
for increasing their terrors there was no difficulty in increasing
the hardships. The " *durus carcer et arcta vita* " — chains and
starvation in a stifling hole—was a favorite device for extracting
confession from unwilling lips. We shall meet hereafter an atrocious instance of this inflicted on a witness, as early as 1263,
when the ruin of the great house of Foix was sought. It was
pointed out that judicious restriction of diet not only reduced the
body but weakened the will, and rendered the prisoner less able

---

* Eymeric. Direct. Inquis. 514, 521.—Concil. Biterrens. ann. 1246, Append. c.
17.—Innoc. PP. IV. Bull. *Illius vicis*, 12 Nov. 1247.—Lib. Confess. Inq. Albiens.
(MSS. Bib. Nat., fonds latin, 11847).—Bernard. Guidon. Practica P. v. (Doat,
XXX.).—Doctrina de modo procedendi (Martene Thesaur. V. 1795).—Molinier,
l'Inq. dans le midi de la France, p. 330.—Archives de l'Inq. de Carcass. (Doat,
XXVII. 7 sqq.).—Lib. Sententt. Inq. Tolosan. pp. 22, 76, 102, 118–50, 158–62,
184, 216–18, 220–1, 228, 244–8, 266–7, 282–5.—Archives de l'Inq. de Carcassonne
(Doat, XXXIV. 89).—Archives de l'hôtel-de-ville d'Albi (Doat, XXXIV. 45).—
Coll. Doat, XXXIV. 189.

to resist alternate threats of death and promises of mercy. Starvation, in fact, was reckoned as one of the regular and most efficient methods to subdue unwilling witnesses and defendants. In 1306 Clement V. declared, after an official investigation, that at Carcassonne prisoners were habitually constrained to confession by the harshness of the prison, the lack of beds, and the deficiency of food, as well as by torture.*

With all these resources at their command, it might seem superfluous for inquisitors to have recourse to the vulgar and ruder implements of the torture-chamber. The rack and strappado, in fact, were in such violent antagonism, not only with the principles of Christianity, but with the practices of the Church, that their use by the Inquisition, as a means of furthering the faith, is one of the saddest anomalies of that dismal period. I have elsewhere shown how consistently the Church opposed the use of torture, so that, in the barbarism of the twelfth century, Gratian lays it down as an accepted rule of the canon law that no confession is to be extorted by torment. Torture, moreover, except among the Wisigoths, had been unknown among the barbarians who founded the commonwealths of Europe, and their system of jurisprudence had grown up free from its contamination. It was not until the study of the revived Roman law, and the prohibition of ordeals by the Lateran Council of 1215, which was gradually enforced during the first half of the thirteenth century, that jurists began to feel the need of torture and accustom themselves to the idea of its introduction. The earliest instances with which I have met occur in the Veronese Code of 1228 and the Sicilian Constitutions of Frederic II. in 1231, and in both of these the references to it show how sparingly and hesitatingly it was employed. Even Frederic, in his ruthless edicts, from 1220 to 1239, makes no allusion to it, but, in accordance with the Verona decree of Lucius III., prescribes the recognized form of canonical purgation for the trial of all suspected heretics. Yet it rapidly won its way in Italy, and when Innocent IV., in 1252, published his bull *Ad extirpanda*, he adopted it, and authorized its use for the discovery of

---

* Archives de l'Inq. de Carcassonne (Doat, XXXI. 57).—Vaissette, III. Pr. 551–3.—Tract. de Paup. de Lugd. (Martene Thesaur. V. 1787).—Joann. Andreæ Gloss. sup. c. 1, Clement. v. 3.—Bernard. Guidon. Practica P. v. (Doat. XXX.). —Arch. de l'Inq. de Carcassonne (Doat, XXXIV. 45).

heresy. A decent respect for the old-time prejudices of the Church, however, forbade him to allow its administration by the inquisitors themselves or their servitors. It was the secular authorities who were ordered to force all captured heretics to confess and accuse their accomplices, by torture which should not imperil life or injure limb, "just as thieves and robbers are forced to confess their crimes and accuse their accomplices." The unrepealed canons of the Church, in fact, prohibited all ecclesiastics from being concerned in such acts, and even from being present where torture was administered, so that the inquisitor whose zeal should lead him to take part in it was thereby rendered "irregular" and unfit for sacred functions until he could be "dispensed" or purified. This did not suit the policy of the institution. Possibly outside of Italy, where torture was as yet virtually unknown, it found difficulty in securing the co-operation of the public officials; everywhere it complained that this cumbrous mode of administration interfered with the profound secrecy which was an essential characteristic of its operations. But four years after the bull of Innocent IV., Alexander IV., in 1256, removed the difficulty with characteristic indirection by authorizing inquisitors and their associates to absolve each other, and mutually grant dispensations for irregularities—a permission which was repeatedly reiterated, and which was held to remove all impediment to the use of torture under the direct supervision of the inquisitor and his ministers. In Naples, where the Inquisition was but slenderly organized, we find the public officials used by it as torturers until the end of the century, but elsewhere it speedily arrogated the administration of torment to its own officials. Even in Naples, however, Frà Tomaso d'Aversa is seen, in 1305, personally inflicting the most brutal tortures on the Spiritual Franciscans; and when he found it impossible in this manner to make them convict themselves, he employed the ingenious expedient of starving for a few days one of the younger brethren, and then giving him strong wine to drink; when the poor wretch was fuddled there was no difficulty in getting him to admit that he and his twoscore comrades were all heretics.*

---

* Superstition and Force, 3d Ed. 1878, pp. 419-20. — Lib. Jur. Civ. Veronæ, ann. 1228, c. 75. — Constit. Sicular. Lib. I. Tit. 27.—Frid. II. Edict. 1220, § 5. —

Torture saved the trouble and expense of prolonged imprison‑ ment; it was a speedy and effective method of obtaining what revelations might be desired, and it grew rapidly in favor with the Inquisition, while its extension throughout secular jurispru‑ dence was remarkably slow. In 1260 the charter granted by Al‑ phonse of Poitiers to the town of Auzon specially exempts the accused from torture, no matter what the crime involved. This shows that its use was gradually spreading, and already, in 1291, Philippe le Bel felt himself called upon to restrain its abuses; in letters to the seneschal of Carcassonne he alludes to the newly-in‑ troduced methods of torture in the Inquisition, whereby the inno‑ cent were convicted and scandal and desolation pervaded the land. He could not interfere with the internal management of the Holy Office, but he sought a corrective in forbidding indiscriminate ar‑ rests at the sole bidding of the inquisitors. As might be expected, this was only a palliative; callous indifference to human suffering grows by habit, and the misuse of this terrible method of coercion continued to increase. When the despairing cry of the population induced Clement V. to order an investigation into the iniquities of the Inquisition of Carcassonne, the commission issued to the cardinals sent thither in 1306 recites that confessions were extort‑ ed by torture so severe that the unfortunates subjected to it had only the alternative of death; and in the proceedings before the commissioners the use of torture is so frequently alluded to as to leave no doubt of its habitual employment. It is a noteworthy fact, however, that in the fragmentary documents of inquisitorial proceedings which have reached us the references to torture are singularly few. Apparently it was felt that to record its use

---

Innoc. PP. IV. Bull. *Ad extirpanda*, § 26.—Concil. Autissiodor. ann. 578 c. 33.— Concil. Matiscon. II. ann. 585 c. 19. — Alex. PP. IV. Bull. *Ut negotium*, 7 Julii, 1256 (Doat, XXXI. 196) ; Ejusd. Bull. *Ne inquisitionis*, 19 Apr. 1259. — Urban. PP. IV. Bull. *Ut negotium*, 1260, 1262 (Ripoll, I. 430; Mag. Bull. Rom. I. 132).— Clement. PP. IV. Bull. *Ne inquisitionis*, 13 Jan. 1266. — Bern. Guidon. Pract. P. IV. (Doat. XXX.). — Pegnæ Comment. in Eymeric. p. 593. — Archivio di Napoli, MSS. Chioccarello, T. VIII.—Historia Tribulationum (Archiv für Litt. u. Kirch‑ engeschichte, 1886, p. 324).

The earliest allusion to the use of torture in Languedoc is in 1254, when St. Louis forbade its use on the testimony of a single witness, even in the case of poor persons.—Vaissette, Éd. Privat, VIII. 1348.

would in some sort invalidate the force of the testimony. Thus, in the cases of Isarn Colli and Guillem Calverie, mentioned above, it happens to be stated that they retracted their confessions made under torture, but in the confessions themselves there is nothing to indicate that it had been used. In the six hundred and thirty-six sentences borne upon the register of Toulouse from 1309 to 1323 the only allusion to torture is in the recital of the case of Calverie, but there are numerous instances in which the information wrung from the convicts who had no hope of escape could scarce have been procured in any other manner. Bernard Gui, who conducted the Inquisition of Toulouse during this period, has too emphatically expressed his sense of the utility of torture on both principals and witnesses for us to doubt his readiness in its employment.*

The result of Clement's investigation in 1306 led to an effort at reform which was agreed to in the Council of Vienne in 1311, but with customary indecision Clement delayed the publication of the considerable body of legislation adopted by the council until his death, and it was not issued till October, 1317, by his successor John XXII. Among the abuses which he sought to limit was that of torture, and to this end he ordered that it should not be administered without the concurrent action of bishop and inquisitor if this could be had within the space of eight days. Bernard Gui emphatically remonstrated against this as seriously crippling the efficiency of the Inquisition, and he proposed to substitute for it the meaningless phrase that torture should only be used with mature and careful deliberation, but his suggestion was unheeded, and the Clementine regulation remained the law of the Church.†

The inquisitors, however, were too little accustomed to restraint in any form to submit long to this infringement on their privileges. It is true that disobedience rendered the proceedings void, and the unhappy wretch who was unlawfully tortured without episcopal

---

* Chassaing, Spicilegium Brivatense, p. 92. — Vaissette, IV. Pr. 97-8. — Archives de l'hôtel-de-ville d'Albi (Doat, XXXIV. 45 sqq.). — Lib. Confess. Inq. Albiens. (MSS. Bib. Nat., fonds latin, 11847).—Lib. Sententt. Inq. Tolosan. pp. 46-78, 132, 169-74, 180-2, 266-7. — Bern. Guidon. Practica P. IV. v. (Doat, XXX.).

† C. 1, § 1, Clement. v. 3.—Bern. Guidon. Gravamina (Doat, XXX. 100, 120). —Eymeric. Direct. Inq. p. 422.—Zanchini Tract. de Hæret. c. xv

consultation could appeal to the pope, but this did not undo the work; Rome was distant, and the victims of the Inquisition for the most part were too friendless and too helpless to protect themselves in such illusory fashion. In Bernard Gui's " Practica," written probably about 1328 or 1330, he only speaks of consultation with experts, making no allusions to bishops; Eymerich adheres to the Clementines, but his instructions as to what is to be done in case of their disregard shows how frequent was such action; while Zanghino boldly affirms that the canon is to be construed as permitting torture by either bishop or inquisitor. In some proceedings against the Waldenses of Piedmont in 1387, if the accused did not confess freely on a first examination an entry was made that the inquisitor was not content, and twenty-four hours were given the prisoner to amend his statements; he would be tortured and brought back next morning in a more complying frame of mind, when a careful record would be made that his confession was without torture and aloof from the torture-chamber. Cunning casuists, moreover, discovered that Clement had only spoken of torture in general and had not specifically alluded to witnesses, whence they concluded that one of the most shocking abuses of the system, the torture of witnesses, was left to the sole discretion of the inquisitor, and this became the accepted rule. It only required an additional step to show that after the accused had been convicted by evidence or had confessed as to himself, he became a witness as to the guilt of his friends and thus could be arbitrarily tortured to betray them. Even when the Clementines were observed, the limit of eight days enabled the inquisitor to proceed independently after waiting for that length of time.*

While witnesses who were supposed to be concealing the truth

---

* Eymeric. Direct. Inq. pp. 453-5.—Bern. Guidon. Practica P. v. (Doat, XXX.). —Zanchini Tract. de Hæret. c. ix., xiv.—Processus contra Waldenses (Archivio Storico Italiano, No. 38, pp. 20, 22, 24, etc.).—Pauli de Leazariis Gloss. sup. c. 1, Clem. v. 3.—Silvest. Prieriat. de Strigimagar. Mirand. Lib. iii. c. 1.—Bernard. Comens. Lucerna Inquisit. s. vv. *Jejunia, Torturæ.*

That the Clementines had practically fallen into desuetude is shown by Carlo III. of Savoy, in 1506, procuring from Julius II. as a special privilege that in his territories the inquisitors should not send to prison or pronounce sentence without the concurrence of the episcopal ordinaries, and this was enlarged in 1515 by Leo X. by requiring their assent for all arrests.—Sclopis, Antica Legislazione del Piemont, p. 484.

could be tortured as a matter of course, there was some discussion among jurists as to the amount of adverse evidence that would justify placing the accused on the rack. Unless there was some colorable reason to believe that the crime of heresy had been committed, evidently there was no excuse for the employment of such means of investigation. Eymerich tells us that when there are two incriminating witnesses, a man of good reputation can be tortured to ascertain the truth, while if he is of evil repute he can be condemned without it or can be tortured on the evidence of a single witness. Zanghino, on the other hand, asserts that the evidence of a single witness of good character is sufficient for the authorization of torture, without distinction of persons, while Bernardo di Como says that common report is enough. In time elaborate instructions were drawn up for the guidance of inquisitors in this matter, but their uselessness was confessed in the admission that, after all, the decision was to be left to the discretion of the judge. How little sufficed to justify the exercise of this discretion is seen when jurists held it to be sufficient if the accused, on examination, was frightened and stammered and varied in his answers, without any external evidence against him.*

In the administration of torture the rules adopted by the Inquisition became those of the secular courts of Christendom at large, and therefore are worth brief attention. Eymerich, whose instructions on the subject are the fullest we have, admits the grave difficulties which surrounded the question, and the notorious uncertainty of the result. Torture should be moderate, and effusion of blood be scrupulously avoided, but then, what was moderation? Some prisoners were so weak that at the first turn of the pulleys they would concede anything asked them; others so obstinate that they would endure all things rather than confess the truth. Those who had previously undergone the experience might be either the stronger or the weaker for it, for with some the arms were hardened, while with others they were permanently weakened. In short, the discretion of the judge was the only rule.

Both bishop and inquisitor ought rightfully to be present. The prisoner was shown the implements of torment and urged to con-

---

* Eymeric. pp. 480, 592, 614. — Zanchini Tract. de Hæret. c. ix. — Bernardi Comens. Lucerna Inquis. s. vv. *Indicium, Torturæ* No. 19, 25.

fess. On his refusal he was stripped and bound by the executioners and again entreated to speak, with promises of mercy in all cases in which mercy could be shown. This frequently produced the desired result, and we may be assured that the efficacy of torture lay not so much in what was extracted by its use as in the innumerable cases in which its dread, near or remote, paralyzed the resolution with agonizing expectations. If this proved ineffectual, the torture was applied with gradually increased severity. In the case of continued obstinacy additional implements of torment were exhibited and the sufferer was told that he would be subjected to them all in turn. If still undaunted, he was unbound, and the next or third day was appointed for renewal of the infliction. According to rule, torture could be applied but once, but this, like all other rules for the protection of the accused, was easily eluded. It was only necessary to order, not a repetition, but a "continuance" of the torture, and no matter how long the interval, the holy casuists were able to continue it indefinitely; or a further excuse would be found in alleging that additional evidence had been discovered, which required a second torturing to purge it away. During the interval fresh solicitations were made to elicit confession, and these being unavailing, the accused was again subjected to torment either of the same kind as before or to others likely to prove more efficacious. If he remained silent after torture, deemed sufficient by his judges, some authorities say that he should be discharged and that a declaration was to be given him that nothing had been proved against him; others, however, order that he should be remanded to prison and be kept there. The trial of Bernard Délicieux, in 1319, reveals another device to elude the prohibition of repeated torture, for the examiners could at any moment order the torture to satisfy their curiosity about a single point, and thus could go on indefinitely with others.

Any confession made under torture required to be confirmed after removal from the torture-chamber. Usually the procedure appears to be that the torture was continued until the accused signified his readiness to confess, when he was unbound and carried into another room where his confession was made. If, however, the confession was extracted during the torture, it was read over subsequently to the prisoner and he was asked if it were true: there was, indeed, a rule that there should be an interval of twenty-four hours between the torture and the confession, or its confirmation, but this was commonly disregarded. Silence indicated assent, and the length of silence to be allowed for was, as usual, left to the discretion of the judge, with warning to consider the condition of the prisoner, whether young or old, male or female, simple or learned. In any case the record was carefully made that the confession was free and spontaneous, without the pressure of force or fear. If the confession was retracted, the accused could be taken back for a continuance of the torture—not, as we are carefully told, for a repetition—provided always that he had not been "sufficiently" tortured before.*

The question as to the retraction of confession was one which exercised to no small degree the inquisitorial jurists, and practice was not wholly uniform. It placed the inquisitor in a disagreeable position, and, in view of the methods adopted to secure confession, it was so likely to occur that naturally stringent measures were adopted to prevent it. Some authorities draw a distinction between confessions made "spontaneously" and those extorted by torture or its threat, but in practice the difference was disregarded. The most merciful view taken of revocation is that of Eymerich, who says that if the torture had been sufficient, the accused who persistently revokes is entitled to a discharge. In this Eymerich is alone. Some authorities recommend that the accused be forced to withdraw his revocation by repetition of torture. Others content themselves with regarding it as impeding the Inquisition, and as such including it in the excommunication regularly published by parish priests and at the opening of every *auto de fé*, and this excommunication included notaries who might wickedly aid in drawing up such revocations. The general presumption of law, how-

---

* Eymeric. Direct. Inq. pp. 480-2.—MSS. Bib. Nat., fonds latin, No. 4270, fol. 101, 146.—Responsa prudentum (Doat, XXXVII. 83 sqq.).—Bernardi Comens. Lucerna Inquis. s. vv. *Confessio, Torturæ.*

The care with which the inquisitors concealed the means by which confessions were procured is illustrated in the ratification obtained from Guillem Salavert in 1303, of his confession made three years before. He is made to declare it "esse veram, non factam vi tormentorum, amore, gratia, odio, timore, vel favore alicujus, non subornatus nec inductus minis vel blanditiis, seu seductus per aliquem, non amens nec stultus sed bona mente," etc. (MSS. Bib. Nat., fonds latin, No. 11847). Yet Salavert belonged to a group of victims on whom, as we shall see hereafter, torture was unsparingly used.

ever, was that the confession was true and the retraction a perjury, and the view taken of such cases was that the retraction proved the accused to be an impenitent heretic, who had relapsed after confession and asking for penance. As such there was nothing to be done with him but to hand him over to the secular arm for punishment without a hearing. It is true, that in the case of Guillem Calverie, thus condemned in 1319 by Bernard Gui for withdrawing his confession, the culprit was mercifully allowed fifteen days in which to revoke his revocation, but this was a mere exercise of the discretion customarily lodged with the inquisitor. How strictly the rule was construed which regarded revocation as relapse is seen in the remark of Zanghino, that if a man had confessed and abjured and been set free under penance, and if he subsequently remarked in public that he had confessed under fear of expense or to avoid heavier punishment, he was to be regarded as an impenitent heretic, liable to be burned as a relapsed. We shall see hereafter the full significance of this point in its application to the Templars. There was an additional question of some nicety which arose when the retracted confession incriminated others besides the accused; in this case the most merciful view taken was that, if it was not to be held good against them, the one who confessed was liable to punishment for false-witness. As no confession was sufficient which did not reveal the names of partners in guilt, those inquisitors who did not regard revocation as relapse could at least imprison the accused for life as a false witness.*

The inquisitorial process as thus perfected was sure of its victim. No one whom a judge wished to condemn could escape. The form in which it became naturalized in secular jurisprudence was less arbitrary and effective, yet Sir John Fortescue, the chancellor of Henry VI., who in his exile had ample opportunity to observe its working, declares that it placed every man's life or limb at the mercy of any enemy who could suborn two unknown witnesses to swear against him.†

---

* Eymeric. Direct. Inquis. p. 481.—Bernardi Comens. Lucerna Inquis. s. vv. *Confessio, Impœnitens, Torturæ* No. 48.—Responsa prudentum (Doat, XXXVII. 83 sqq.).—Arch. de l'Inq. de Carcass. (Doat, XXVII. 126; XXXII. 251).—Lib. Sententt. Inq. Tolosan. pp. 266–7.—Zanchini Tract. de Hæret. c. xxiii.

† Fortescue de Laudibus Legum Angliæ, c. xxvii.

CHAPTER IV.

WE have seen in the foregoing chapter the inevitable tendency of the inquisitorial process to assume the character of a duel between the judge and the accused with the former as the assailant. This deplorable result was the necessary outcome of the system and of the task imposed upon the inquisitor. He was required to penetrate the inscrutable heart of man, and professional pride perhaps contributed as much as zeal for the faith in stimulating him to prove that he was not to be baffled by the unfortunates brought before him in judgment.

In such a struggle as this the testimony of witnesses, for the most part, counted for little except as a basis for arrest and prosecution, and for threatening the accused with the unknown mass of evidence against him, and for this the slightest breath of scandal, even from a single person notoriously foul-mouthed, sufficed, without calling witnesses.* The real battlefield was the prisoner's conscience, and his confession the prize of victory. Yet the subject of evidence as treated by the Inquisition is not wholly to be passed over, for it affords fresh illustration of the manner in which the practice of construing everything "in favor of the faith" led to the development of the worst body of jurisprudence invented by man, and to the habitual perpetration of the foulest injustice. The matter-of-course way in which rules destructive of every principle of fairness are laid down by men presumably correct in the ordinary affairs of life affords a wholesome lesson as to the power of fanaticism to warp the intellect of the most acute.

This did not arise from any peculiar laxity of practice in the ordinary ecclesiastical courts. Their procedure, based upon the civil law, accepted and enforced its rules as to the admission of

---

* Bernardi Comens. Lucerna Inquisit. s. vv. *Infamia, Inquisitores* No. 7.

evidence, and the onus of proof lay upon the assertor of a fact. Innocent III., in his instructions as to the Cathari of La Charité, reminded the local authorities that even violent presumptions were not proof, and were insufficient for condemnation in a matter so heinous—a rule which was embodied in the canon law, where it became for the inquisitors merely an excuse for obtaining certitude by extorting confession. How completely they felt themselves emancipated from all wholesome restraint is shown by the remarks of Bernard Gui—" The accused are not to be condemned unless they confess or are convicted by witnesses, though not according to the ordinary laws, as in other crimes, but according to the private laws or privileges conceded to the inquisitors by the Holy See, for there is much that is peculiar to the Inquisition." *

From almost the inception of the Holy Office there was an effort to lay down rules as to what constituted evidence of heresy; but the Council of Narbonne, in 1244, winds up an enumeration of the various indications by saying that it is sufficient if the accused can be shown to have manifested by any word or sign that he had faith or belief in heretics or considered them to be "good men" (bos homes). The kind of testimony received was as flimsy and impalpable as the facts, or supposed facts, sought to be proved. In the voluminous examinations and depositions which have reached us from the archives of the Inquisition we find the witnesses allowed and encouraged to say everything that may occur to them. Great weight was attached to popular report or belief, and to ascertain this the opinion of the witness was freely received, whether based on knowledge or prejudice, hearsay evidence, vague rumors, general impressions, or idle gossip. Everything, in fact, that could affect the accused injuriously was eagerly sought and scrupulously written down. In the determined effort to ruin the seigneurs de Niort, in 1240, of the one hundred and eight witnesses examined scarce one was able to speak of his own knowledge as to any act of the accused. In 1254 Arnaud Baud of Montréal was qualified as "suspect" of heresy because he continued to visit his mother and aided her in her need after she had been hereticated, though there was absolutely nothing else against him; only delivering her

---

* Fournier, Les officialités an moyen âge, pp. 177-8.—C. 14 Extra ii. 23.— Bern. Guidon. Practica P. iv. (Doat, XXX.).

up to be burned would have cleared him. It became, in fact, a settled principle of law that either husband or wife knowing the other to be a heretic and not giving information within a twelve-month was held to be a consenting party without further evidence, and was punishable as a heretic.*

Naturally the conscientious inquisitor recognized the vicious circle in which he moved and sought to satisfy himself that he could designate infallible signs which would justify the conclusion of heresy. There is ample store of such enumerated. Thus for the Cathari it sufficed to show that the accused had venerated one of the perfected, had asked a blessing, had eaten of the blessed bread or had kept it, had been voluntarily present at an heretication, had entered into the *covenansa* to be hereticated on the death-bed, etc. For the Waldenses such indications were considered to be the confessing of sins to and accepting penance from those known not to be regularly ordained by an orthodox bishop, praying with them according to their rites by bending the knees with them on a bench or other inclined object, being present with them when they pretended to make the Host, receiving "peace" from them, or blessed bread. All this was easily catalogued, but beyond it lay a region of doubt concerning which authorities differed. The Council of Albi, in 1254, declared that entering a house, in which a heretic was known to be, converted simple suspicion into vehement; and Bernard Gui mentions that some inquisitors held that visiting heretics, giving them alms, guiding them in their journeys, and the like was sufficient for condemnation, but he agrees with Gui Foucoix in not so considering it, as all this might be done through carnal affection or for hire. The heart of man, he adds, is deep and inscrutable, but he seeks to satisfy himself for attempting the impossible by arguing that all which cannot be explained favorably must be admitted as adverse proof. It is a noteworthy fact that in long series of interrogations there will frequently be not a single question as to the belief of the party making confession. The whole energy of the inquisitor was directed to obtaining statements of external acts. The upshot of it all necessarily was that almost

---

* Concil. Narbonn. ann. 1244 c. 29.—Trésor des chartes du roi en Carcassonne (Doat, XXI. 34).—Molinier, L'Inquisition dans le midi de la France, p. 342.— Livres de Jostice et de Plet, Liv. I. Tit. iii. § 7.

everything was left to the discretion of the inquisitor, whose temper had more to do with the result than the proof of guilt or its absence. How insignificant were the tokens on which a man's fate might depend may be understood by a single instance. In 1234 Accursio Aldobrandini, a Florentine merchant in Paris, made the acquaintance of some strangers with whom he conversed several times, giving their servant on one occasion ten sols, and bowing to them when they met, out of politeness. This latter act was equivalent to the "veneration" which was the crucial test of heresy, and when he chanced to learn that his new acquaintances were heretics he felt himself lost. Hastening to Rome, he laid the matter before Gregory IX., who exacted bail of him and sent a commission to the Bishop of Florence to investigate the antecedents of Accursio. The report was examined by the cardinals of Ostia and Preneste and found to be emphatic in commending his orthodoxy, so he escaped with a penance prescribed by Raymond of Pennaforte, the papal penitentiary, and Gregory wrote to the inquisitors of Paris not to molest him. Under such a system the most devout Catholic could never feel safe for a moment.*

Yet in spite of all these efforts to define the indefinable, it was in the very nature of things that absolute certitude could not, in a vast range of cases, be reached except through confession. In order, therefore, to avert the misfortune of acquitting those who could not be brought to confess, it became necessary to invent a new crime—that known as "suspicion of heresy." This opened a wide field for the endless subtleties and refinements in which the jurists of the schools delighted, rendering their so-called science of law a worthy rival of scholastic theology. Suspicion thus was primarily divided into three grades, designated as light, vehement, and violent, and the glossators revel in defining the amount and quality of evidence which renders the accused guilty of either of these, with the usual result that practically the matter was left to the discretion of the tribunal. That a man against whom nothing substantial was proved should be punished merely because he was suspected of guilt may seem to modern eyes a scant measure of jus-

---

* Concil. Albiens. ann. 1254 c. 27.—Guid. Fulcod. Quæst. IX.—Bern. Guidon. Practica P. IV. (Doat, XXX.).—Lib. Confess. Inq. Albiens. (MSS. Bib. Nat., fonds latin, 11847).—Ripoll, I. 72.

tice; but to the inquisitor it appeared a wrong to God and man that any one should escape against whose orthodoxy there rested a shadow of a doubt. Like much else taught by the Inquisition, this found its way into general criminal law, which it perverted for centuries.*

Two witnesses were usually assumed to be necessary for the condemnation of a man of good repute, though some authorities demanded more. Yet when a case threatened to fail for lack of testimony, the discretion of the inquisitor was the ultimate arbitrator; and it was agreed that if two witnesses to the same fact could not be had, single witnesses to two separate facts of the same general character would suffice. When there was only one witness in all, the accused was still put on his purgation. With the same determination to remove all obstacles in the way of conviction, if a witness revoked his testimony it was held that if his evidence had been favorable to the accused, the revocation annulled it; if adverse, the revocation was null.†

The same disposition to construe everything in favor of the faith governed the admissibility of witnesses of evil character. The Roman law rejected the evidence of accomplices, and the Church had adopted the rule. In the False Decretals it had ordered that no one should be admitted as an accuser who was a heretic or suspected of heresy, was excommunicate, a homicide, a thief, a sorcerer, a diviner, a ravisher, an adulterer, a bearer of false witness, or a consulter of diviners and soothsayers. Yet when it came to prosecuting heresy all these prohibitions were thrown to the winds. As early as the time of Gratian, infamous and heretical witnesses were receivable against heretics. The edicts of Frederic II. rendered heretics incapable of giving testimony, but this disability was removed when they testified against heretics.

---

* Eymeric. Direct. Inq. pp. 376–81.—Zanchini Tract. de Hæret. c. iii.

† Archidiaconi Gloss. super c. xi. § 1 Sexto v. 2.—Joann. Andreæ Gloss. sup. c. xiii. § 7 Extra v. 7.—Eymeric. Direct. Inquis. pp. 445, 615–16.—Guid. Fulcodii Quæst. xiv.—Zanchini Tract. de Hæret. c. xiii., xiv.—Bern. Guidon. Practica P. iv. (Doat, XXX.).

In the lay courts, if a witness swore to the innocence of the accused and subsequently changed his testimony, the first statement was held good and the second was rejected, but in cases of heresy the incriminating evidence was always received.—Ponzinibii de Lamiis c. 84.

That there was some hesitation on this point we see in the Legatine Inquisition held in Toulouse in 1229, where it is recorded that
Guillem Solier, a converted heretic, was restored in fame in order
to enable him to bear witness against his former associates, and
even as late as 1260 Alexander IV. was obliged to reassure the
French inquisitors that they could safely use the evidence of heretics; but the principle became a settled one, adopted in the canon
law, and constantly enforced in practice. Without it, in fact, the
Inquisition would have been deprived of its most fruitful means of
tracking heretics. It was the same with excommunicates, perjur-
ers, infamous persons, usurers, harlots, and all those who, in the
ordinary criminal jurisprudence of the age, were regarded as incapable of bearing witness, yet whose evidence was receivable
against heretics. All legal exceptions were declared inoperative
except that of mortal enmity.*

In the ordinary criminal law of Italy no evidence was received
from a witness under twenty, but in cases of heresy such testimony
was taken, and, though not legal, it sufficed to justify torture. In
France the distinction seems to have been less rigidly defined, and
the matter probably was left, like so much else, to the discretion
of the inquisitors. As the Council of Albi specifies seven years as
the period at which all children were ordered to be made to attend
church and learn the Creed, Paternoster, and Salutation to the
Virgin, it may be safely assumed that below that age they would
hardly be admitted to give testimony. In the records of the Inquisition the age of the witness is rarely stated, but I have met
with one case, in 1244, after the capture of the pestilent nest of
heretics at Montségur, where the Inquisition gathered so goodly a

---

* C. 17 Cod. IX. ii. (Honor. 423).—Pseudo-Julii Epist. II. c. 18 (Gratiani Decret.
P. II. caus. V. Q. 3, c. 5.—Pseudo-Eutychiani Epist. ad Episcopp. Siciliæ.—Gra-
tiani Comment. in Decret. P. II. caus. II. Q. 7, c. 22 ; caus. VI. Q. 1, c. 19.—Hist.
Diplom. Frid. II. T. IV. pp. 299–300.—Guill. Pod. Laur. c. 40.—Alex. PP. IV.
Bull. *Consuluit*, 6 Mai. 1260 (Doat, XXXI. 205) ; Ejusd. Bull. *Quod super nonnullis*,
9 Dec. 1257 ; 15 Dec. 1258.—C. 5 Sexto V. 2.—C. 8 § 3 Sexto V. 2.—Concil. Biter-
rens. ann. 1246 c. 12.—Jacob. Laudun. Orat. in Conc. Constant. (Von der Hardt
III. 60).—MSS. Bib. Nat., fonds latin, No. 14930, fol. 221.—Zanchini Tract. de
Hæret. c. xi., xiii.—Eymeric. Direct. Inq. pp. 602–6.

Under the contemporary English law, criminals and accomplices were rejected as accusers, even in high-treason (Bracton, Lib. III. Tract. ii. cap. 3, No. 1).

harvest, when the age of a witness, Arnaud Olivier, happens to be mentioned as ten years. He admitted having been a Catharan "believer" since he had reached the age of discretion, and thus was responsible for himself and others. His evidence is gravely recorded against his father, his sister, and nearly seventy others; and in it he is made to give the names of sixty-six persons who were present about a year before at the sermon of a Catharan bishop. The wonderful exercise of so young a memory does not seem to have excited any doubts as to the validity of his testimony, which must have been held conclusive against the unfortunates enumerated, as he stated that they all "venerated" their prelate.*

Wives and children and servants were not admitted to give evidence in favor of the accused, but their testimony if adverse to him was welcomed, and was considered peculiarly strong. It was the same with the heretic, who, as we have seen, was freely admitted as an adverse witness, but who was rejected if appearing for the defence. In short, the only exception which could be taken to an accusing witness was malignity. If he was a mortal enemy of the prisoner it was presumed that his testimony was rather the prompting of hate than zeal for the faith, and it was required to be thrown out. In the case of the dead, the evidence of a priest that he had shriven the defunct and administered the *viaticum* went for nothing; but if he testified that the departed had confessed to being a heretic, had recanted, and had received absolution, then his bones were not exhumed and burned, but the heirs had to endure such penance of fine or confiscation as would have been inflicted on him if alive.†

Of course no witness could refuse to give evidence. No privilege or vow or oath released him from the duty. If he was unwilling and paltered or prevaricated and equivocated, there was the gentle persuasion of the torture-chamber, which, as we have seen,

---

* Bernardi Comens. Lucerna Inquisit. s. v. *Testis*, No. 14.—Concil Albiens. ann. 1254 c. 18.—Coll. Doat, XXII. 237 sqq.

In the German feudal law of the period no witness was admitted below the age of eighteen.—Sächsisches Lehenrechtbuch, c. 49 (Daniels, Berlin, 1863, p. 113).

† Eymeric. Direct. Inq. pp. 611-13.—Concil. Narbonn. ann. 1244 c. 25.—Concil. Biterrens. ann. 1246 c. 14.—Arch. de l'Inq. de Carcass. (Doat, XXXI. 149).

was even more freely used on witnesses than on principals. It was the ready instrument by which any doubts as to the testimony could be cleared up ; and it is fair to attribute to the sanction of this terrible abuse by the Inquisition the currency which it so long enjoyed in European criminal law. Even the secrecy of the confessional was not respected in the frenzied effort to obtain all possible information against heretics. All priests were enjoined to make strict inquiries of their penitents as to their knowledge of heretics and fautors of heresy. The seal of sacramental confession could not be openly and habitually violated, but the result was reached by indirection. When the confessor succeeded in learning anything he was told to write it down and then endeavor to induce his penitent to reveal it to the proper authorities. Failing in this, he was, without mentioning names, to consult God-fearing experts as to what he ought to do—with what effect can readily be conjectured, since the very fact of consulting as to his duty shows that the obligation of secrecy was not to be deemed absolute.*

After this glimpse at the inquisitorial system of evidence, we hardly need the assurance of the legists that less was required for conviction in heresy than in any other crime, and inquisitors were instructed that slender testimony was sufficient to prove it— "*probatur quis hœreticus ex levi causa.*" Yet evil as was all this, the crowning infamy of the Inquisition in its treatment of testimony was withholding from the accused all knowledge of the names of the witnesses against him. In the ordinary courts, even in the inquisitorial process, their names were communicated to him along with the evidence which they had given, and it will be remembered that when the Legate Romano held his inquest at Toulouse, in 1229, the accused followed him to Montpellier with de-

---

* Guid. Fulcod. Quæst. viii.—Pegnæ Comment. in Eymeric. p. 601.—Zanchini Tract. de Hæret. c. xiii.—Doctrina de modo procedendi (Martene Thesaur. V. 1802).

Heresy, of course, was a "reserved" case for which the ordinary confessor could not give absolution. Thus a man of Realmont in Albigeois who repented of having been present at a Catharan conventicle went to a Franciscan and confessed, accepting the penance imposed of the minor pilgrimages and some other penitential acts. On his return from their performance, however, he was seized by the Inquisition, tried and imprisoned.—Vaissette, IV. 41.

mands to see the names of those who had testified against them, when the cardinal recognized their right to this, but eluded it by showing merely a long list of all the witnesses who had appeared during the whole inquest, giving as an excuse the danger to which they were exposed from the malevolence of those who had suffered by their evidence. That there was some risk incurred by those who destroyed their neighbors is true; the inquisitors and chroniclers mention that assassinations from this cause sometimes occurred—six being reported in Toulouse between 1301 and 1310. It would have been strange had this not been the case, nor was the chance of such wild justice altogether an unwholesome check upon the security of malevolence. Yet that so flimsy an excuse should have been systematically put forward shows merely that the Church recognized and was ashamed of its plain denial of justice, since no such precaution was deemed necessary in other criminal affairs. Already in 1244 and 1246 the councils of Narbonne and Béziers order the inquisitors not to indicate in any manner the names of the witnesses, alleging as a reason the " prudent wish " of the Holy See, although in the instructions of the Cardinal of Albano the saving clause of risk is expressed. When Innocent IV. and his successors regulated the inquisitorial procedure, the same limitation to cases in which divulging the names would expose the witnesses to danger was sometimes omitted and sometimes repeated, and when Boniface VIII. embodied in the canon law the rule of withholding the names he expressly cautioned bishops and inquisitors to act with pure intentions, not to withhold the names when there was no peril in communicating them, and if the peril ceased they were to be revealed. Yet it is impossible to regard all this as more than a decent veil of hypocrisy to cover recognized injustice, for it was a flagrant fact that inquisitors everywhere treated these exhortations as the councils of Narbonne and Béziers had treated the limitations prescribed by the Cardinal of Albano. Although in the inquisitorial manuals the limitation of risk is usually mentioned, the instructions with regard to the conduct of the trials always assume as a matter of course that the prisoner is kept in ignorance of the names of the witnesses against him. As early as the time of Gui Foucoix that jurist treats it as the universal practice; a nearly contemporary MS. manual lays it down as an invariable rule; and in the later periods we are coolly

informed by both Eymerich and Bernardo di Como that cases were
rare in which risk did not exist; that it was great when the accused was rich and powerful, but greater still when he was poor
and had friends who had nothing to lose. Eymerich evidently
considers it much more decent to refuse the names than to adopt
the expedients of some over-conscientious inquisitors who furnished,
like Cardinal Romano, the names written on a different piece of
paper and so arranged that their identification with their evidence
was impossible, or who mixed up other names with those of the
witnesses so as to confuse hopelessly the defence. Occasionally a
less disreputable but almost equally confusing plan was adopted,
in swearing a portion of the witnesses in the presence of the accused, while examining them in his absence. Thus in the trial of
Bernard Délicieux, in 1319, out of forty-eight witnesses whose depositions are recorded, sixteen were sworn in his presence; in that
of Huss, in 1414, it is mentioned that fifteen witnesses at one time
were taken to his cell that he might see them sworn.*

From this withholding of names it was but a step to withholding the evidence altogether, and that step was sometimes taken.
In truth the whole process was so completely at the arbitrary discretion of the inquisitor, and the accused was so wholly without
rights, that whatever seemed good in the eyes of the former was
allowable in the interest of the faith. Thus we are told that if a
witness retracted his evidence, the fact should not be made known
to the defendant lest it should encourage him in his defence, but
the judge is recommended to bear it in mind when rendering

---

* Bernardi Comens. Lucerna Inquisit. s. v. *Probatio*, No. 3.—Archidiac. Gloss.
sup. c. xi. § 1 Sexto v. 2.—Guill. Pod. Laur. c. 40.—Bern. Guidon. Gravamina
(Doat, XXX. 102).—Concil. Narbonn. ann. 1244 c. 22.—Concil. Biterrens. ann.
1246 c. 4, 10.—Arch. de l'Inq. de Carc. (Doat, XXXI. 5).—Innoc. PP. IV. Bull.
Cum negotium, 9 Mart. 1254; Ejusd. Bull. *Ut commissum*, 21 Jun. 1254.—Alex.
PP. IV. Bull. *Licet vobis*, 7 Dec. 1255; Ejusd. Bull. *Præ cunctis*, § 6, 9 Nov.
1256; Ejusd. Bull. *Super extirpatione*, § 9, 1258.—Clem. PP. IV. Bull. *Licet ex
omnibus*, 17 Sep. 1265.—Ejusd. Bull. *Præ cunctis*, 23 Feb. 1266.—Guid. Fulcod.
Quæst. xv.—MSS. Bib. Nat., fonds latin, No. 14930, fol. 221.—C. 20 Sexto v. 2.—
Bern. Guidon. Practica P. iv. (Doat, XXX.). — Responsa Prudentum (Doat,
XXXVII.). — Eymeric. Direct. Inq. pp. 450, 610, 614, 626, 627. Cf. Pegnæ
Comment. pp. 627-8.—MSS. Bib. Nat., fonds latin, No. 4270.—Bernardi Comens,
Lucerna Inquisit. s. v. *Nomina.* — Mladenovic Relatio (Palacky Documenta
Joannis Hus, pp. 252-3).

judgment. The tender care for the safety of witnesses even went so far that it was left to the conscience of the inquisitor whether or not to give the accused a copy of the evidence itself if there appeared to be danger to be apprehended from doing so. Relieved from all supervision, and practically not subject to appeals, it may be said that there were no rules which the inquisitor might not suspend or abrogate at pleasure when the exigencies of the faith seemed to require it.*

Among the many evils springing from this concealment, which released witnesses and accusers from all responsibility, not the least was the stimulus which it afforded to delation and the temptation created to gratify malice by reckless perjury. Even without any special desire to do mischief, an unfortunate, whose resolution had been broken down by suffering and torture, when brought at last to confess, might readily be led to make his story as satisfactory as possible to his tormentors by mentioning all names that might occur to him as being present at conventicles and heretications. There can be no question that the business of the Inquisition was greatly increased by the protection which it thus afforded to informers and enemies, and that it was made the instrument of an immense amount of false-witness. The inquisitors felt this danger and frequently took such precautions as they could without trouble, by warning a witness of the penalties incurred by perjury, making him obligate himself in advance to endure them, and rigidly questioning him as to whether he had been suborned. Occasionally, also, we find a conscientious judge like Bernard Gui carefully sifting evidence, comparing the testimony of different witnesses, and tracing out incompatibilities which proved that one at least was false. He accomplished this twice, once in 1312 and again in 1316, the earlier case presenting some peculiar features. A man named Pons Arnaud came forward spontaneously and accused his son Pierre of having endeavored to have him hereticated when laboring under apparently mortal sickness. The son denied it. Bernard, on investigation, found that Pons had not been sick at the date specified, and that there had been no heretics at the place named. Armed with this informa-

---

* Responsa Prudentum (Doat, XXXVII.). — Bernardi Comens. Lucerna Inquis. s. v. *Tradere.*—Zanchini Tract. de Hæret. c. ix.

tion he speedily forced the accuser to confess that he had fabricated the story to injure his son. Creditable as is this case to the inquisitor, it is hideously suggestive of the pitfalls which lay around the feet of every man; and no less so is an instance in which Henri de Chamay, Inquisitor of Carcassonne, in 1329, resolutely traced out a conspiracy to ruin an innocent man, and had the satisfaction of forcing five false-witnesses to confess their guilt. Rare instances such as these, however, offered but a feeble palliation for the inherent vices of the system, and in spite of the severe punishment meted out to those who were discovered, the crime was of very frequent occurrence. The security with which it could be committed renders it safe to assume that detection occurred in a very small proportion of the cases; so when among the scanty documents that have reached us we see six false-witnesses (of whom two were priests and one a clerk), sentenced at an *auto de fé* held at Pamiers in 1323; four at Narbonne in December, 1328; one, a few weeks after, at Pamiers; four more at Pamiers in January, 1329, and seven (one of whom was a notary) at Carcassonne in September, 1329, we may conclude that if the full records of the Inquisition were accessible, the list would be a frightful one, and would suggest an incalculable amount of injustice which remained undiscovered. We do not need the admission of Eymerich that witnesses are found frequently to conspire together to ruin an innocent man, and we may well doubt his assurance that persistent scrutiny by the inquisitor will detect the wrong. There is, perhaps, only a consistent exhibition of inquisitorial logic in the dictum of Zanghino, that a witness who withdraws testimony adverse to a prisoner is to be punished for false-witness, while his testimony is to stand, and to receive full weight in rendering judgment.*

A false-witness, when detected, was treated with as little mercy as a heretic. As a symbol of his crime two pieces of red cloth in the shape of tongues were affixed to his breast and two to his back, to be worn through life. He was exhibited at the church-doors on a scaffolding during divine service on Sundays, and was

---

* Lib. Confess. Inq. Albiens. (MSS. Bib. Nat., fonds latin, 11847).—Lib. Sententt. Inq. Tolosan. pp. 96–7, 180, 393.—Arch. de l'Inq. de Carcass. (Doat, XXVII. 118, 133, 140, 149, 178, 204–16).—Eymeric. Direct. Inq. p. 521.—Zanchini Tract. de Hæret. c. xiv.

usually imprisoned for life. The symbol was changed to that of
a letter in the case of Guillem Maurs, condemned in 1322 for conspiring with others to forge letters of the Inquisition whereby
some parties were to be cited for heresy with the view of extorting hush-money from them. As the degree of criminality varied,
so there were differences in the severity of punishment. Those
condemned in Pamiers in 1323 were let off without incarceration.
The four at Narbonne, in 1328, were regarded as peculiarly culpa-
ble, having been suborned by enemies of the accused, and they
were accordingly condemned to the severest form of imprisonment, on bread and water, with chains on hands and feet. The
assembly of experts held at Pamiers for the *auto* of January, 1329,
decided that, in addition to imprisonment, either lenient or harsh,
according to the gravity of the offence, the offenders should make
good any damage accruing to the accused. This was an approach
to the *talio*, and the principle was fully carried out in 1518 by
Leo X. in a rescript to the Spanish Inquisition, authorizing the
abandonment to the secular arm of false witnesses who had succeeded in inflicting any notable injury on their victims. The expressions used by the pope justify the conclusion that the crime
was still frequent. Zanghino tells us that in his time there was
no defined legal penalty, and that the false witness was to be punished at the discretion of the inquisitor—another instance of the
tendency which pervades the whole inquisitorial jurisprudence, to
fetter the tribunals with as few rules as possible, to clothe them
with arbitrary power, and trust to God, in whose name and for
whose glory they professed to act, to inspire them with the wisdom necessary for the discharge of their irresponsible trust.*

---

* Lib. Sententt. Inq. Tolosan. pp. 297, 393.—Arch. de l'Inq. de Carcassonne
(Doat, XXVII. 119, 133, 140, 241).—Pegnæ Comment. in Eymeric. p. 625.—Zanchini Tract. de Hæret. c. xiv.

CHAPTER V.

THE DEFENCE.

FROM the preceding sketch of the inquisitorial process it may readily be inferred that scant opportunities for defence were allowed by the Holy Office. It was in the very nature of the process that all the preliminary proceedings were taken in secrecy and without the knowledge of the accused. The case against him was made up before his arrest, and he was examined, urged to confess, and perhaps imprisoned for years and tortured, before he was allowed to know what were the charges against him. It was only after a confession had been extorted from him, or the inquisitor despaired of extorting one, that he was furnished with the evidence against him, and even then the names of the witnesses were habitually suppressed. All this is in cruel contrast with the righteous care to avoid injustice prescribed for the ordinary episcopal courts. In them the Council of Lateran orders that the accused shall be present at the inquisition against him, unless he contumaciously absents himself; the charges are to be explained to him, that he may have the opportunity of defending himself; the witnesses' names, with their respective evidence, are to be made public, and all legitimate exceptions and answers be admitted, for suppression of names would invite slander, and rejection of exceptions would admit false testimony.* The suspected heretic, however, was prejudged. The effort of the inquisitor was not to avoid injustice, but to force him to admit his guilt and seek reconciliation with the Church. To accomplish this effectually the facilities for defence were systematically reduced to a minimum.

---

* Concil. Lateran IV. ann. 1215 c. 8.

So, in 1254, St. Louis orders that in all criminal cases where the inquisitorial process is used, the whole proceedings shall be submitted to the accused.—Vaissette, Éd. Privat, VIII. 1348.

It is true that, in 1246, the Council of Béziers lays down the
rule that the accused shall have proper opportunities for defence,
including necessary delays and the admission of exceptions and
legitimate replies; but if this were intended as a check on the
arbitrary operations which already characterized the Inquisition,
it was wholly disregarded. In the first place, the secrecy of the
tribunal enabled the judge to do as he might think best. In the
second place, the only possible remaining check to arbitrary action was removed by denying to the accused the advantage of
counsel. Then, as now, the intricacy of legal forms rendered the
trained advocate a necessity to every man on trial; the layman,
ignorant of his rights, and of the method of enforcing them, was
utterly helpless. So thoroughly was this understood that in the
ecclesiastical courts it was frequently a custom to furnish advocates gratuitously to poor men unable to employ them, and in the
charter granted by Simon de Montfort, in 1212, to his newly-acquired territories, it was provided that justice should always be
gratuitous, and that counsel should be provided by the court for
pleaders too poor to retain them. When this right thus was recognized in the most trifling cases, to refuse it to those who were
battling for their lives before a tribunal in which the judge was
also prosecutor, was more than the Church at first dared openly
to do, but it practically reached the result by indirection. Innocent III., in a decretal embodied in the canon law, had ordered
advocates and scriveners to lend no aid or counsel to heretics and
their defenders, or to undertake their causes in litigation. This,
which was presumably intended as one of the disabilities inflicted
on defiant and acknowledged heretics, was readily applied to the
suspect who were not yet convicted, and who were struggling to
prove their innocence, for their guilt was always assumed in advance. The councils of Valence and Albi, in 1248 and 1254, while
ordering inquisitors not to embarrass themselves with the vain
jangling of lawyers in the conduct of the prosecution, significantly make reference to this provision of the canon law as applicable to counsel who might be so hardy as to aid the defence.
That this became a settled and recognized principle is shown by
Bernard Gui's assertion that advocates who excuse and defend
heretics are to be held guilty of fautorship of heresy — a crime
which became heresy itself if satisfaction at the discretion of the

inquisitor was not rendered within a twelvemonth. When to this we add the perpetually reiterated commands to the inquisitors to proceed without regard to legal forms or the wrangling of advocates, and the notice to notaries that he who drew up the revocation of a confession was excommunicated as an impeder of the Inquisition, it will readily be seen that there was no need of formally refusing counsel to the accused, and that there was no practical benefit permitted from the admission of the barren generality that one who believed a heretic to be innocent and endeavored to prove him so was not on that account liable to punishment. Eymerich is careful to specify that the accused has the right to employ counsel, and that a denial of this justifies an appeal, but then he likewise states that the inquisitor can prosecute any advocate or notary who undertakes the cause of heretics; and a century earlier a manuscript manual for inquisitors directs them to prosecute as defenders of heresy any advocates who take such cases, with the addition that if they are clerks they are to be perpetually deprived of their benefices. It is no wonder, therefore, that finally inquisitors adopted the rule that advocates were not to be allowed in inquisitorial trials. This injustice had its compensation, however, for the employment of counsel, in fact, was likely to prove as dangerous to the defendant as to his advocate, for the Inquisition was entitled to all accessible information, and could summon the latter as a witness, force him to surrender any papers in his hands, and reveal what had passed between him and his client. Such considerations, however, are rather theoretical than practical, for it may well be doubted whether, in the ordinary course of the Inquisition, counsel for the defence ever appeared before it. The terror that it inspired is well illustrated by the circumstance that when, in 1300, Friar Bernard Délicieux was commissioned by his Franciscan provincial to defend the memory of Castel Fabri, and Nicholas d'Abbeville, the Inquisitor of Carcassonne, rudely refused him even an audience, he could find no notary in the city who dared to assist him in drawing up a legal protest; every one feared arrest and prosecution if he took the least part in an opposition to the dreaded inquisitor, and Bernard had to wait ten or twelve days until he could bring a notary from a distance to perform the simplest formality. The local officials might well hesitate to incur the wrath of Nicholas, for a few years before he had cast in jail a notary who had ventured to draw up an appeal of the inhabitants of Carcassonne to the king.*

All this is interesting as an illustration of the spirit which pervaded every act of the Inquisition, but in reality no advocate could be of material service to the accused, save in the most exceptional cases. The men who organized the Holy Office knew too well what they wanted to leave open any possibilities of which even the shrewdest advocate could take advantage, and it was admitted on all hands as a recognized fact that there was no method of defence save disabling the witnesses for the prosecution. It has been seen that enmity was the only source of disability in a witness, and this had to be mortal—there must have been bloodshed between the parties, or other cause sufficient to induce one to seek the life of the other. If, therefore, the case rested on witnesses of this kind, their testimony had to be rejected and the prosecution fell. As this was the only possible mode of escape, the cruelty of withholding from the prisoner the names of the adverse witnesses becomes doubly conspicuous. He was forced to grope around in the dark and blindly name such persons as he imagined might have a hand in his misfortunes. If he failed to hit upon any who appeared in the case, the evidence against him was conclusive, as far as it went. If he chanced to name some of the witnesses, he was interrogated as to the causes of enmity; the inquisitor examined into the facts of the alleged quarrel, and decided as he saw fit as to the retention or the rejection of their testimony. Conscientious jurists like Gui Foucoix and inquisitors like Eymerich warned their brethren that as the accused had so slender a chance of guessing the sources of evidence, the judge ought to investigate for himself and discard any that seemed to be the product of malice; but there were others who sought rather to deprive the poor wretch of every straw that might postpone his sinking. One device was to ask him, as though

---

* Concil. Biterrens. ann. 1246, Append. c. 8. — Concil. Campinacens. ann. 1238 c. 14. — Contre le Franc-Alleu sans Tiltre, Paris, 1629, p. 216. — Fournier, Les Officialités, etc. p. 289. — C. 11, Extra v. 7.—Concil. Valentin. ann. 1248 c. 11.—Concil. Albiens. ann. 1254 c. 23.—Bernard. Guidon. Practica. P. IV. (Doat, XXX.).—Eymeric. Direct. Inquis. pp. 446, 452, 565, 568.—MSS. Bib. Nat., fonds latin, No. 14930, fol. 220.—Bernardi Comens. Lucerna Inquisitor. s. vv. *Advocatus, Defensor.* — C. 13, § 7, Extra v. 7. — Alex. PP. IV. Bull. *Cupientes*, 4 Mart. 1260.—Arch. de l'Inq. de Carcassonne (Doat, XXXIV. 123).—Vaissette, IV. 72.

casually, at the end of his examination, whether he had any enemies who would so disregard the fear of God as to accuse him falsely, and if, thus taken unawares, he replied in the negative, he debarred himself from any subsequent defence; or the most damaging witness would be selected and the prisoner be asked if he knew him, when a denial would estop him from claiming enmity. It is easy to imagine other tricks by which shrewd and experienced inquisitors could save themselves the trouble of admitting the accused to even the nugatory form of defence to which alone he was entitled. As to allowing him to call witnesses in his favor, except to prove enmity of the accusers, it was never thought of in ordinary cases. By a legal fiction, the inquisitor was supposed to look at both sides of the case, and to take care of the defence as well as of the prosecution. If the accused failed to guess the names of enemies among the witnesses and to disable their testimony, he was condemned.*

In England, under the barbarous custom of the *peine forte et dure*, a prisoner who refused to plead either guilty or not guilty was pressed to death, because the trial could not go on without either confession or defence. Cruel as was this expedient, it was the outcome of a manly sense of justice, which based its procedure on the rule that the worst felon should have a fair opportunity to prove his innocence. Far worse was the system of the Inquisition, which was equally resolved that its culprits should have no such easy method of escape as a refusal to plead. It had no scruples as to proceeding in such cases, and the obstinacy of the accused only simplified matters. The refusal was an act of contumacy, equivalent to disobeying a summons to appear, or it was held to be tantamount to a confession, and the obdurate prisoner was forthwith handed over to the secular arm as an impenitent heretic, fit only for the stake. The use of torture, however, rendered such cases rare.†

---

* Guid. Fulcod. Quæst. xv.—Eymeric. Direct. Inq. pp. 446, 450, 607, 610, 614. —Zanchini Tract. de Hæret. c. ix., xli.—Litt. Petri Albanens. (Doat, XXXI. 5).

In the register of the Inquisition of Carcassonne from 1249 to 1258 M. Molinier has found two cases in which the accused was allowed to introduce evidence in his favor. In one of these G. Vilanière called two witnesses to prove an alibi; in the other Guillem Nègre brought forward a letter of reconciliation and penitence. In neither case was the defendant successful (L'Inq. dans le midi de la France, p. 346).

† Coll. Doat, XXXI. 149.—Bernardi Comens. Lucerna Inquisit. s. v. *Taciturnitas.*

The enviable simplicity which the inquisitorial process thus assumed in the absence of counsel and of all practical opportunities for defence can perhaps best be illustrated by one or two cases. Thus in the Inquisition of Carcassonne, June 19, 1252, P. Morret is called up and asked if he wishes to defend himself against the matters found in the *instructio* or indictment against him. He has nothing to allege except that he has enemies, of whom he names five. Apparently he did not happen to guess any of the witnesses, for the case proceeded by reading the evidence to him, after which he is again asked thrice if he has anything further to say. To this he replies in the negative, and the case ends by assigning January 29 for the rendering of sentence. Two years later, in 1254, at Carcassonne, a certain Bernard Pons was more lucky, for he happened to guess aright in naming his wife as an inimical witness, and we have the proceedings of the inquest held to determine whether the enmity was mortal. Three witnesses are examined, all of whom swear that she is a woman of loose character; one deposes that she had been taken in adultery by her husband; another that he had beaten her for it, and the third that he had recently heard her say that she wished her husband dead that she might marry a certain Pug Oler, and that she would willingly become a leper if that would bring it about. This would certainly seem sufficient, but Pons appears nevertheless not to have escaped. So thoroughly hopeless, indeed, was the prospect of any effort at defence, that it frequently was not even attempted, and the accused, like Arnaud Fabri at Carcassonne, August 26, 1252, when asked if he wished a copy of the evidence against him, would despairingly decline it. It was a customary formula in a sentence to state that the convict had been offered opportunity for defence and had not availed himself of it, showing how frequently this was the case.*

In the case of prosecution of the dead, the children or the heirs were scrupulously cited to appear and defend his memory, as they were necessarily parties to the case through the disabilities and confiscation following upon condemnation. Proclamation was also

---

* Registre de l'Inq. de Carcassonne (MSS. Bib. Nat., fonds latin, Nouv. Acquis. 139, f. 33, 44, 62).—Practica super Inquisitione (MSS. Bib. Nat., fonds latin, No. 14930, fol. 212).

made publicly in the churches inviting any one else who chose to appear or who had any interest in the matter by reason of holding property of the deceased; and then a third public notice was given that if no one came forward on the day named, definitive sentence would be rendered. Thus in a case occurring in 1327, Jean Duprat, Inquisitor of Carcassonne, orders the priests of all the churches in the dioceses of Carcassonne, Narbonne, and Alet to publish the notice during divine service on every Sunday and feast-day till the day of hearing, and to send him a notarial attestation of their action. The sentences in these cases are careful to recite these notices so sedulously served on all concerned; but notwithstanding this display of a desire to do exact justice, the proceedings were quite as hollow a mockery as those against the living. That it was so recognized is seen at the *auto* of 1309 at Toulouse, where there were four dead persons sentenced, and it is stated that in one case no one appeared, and in the other three the heirs obeyed the citation but renounced all defence. In the case of Castel Fabri, before alluded to, at Carcassonne, in 1300, where the estate was very large, the heirs appeared, but were denied all opportunity of defence by Nicholas d'Abbeville, the inquisitor; and in that of Pierre de Tornamire, though the heirs, as we have seen, succeeded in reversing the judgment through the gross informality of the proceedings, it was not until after a struggle which lasted for thirty-two years, during which time the estate must have been sequestrated. Sometimes, when death-bed heretications had occurred, the children put in the plea of *non compos*, which was admitted to be good, but as none of the family were allowed to testify, and only disinterested witnesses of approved orthodoxy were received, instances of success must have been rare indeed.*

Practically every avenue of escape was closed to those who fell into the hands of the inquisitor. Technically the accused had a right, as in other cases, to recuse his judge, but this was a dangerous experiment, and we hardly need the assurance of Bernardo di

---

* Concil. Biterrens. ann. 1246, Append. c. 18.—Doctrina de modo procedendi (Martene Thesaur. V. 1813).—Coll. Doat, XXVII. 97-8; XXIX. 27; XXXIV. 123; XXXV. 61; XXXVIII. 166.—Lib. Sententt. Inquis. Tolosan. pp. 33-4.— Molinier, L'Inquis. dans le midi de la France, p. 287.—Alex. PP. IV. Bull. *Olim ex parte*, 24 Sept.; 13 Oct. 1258; Urbani PP. IV. Bull. *Idem*, 21 Aug. 1262 (Mag. Bull. Rom. I. 117).

Como that it was virtually unknown. Ignorance was no defence, and its mere assertion, according to Bernard Gui, only rendered a man worthy of condemnation along with his master, the father of lies. Persistent denial of the offence charged, even when accompanied with profession of faith and readiness to submit to the mandates of the Church, was obstinacy and impenitence which precluded all hope of mercy. Even suicide in prison was equivalent to confession of guilt without repentance. It is true that insanity or drunkenness might be urged in extenuation of the utterance of heretical words, and this might mitigate the sentence, if there were due contrition and seeking for reconciliation, but admission of the conclusion at which the inquisitor had arrived from his *ex parte* inquest was the predetermined result, and the only alternative to this was abandonment to the secular arm.*

That plain-spoken friar, Bernard Délicieux, uttered the literal truth when he declared, in the presence of Philippe le Bel and all his court, that if St. Peter and St. Paul were accused of " adoring " heretics and were prosecuted after the fashion of the Inquisition, there would be no defence open for them. Questioned as to their faith, they would answer like masters in theology and doctors of the Church, but when told that they had adored heretics, and they asked what heretics, some names, common in those parts, would be mentioned, but no particulars would be given. When they would ask for statements as to time and place, no facts would be furnished, and when they would demand the names of the witnesses these would be withheld. How, then, asked Bernard, could the holy apostles defend themselves, especially when any one who wished to aid them would himself be attacked as a fautor of heresy. It was so. The victim was enveloped in a net from which there was no escape, and his frantic struggles only twisted it more tightly around him.†

Theoretically, indeed, an appeal lay to the pope from the Holy Office, and to the metropolitan from the bishop, for denial of jus-

---

* Bernardi Comens. Lucerna Inquisit. s. v. *Recusatio.*—Bern. Guidon. Practica P. iv. (Doat, XXX.).—Zanchini Tract. de Hæret. c. ii., vii.—Concil. Narbonn. ann. 1244 c. 26.—Concil. Biterrens. ann. 1246 c. 9.—Eymeric. Direct. Inq. p. 572.

† MSS. Bib. Nat., fonds latin, No. 4270, fol. 139.

tice or irregularity of procedure, but it had to be made before sentence was rendered, as condemnation was final. Possibly this may have held out some prospect of benefit in the case of bishops exercising their inquisitorial jurisdiction. In that of inquisitors, when "*apostoli*," or letters remanding the case to the Holy See, were demanded, it rested with them to grant affirmative ("reverential") ones, or negative ones. The former admitted the transfer of the case; the latter kept it in the inquisitor's hands unless it was formally taken from him by the pope. This, it is safe to say, could rarely happen, and, as the proceeding was an intricate one, it could only be resorted to by experts. A man like Master Eckart, supported by the whole Dominican Order, could undertake it, even though in the end he fared no better at the hands of John XXII. than he would have done at those of the Archbishop of Cologne. So when, in 1323, the Sire de Partenay, one of the most powerful nobles of Poitou, was cited for heresy by Friar Maurice, the Inquisitor of Paris, and was thrown into the Temple by Charles le Bel, he appealed from Maurice as a judge prejudiced by personal hatred. Charles sent him under guard to John XXII. at Avignon, who at first refused to entertain the appeal, but at length, by the influential intercession of Partenay's friends, was induced to appoint several bishops as assessors to the inquisitor, and after long-protracted proceedings the interest of Partenay was sufficient to obtain his liberation. Cases like these, however, are wholly exceptional and have no bearing upon the thousands of humble folk and "*petite noblesse*" who filled the prisons of the Inquisition and figured in its *autos de fé*. The manuals for inquisitors, indeed, make no scruple in instructing them as to the devices and deceits by which they can elude all attempts to appeal when through disregard of rules they have exposed themselves to it.*

There was another class of cases, however, in which the interference of the pope occasionally gave relief, for the Holy See was autocratic and could set aside all rules. The curia was always greedy for money, and, outside of Italy, had no share in the confiscations. It can, therefore, readily be imagined that men of

---

* Pegnæ Comment. in Eymeric. p. 675.—Zanchini Tract. de Hæret. c. xxix.— Eymeric. Direct. Inq. pp. 453–55.—Grandes Chroniques. ann. 1323.—Guill. Nangiac. Contin. ann. 1323.—Chron. de Jean de S. Victor. Contin. ann. 1323.—Bernardi Comens. Lucerna Inquisitor. s. vv. *Appellatio, Exceptio* No. 2.

wealth whose whole property was at stake might well consent to divide it with the papal court, whose all-powerful intervention would thereby be secured. As early as 1245 the bishops of Languedoc are found complaining to Innocent IV. of the number of heretics who thus obtain exemption. Not only those undergoing trial, but those fearing to be cited, those excommunicated for contumacy, or legitimately sentenced, escape the jurisdiction of the Inquisition and enjoy immunity on the strength of letters granted by the papal penitentiaries. I have met with a number of special cases of this interference of the Holy See with the Holy Office, one at least of which indicates the means of persuasion employed. In letters of December 28, 1248, the papal penitentiary Algisius orders the release, without confiscation, of six prisoners of the Inquisition who had confessed to heresy, one of the reasons assigned being the liberal contributions which they had made to the cause of the Holy Land. It is no wonder that the inquisitors sometimes grew mutinous under this aggravating interference, of which they could so readily guess the motive, and, on one occasion at least, they gave the curia a lesson. Some inhabitants of Limoux, in 1249, condemned to wear crosses and perform heavy penances, obtained from Innocent IV. an order for their mitigation, whereupon the inquisitors, in their irritation, went a step further and absolved the penitents without reserve. Accepting this rebuke, Innocent commanded the original sentence to be reimposed, and the unlucky culprits gained nothing by their effort. Less questionable was the interference, in 1255, of Alexander IV. in the case of Aimeric de Bressols of Castel-Sarrazin, who had been condemned for heretical acts committed thirty years before. He represented that he had performed most of the penance enjoined on him and that he was unable, through old age and poverty, to accomplish the rest, whereupon the pope mercifully authorized the Inquisitors to commute it into other pious works. A somewhat remarkable case occurred in 1371, when Gregory XI. authorized the Inquisitor of Carcassonne to release Bidon de Puy-Guillem, condemned to perpetual imprisonment, and repentant, the reason given for papal intervention being that there existed no other power to commute the sentence.*

* Vaissette, III. 462; Pr. 447.—Coll. Doat, XXXI. 152, 169, 283; XXXII. 69; XXXV. 134.—Potthast No. 10292, 10311, 10317, 18723, 18895.—Ripoll, I. 287.—Coll. Doat, XXXV. 134.

This kind of papal intervention, however, was in contravention of the law and not in its fulfilment, and need not be weighed in considering the results of the inquisitorial process. That result, as might be expected, was condemnation in some form or other so uniformly that it may be regarded as inevitable. In the register of Carcassonne from 1249 to 1258, comprising about two hundred cases, there does not occur a single instance of a prisoner discharged as innocent. It is true that the interrogatory of Alizaïs Debax, March 27, 1249, is followed by the note "she was not heard a second time because she was considered innocent," but this apparent exception is nullified by a second memorandum "*crucesignata est*"—she was condemned to the public infamy of wearing crosses, probably to confirm the popular impression that the Inquisition never missed its mark. A man against whom there was no evidence to justify conviction and who yet would not confess himself guilty, was kept in prison indefinitely at the discretion of the inquisitor; at length, if the proof against him was only incidental and not direct, and the suspicion was light, he might be mercifully discharged under bail, with orders to stand at the door of the Inquisition from breakfast-time until dinner, and from dinner until supper, until some further testimony should turn up against him, and the inquisitor be able to prove the guilt so confidently assumed. On this side of the Alps it was a recognized rule that no one should be acquitted. The utmost stretch of justice, when the accusation failed entirely, was a sentence of not proven. The charges were simply declared not to be substantiated, and the inquisitors were carefully warned never to pronounce a man innocent, so that there might be no bar to subsequent proceedings in case of further evidence. Possibly in Italy, in the fourteenth century, this rule may have been neglected, for Zanghino gives a formula of acquittal, based, significantly enough, on the evidence being proved to be malicious.*

Clement V. recognized the injustice wrought under this system when he embodied in the canon law a declaration that inquisitors abused to the injury of the faithful the wise provisions made for the defence of the faith; when he forbade them from falsely con-

* Molinier, L'Inquisition dans le midi de la France, pp. 332-33.—Responsa Prudentum (Doat, XXXVII.).—Bern. Guidon. Practica P. v. (Doat, XXX.).—Eymeric. Direct. Inquis. p. 474.—Zanchini Tract. de Hæret. c. xli.

victing any one, or acting either for or against the accused through love, hate, or the hopes of gain, under penalty of *ipso facto* excommunication, removable only by the Holy See. Bernard Gui hotly denied these assertions, which he declared to be precisely those with which the heretics defamed the Holy Office to its great damage. To impute heresy to the innocent, he said, is worthy of damnation, but none the less so is it to slander the Inquisition. In spite, he adds, of the refutation of the accusations brought against it, this canon assumes their truth and the heretics exult over its disgrace. If the heretics exulted, their rejoicings were premature. The Inquisition went its way in the accustomed paths, and Clement's well-meant effort at reform proved wholly unavailing.*

The erection of suspicion into a crime gave ample opportunity for the habitual avoidance of acquittal. This took its origin in the customs of the barbarian and mediæval codes, which required the accused, against whom a probable case was made out, to demonstrate his innocence either by the ordeal, or by the form of purgation known in England as the Wager of Law, in which he produced a prescribed number of his friends to share with him the oath of denial. In the coronation-edict of Frederic II. those who were suspected of heresy were required to purge themselves in this manner, as the Church might demand, under pain of being outlawed, and, if they remained so for a year, of being condemned as heretics. This gave a peculiar and sinister significance to suspicion of heresy which was carefully elaborated and turned to account. Suspicion might arise from many causes, the chief of which was popular rumor and belief. Omission to take the oath abjuring heresy imposed on all the inhabitants of Languedoc, within the term prescribed, was sufficient, or neglect to reveal heretics, or the possession of heretical books. The intricate questions to which this extension of criminality gave rise are fairly illustrated in the discussion of an inquisitor whether those who listened to the instructions of the Waldenses, "Do not lie, nor swear, nor commit fornication, but give to every man his due; go to church, pay your tithes, and the perquisites of the priests," and, knowing this to be good advice, conclude the utterers to be good men—whether such

---

* C. 1 Clement. v. 3.—Bern. Guidon. Gravamina (Doat, XXX. 112).

are to be considered suspect of heresy; and he tells us that after diligent consideration he must decide in the affirmative, and order them to purgation. The difficulty of reducing to practice these intangible speculations was realized by Chancellor Gerson, who admits that due allowance should be made for variations of habits and manners in different places and times, but the ordinary inquisitor was troubled with few such scruples. It was easier to treat the suspect as criminals; to classify suspicion into its three grades of light, vehement, and violent; to prescribe punishment for it, and to inflict the disabilities of heresy on the suspect and their descendants. Even the definition of the three grades of suspicion was abandoned as impossible, and it was left to the arbitrary discretion of the inquisitor to classify each individual case which came before him. Nothing more condemnatory of the whole system can well be imagined than the explanation of Eymerich that suspects are not heretics; that they are not to be condemned for heresy, and that therefore their punishment should be lighter, except in the case of violent suspicion. Against this there was no defence possible, and no evidence to be admitted. The culprit might not be a heretic or entertain any error of belief, but if he would not abjure and give satisfaction (and abjuration included confession), he was to be handed over to the secular arm; if he confessed and sought reconciliation, he was to be imprisoned for life.*

For light and vehement suspicion the accused was ordered to furnish conjurators in his oath of denial. These were to be men

---

* Hist. Diplom. Frid. II. T. II. p. 4.—Concil. Tolosan. ann. 1229 c. 18.—Concil. Albiens. ann. 1254 c. 16.—Concil. Tarraconens. ann. 1242.—Eymeric. Direct. Inquis. pp. 376-8, 380-4, 494-5, 500.—Concil. Biterrens. ann. 1246, Append. c. 31, 36.—Zanchini Tract. de Hæret. v., vii., xx.—Doctrina de modo procedendi (Martene Thesaur. V. 1802).—Gersonis de Protestatione consid. xii.—Bernardi Comens. Lucerna Inquisit. s. v. *Præsumptio*, No. 5.—Isambert, Anc. Loix Françaises, IV. 364.

It is somewhat remarkable that Cornelius Agrippa maintains that the law expressly forbade the Inquisition from meddling with cases involving mere suspicion, or the defending, reception, and favoring of heretics (De Vanitate Scientiarum, cap. xcvi.).—His contemporary, the learned jurist Ponzinibio, calls special attention to the fact that mere suspicion, even when not accompanied by evil report, is sufficient to justify proceedings in case of heresy, though not in other crimes.—(Ponzinibii de Lamiis c. 88).

of his own rank in life, who knew him personally and who swore to their belief in his orthodoxy and in the truth of his exculpatory oath. Their number varied, at the discretion of the inquisitor, with the degree of suspicion to be purged away, from three to twenty or thirty, and even more. In the case of strangers, however, who had no acquaintances, the inquisitor was advised to be moderate. It was no mere idle ceremony, and, as usual, all the chances were thrown against the defendant. If he was unable to procure the required number of compurgators, or neglected to do so within a year, the law of Frederic II. was enforced, and he was usually condemned as a heretic to burning alive; although some inquisitors argued that this was only presumptive, not absolute, proof, and that he could escape the stake by confessing and abjuring—of course being subject to the penance of perpetual prison. If he succeeded and performed his purgation duly, he was by no means acquitted. If the suspicion against him was vehement he could still be punished; even if it was light the fact that he had been suspected was an ineradicable blot. With the curious logical inconsequence characteristic of inquisitorial procedure, in addition to the purgation, he was obliged to abjure the heresy of which he had cleared himself; this abjuration remained of record against him, and in case of a second accusation his escape from the previous one was not reckoned as having proved his innocence, but as an evidence of guilt. If the purgation had been for light suspicion, his punishment now was increased; and if it had been for vehement suspicion, he was now regarded as a relapsed, to whom no mercy could be shown, but who was handed over to the secular arm without a hearing. Practically, however, this injustice is important chiefly as a manifestation of the spirit of the Inquisition; its methods were too thorough to render frequent a recourse to purgation, and Zanghino, when he treats of it, feels obliged to explain it as a custom little known. One case, however, at least, is on record at Angermünde, where the inquisitor Friar Jordan, in 1336, tried by this method a number of persons accused of the mysterious Luciferan heresy, when fourteen men and women who were unable to procure the requisite number of compurgators were duly burned.*

---

* Concil. Tarraconens. ann. 1242.—Eymeric. Direct. Inq. pp. 376-8, 475-6.—

An indispensable formality in all cases in which the culprit was admitted to reconciliation with the Church was abjuration of heresy. Of this there were various forms adapted to the different occasions of its use—whether for suspicion, light, vehement, or violent, or after confession and repentance. It was performed in public, at the *autos de fé*, except in rare cases, such as those of ecclesiastics likely to cause scandal, and it frequently embodied a pecuniary penalty for infraction of its promises, and security for their performance. The principal point to be observed in all was to see that the penitent abjured heresy in general as well as the special heresy with which he had been charged. If this were duly attended to, he could always be handed over to the secular arm without a hearing in case of relapse, except when the abjuration had been for light suspicion. If it were neglected, and he had, for instance, abjured Catharism only, he might subsequently indulge in some other form of heresy, such as Waldensianism or usury, and have the benefit of another chance. The case was one not likely to occur, but the point is interesting as showing how the Inquisition could manifest the most scrupulous attention to form, while discarding in its practice all that entitles the administration of justice to respect. The importance attached to the abjuration is illustrated by a case in the Inquisition of Toulouse in 1310. Sibylla, wife of Bernard Borell, had been forced to confession and abjuration in 1305. Continuing her heretical practices, she was arrested in 1309 and again obliged to confess. As a relapsed heretic she was doomed irrevocably to the stake, but, luckily for her, the abjuration could not be found among the papers of the Holy Office, and though the rest of the record seems to have been accessible, she could only be prosecuted as though for a first offence, and she escaped with imprisonment for life.*

In the case of suspects of heresy who cleared themselves by compurgation, abjuration, of course, did not include confession.

Bernardi Comens. Lucerna Inquis. s. vv. *Practica, Purgatio.*—Albertini Repertor. Inquisit. s. v. *Deficiens.*—Gregor. PP. XI. Bull. *Excommunicamus*, 20 Aug. 1229.—Zanchini Tract. de Hæret. c. vii., xvii.—Martini App. ad Mosheim de Beghardis, p. 537.

* Concil. Narbonn. ann. 1244 c. 6, 12.—Muratori Antiq. Ital. Dissert. LX.—Doctrina de modo procedendi (Martene Thesaur. V. 1800–1).—Eymeric. Direct. Inq. pp. 376, 486–7, 492–8.—Lib. Sententt. Inq. Tolos. pp. 67, 215.

In accusations of heresy, supported by evidence, however, no one could be admitted to abjuration who did not confess that of which he was accused. Denial, as we have seen, was obduracy, punished by the stake, and confession was a condition precedent to admission to abjuration. In ordinary cases, where torture was freely used, confession was almost a matter of course. There were extraordinary cases, however, like that of Huss at Constance, where torture was spared and where the accused denied the doctrines attributed to him. In such cases the necessity of confession prior to abjuration must be borne in mind if we are to understand the inevitable consequences.

CHAPTER VI.

THE SENTENCE.

THE penal functions of the Inquisition were based upon a fiction which must be comprehended in order rightly to appreciate much of its action. Theoretically it had no power to inflict punishment. Its mission was to save men's souls; to recall them to the way of salvation, and to assign salutary penance to those who sought it, like a father-confessor with his penitents. Its sentences, therefore, were not, like those of an earthly judge, the retaliation of society on the wrong-doer, or deterrent examples to prevent the spread of crime; they were simply imposed for the benefit of the erring soul, to wash away its sin. The inquisitors themselves habitually speak of their ministrations in this sense. When they condemned a poor wretch to lifelong imprisonment, the formula in use, after the procedure of the Holy Office had become systematized, was a simple injunction on him to betake himself to the jail and confine himself there, performing penance on bread and water, with a warning that he was not to leave it under pain of excommunication, and of being regarded as a perjured and impenitent heretic. If he broke jail and escaped, the requisition for his recapture under a foreign jurisdiction describes him, with a singular lack of humor, as one insanely led to reject the salutary medicine offered for his cure, and to spurn the wine and oil which were soothing his wounds.*

Technically, therefore, the list of penalties available to the in-

---

* Guid. Fulcod. Quæstt. XIII., XV.—Ripoll, I. 254.—Archives de l'Inq. de Carcassonne (Doat, XXXI. 139).—Archives de l'Évêché d'Albi (Doat, XXXV. 69). — Lib. Sententt. Inq. Tolosan. p. 32. — Eymeric. Direct. Inquis. pp. 465, 643, — Zanchini Tract. de Hæret. c. xx.

In the sentences of Bernard de Caux, 1246-8, though imprisonment is treated as a penance, the expression is more mandatory than in later proceedings (MSS. Bib. Nat., fonds latin, 9992).

quisitor was limited. He never condemned to death, but merely withdrew the protection of the Church from the hardened and impenitent sinner who afforded no hope of conversion, or from him who showed by relapse that there was no trust to be placed in his pretended repentance. Except in Italy, he never confiscated the heretic's property; he merely declared the existence of a crime which, under the secular law, rendered the culprit incapable of possession. At most he could impose a fine, as a penance, to be expended in good works. His tribunal was a spiritual one, and dealt only with the sins and remedies of the spirit, under the inspiration of the Gospels, which always lay open before it. Such, at least, was the theory of the Church, and this must be borne in mind if we would understand what may occasionally seem to be inconsistencies and incongruities—especially in view of the arbitrary discretion which left to the individual inquisitor such opportunity to display his personal characteristics in dealing with the penitents before him. He was a judge in the forum of conscience, bound by no statutes and limited by no rules, with his penitents at his mercy, and no power save that of the Holy See itself could alter one jot of his decrees.*

This sometimes led to a lenity which would be otherwise inexplicable, as in the case of the murderers of St. Peter Martyr. Pietro Balsamo, known as Carino, one of the hired assassins, was caught red-handed, and his escape by bribery from prison created a popular excitement leading to a revolution in Milan. Yet, when recaptured, he repented, was forgiven, and allowed to enter the Dominican Order, in which he peacefully died, with the repute of a "beato;" and though the Church never formally recognized his right to the public worship paid to him in some places, still, in one of the stalls of the martyr's own great church of Sant' Eustorgio, he appears, with the title of the blessed Acerinus, in a chiaroscuro of 1505, among the Dominican saints. Not one, indeed, of those concerned in the assassination appears to have been put to death, and the leading instigator of the crime, Stefano Confalo-

---

* Arch. de l'Évêché d'Albi (Doat, XXXV. 69). — Arch. de l'Inq. de Carcassonne (Doat, XXVII. 232). — Concil. Narbonn. ann. 1234 c. 5. — Concil. Biterrens. ann. 1246, Append. c. 29.—Eymeric. Direct. Inq. pp. 506-7. — Zanchini Tract. de Hæret. c. xvi.—Guid. Fulcod. Quæst. xv.

niere of Aliate, a notorious heretic and fautor of heretics, after repeated abjurations, releases, and relapses, was not fairly imprisoned until 1295, forty-three years after the murder. It was the same when, soon afterwards, the Franciscan inquisitor, Pier da Bracciano, was assassinated, and Manfredo di Sesto, who had hired the assassins, was brought before Rainerio Saccone, the Inquisitor of Milan. He confessed the crime and other offences in aid of heresy, but was only ordered to present himself to the pope and receive penance. Contumaciously neglecting to do this, Innocent IV. merely ordered the magistrates of Italy to arrest and detain him if he should be found.*

Yet the theory which held the Church to be a loving mother unwillingly inflicting wholesome chastisement on her unruly children only lent a sharper rigor to most of the operations of the Inquisition. Those who were obdurate to its kindly efforts were ungrateful and disobedient when ingratitude and disobedience were offences of the most heinous nature. They were parricides whom it was mercy to reduce to subjection, and whose sin only the severest suffering could expiate. We have seen how little the inquisitor recked of human misery in his efforts to detect and convert the heretic, and it is not to be supposed that he would be more tender in his ministrations to the diseased souls asking for absolution and penance—and it was only the penitent who had confessed and abjured his sin who came before the judgment-seat for punishment. All others were left to the secular arm.

The flimsiness of this theory, however, is manifest from the fact that it was not only heretics—those who consciously erred in matters of faith—who were subjected to the jurisdiction and chastisement of the Inquisition. Fautors, receivers, and defenders— those who showed hospitality, gave alms, or sheltered or assisted heretics in any way, or neglected to denounce them to the authorities, or to capture them when occasion offered, also rulers who omitted to execute the laws against heresy, however orthodox themselves, incurred suspicion of heresy, simple, vehement, or violent. · If violent, it was tantamount to heresy; if simple or vehe-

---

* Tamburini, Istoria dell' Inquisizione, I. 492–502. — Bern. Corio, Hist. di Milano, ann. 1252.—Arch. de l'Inq. de Carcassonne (Doat, XXXI. 201).—Ripoll, I. 244, 280, 389.

ment, we have seen how readily it might, by failure of purgation, or by repetition, grow into technical heresy and relapse, incurring the gravest penalties, including relaxation to the secular arm. Not less conclusive to the real import of the inquisitorial organization is the argument of Zanghino, that if a heretic repents, confesses to his priest, accepts and performs penance and receives absolution, however he may be relieved from hell and pardoned in the sight of God, he is not released from temporal punishment, and is still subject to prosecution by the Inquisition. It would not abandon its prey, while yet it could not impugn the efficacy of the sacrament of penitence, and such difficulties were eluded by forbidding priests to take cognizance of heresy, which was reserved for bishops and inquisitors.*

The penances customarily imposed by the Inquisition were comparatively few in number. They consisted, firstly, of pious observances — recitation of prayers, frequenting of churches, the discipline, fasting, pilgrimages, and fines nominally for pious uses, such as a confessor might impose on his ordinary penitents. These were for offences of trifling import. Next in grade are the "*pœnœ confusibiles*"—the humiliating and degrading penances, of which the most important was the wearing of yellow crosses sewed upon the garments; and, finally, the severest punishment among those strictly within the competence of the Holy Office, the "*murus*," or prison. Confiscation, as I have said, was an incident, and the stake, like it, was the affair of the secular power; and though both were really controlled by the inquisitor, they will be more conveniently considered separately. The Councils of Narbonne and Béziers, in addition, prescribe a purely temporal punishment— banishment, either temporary or perpetual—but this would appear to have been so rarely employed that it may be disregarded, although in the earlier period it occasionally occurs in sentences, or is found among the penances to which repentant heretics pledged themselves to submit.†

---

* Concil. Tarraconens. ann. 1242. — Innoc. PP. IV. Bull. *Noverit universitas,* 1254 (Mag. Bull. Rom. I. 103). — Bern. Guidon. Practica P. IV. (Doat, XXX.).— Eymeric. Direct. Inquis. pp. 368–72, 376–8.—Zanchini Tract. de Hæret. c. xxxiii.
† Concil. Narbonn. ann. 1244 c. 3.—Concil. Biterrens. ann. 1246, Append. c. 28.—Coll. Doat, XXI. 200.—MSS. Bib. Nat., fonds latin, No. 9992.

The sin of heresy was too grave to be expiated simply by contrition and amendment. While the Church professed to welcome back to her bosom all her erring and repentant children, the way of the transgressor was made hard, and his offence could only be washed away by penances severe enough to prove the robustness of his convictions. Before the Inquisition was founded, about 1208, St. Dominic, while acting under the authority of the Legate Arnaud, converted a Catharan named Pons Roger, and prescribed for him a penance which has chanced to be preserved. It will give us an insight into what were considered reasonable terms of readmission to the Church, at a time when it was straining every nerve to win the heretics back, and before it had fairly resorted to the use of force. On three Sundays the penitent is to be stripped to the waist and scourged by the priest from the entrance of the town of Tréville to the church-door. He is to abstain forever from meat and eggs and cheese, except on Easter, Pentecost, and Christmas, when he is to eat of them in sign of his abnegation of his Manichæan errors. For twoscore days, twice a year, he is to forego the use of fish, and for three days in each week that of fish, wine, and oil, fasting, if his health and labors will permit. He is to wear monastic vestments, with a small cross sewed on each breast. If possible, he is to hear mass daily, and on feast-days to attend church at vespers. Seven times a day he is to recite the canonical hours, and, in addition, the Paternoster ten times each day and twenty times each night. He is to observe the strictest chastity. Every month he is to show this paper to the priest, who is to watch its observance closely, and this mode of life is to be maintained until the legate shall see fit to alter it, while for infraction of the penance he is to be held as a perjurer and a heretic, and be segregated from the society of the faithful.[*]

This shows how the various forms of penance were mingled together at the discretion of the ghostly father. The same is seen in an exceedingly lenient sentence imposed in 1258 by the inquisitors of Carcassonne on Raymond Maria, who had confessed to various acts of heresy committed twenty or thirty years before, and who, for other reasons, had strong claims for merciful treatment. It further illustrates the practice of compounding pious

---

[*] Paramo de Orig. Offic. S. Inquis. Lib. II. Tit. i. c. 2, § 6.—Martene Thesaur. I. 802.—Coll. Doat, XXXI. 1.

observances for money. Raymond is ordered to fast from the Friday after Michaelmas until Easter, and to eat no meat on Saturdays, but he can redeem the fast by giving a denier to a poor man. Every day he is to recite seven times the Paternoster and Ave Maria. Within three years he is to visit the shrines of St. Mary of Roche-amour, St. Rufus of Aliscamp, St. Gilles of Vauverte, St. William of the Desert, and Santiago de Compostella, bringing home testimonial letters from the rector of each church; and in lieu of other penances he is to give six livres Tournois to the Bishop of Albi to aid in building a chapel. He is to hear mass at least every Sunday and feast-day, and to abstain from all work on those days. Another penance belonging to the same general category is that inflicted on a Carthusian monk of la Loubatière who was guilty of Spiritual Franciscanism. He was ordered not to leave the abbey for three years, and during that time not to speak except in extreme necessity. For a year he was to confess daily in the presence of his brethren that John XXII. was the true pope and entitled to obedience; and, in addition, he was to undergo certain fasts and perform certain recitations of the liturgy and psalter. Penances of this character could be varied *ad infinitum* at the caprice of the inquisitor.*

In all this there is no mention of flagellation, but that was so general a feature of penance that it is frequently taken for granted in prescribing pilgrimages and attendance at church. We have seen Raymond of Toulouse submitting to it, and however abhorrent it may be to our modern ideas, it did not carry with it that sense of humiliation which to us appears inseparable from it. In the lightest penalties provided for voluntary converts, coming forward within the time of grace, the Councils of Narbonne and Béziers, in 1244 and 1246, and that of Tarragona, in 1242, order the discipline. It was no light matter. Stripped as much as decency and the inclemency of the weather would permit, the penitent presented himself every Sunday, between the Epistle and the Gospel, with a rod in his hand, to the priest engaged in celebrating mass, who soundly scourged him in the presence of the congregation, as a fitting interlude in the mysteries of divine service. On the first Sunday in every month, after mass, he was to visit, similarly

---

* Archives de l'Inq. de Carcassonne (Doat, XXXI. 255).—Coll. Doat, XXVII. 136.

equipped, every house in which he had seen heretics, and receive the same infliction; and on the occasion of every solemn procession he was to accompany it in the same guise, to be beaten at every station and at the end. Even when the town happened to be placed under interdict, or himself to be excommunicated, there was to be no cessation of the penance, and apparently it lasted as long as the wretched life of the penitent, or at least until it pleased the inquisitor to remember him and liberate him. That this was no idle threat is shown by these precise details occurring in a formula given by Bernard Gui, about 1330, for the release from prison of penitents who by patience and humility in their captivity have earned a mitigation of their punishment, and virtually the same formula was employed immediately after the organization of the Inquisition.*

The pilgrimages, which were regarded as among the lightest of penances, were also mercies only by comparison. Performed on foot, the number commonly enjoined might well consume several years of a man's life, during which his family might perish. A frequent injunction by Pierre Cella, one of the most moderate of inquisitors, comprehended Compostella and Canterbury, with perhaps several intermediate shrines, and in one case a man over ninety years of age was ordered to perform the weary tramp to Compostella simply for having consorted with heretics. These pilgrimages were not without peril and hardship, although the hospitality exercised by the numerous convents on the road enabled the poorest pilgrim to sustain life. Still, pilgrimages were so habitual a feature of mediæval habits, and entered so frequently into ordinary penance, that their use by the Inquisition was inevitable. When the yearning for salvation was so strong that two hundred thousand pilgrims arriving in Rome in a single day is said to have been no uncommon occurrence during the Jubilee of 1300, the penitent who escaped with the performance of such pious observances might well regard himself as mercifully treated.†

The penitential pilgrimages of the Inquisition were divided

---

* Concil. Tarraconens. ann. 1242.—Concil. Narbonnens. ann. 1244 c. 1.—Concil. Biterrens. ann. 1246, Append. c. 6.—Bern. Guidon. Practica (Doat, XXIX. 54). —MSS. Bib. Nat., fonds latin, No. 14930, fol. 214.

† Coll. Doat, XXI. 222.—Wadding. Annal. ann. 1300, No. 1.—Cf. Molinier, L'Inq. dans le midi de la France, pp. 400-1.

into two classes—the greater and the less. In Languedoc the greater pilgrimages were customarily four—to Rome, Compostella, St. Thomas of Canterbury, and the Three Kings of Cologne. The smaller were nineteen in number, extending from shrines of local celebrity to Paris and Boulogne-sur-mer. The cases in which they were employed may be estimated by the sentence passed by Bernard Gui, in 1322, on three culprits whose only offence was that, some fifteen or twenty years before, they had seen Waldensian teachers in their fathers' houses without knowing what they were. Commencing within three months, the penitents were required to perform seventeen of the minor pilgrimages, reaching from Bordeaux to Vienne, bringing back, as usual, from each shrine testimonial letters of the visit. In this case it is specified that they were not obliged to wear the crosses, and I think it probable that this exempted them from scourging at each of the shrines, to which penitents with crosses would naturally be subjected. In one case, occurring in 1308, a culprit was excused from pilgrimages on account of his age and weakness, and was only required to make two visitations a year in the city of Toulouse. Considerate humanity such as this is not sufficiently common in the annals of the Inquisition for an example of it to be passed in silence.*

At the inception of the Inquisition the pilgrimage universally ordered for men was that to Palestine, as a crusader. Indeed, the legate, Cardinal Romano, commanded this for all who were suspect of heresy. It seems to have been felt that the best use to which a heretic could be put, if he was to escape the fagot, was to make him aid in the defence of the Holy Land—a service of infinite hardship and peril. In the wholesale persecutions in Languedoc the numbers of these unwilling crusaders were so great that alarm was excited lest they should pervert the faith in the land of its origin, and about 1242 or 1243 a papal prohibition was issued, forbidding it for the future. The Council of Béziers, in 1246, commits to the discretion of the inquisitors whether penitents shall serve beyond seas, or send a man-at-arms to represent them, or fight the battles of the faith nearer home, against heretics or Saracens. The term of service was also left to the inquisitors, but

---

* Arch. de l'Inq. de Carcassonne (Doat, XXXVII. 11).—Lib. Sententt. Inq. Tolosan. pp. 1, 340-1.

was usually for two or three years, though sometimes for seven or eight, and those who went to Palestine, if they were so fortunate as to return, were obliged to bring back testimonial letters from the Patriarch of Jerusalem or Acre. When Count Raymond was preparing to fulfil his long-delayed vow of a crusade, in his eagerness for recruits he procured in 1247, from Innocent IV., a bull empowering the Archbishop of Ausch and Bishop of Agen, within Raymond's dominions, to commute into a pilgrimage beyond seas the penance of temporary crosses and prison, and even when these were perpetual, if the consent could be had of the inquisitor who had uttered the sentence; and the following year this was extended to those in the territories of the Counts of Montfort. Under this impulsion, the penance of crusading became common again. There is extant a notice given by the inquisitors of Carcassonne, October 5, 1251, in the church of St. Michael, to those wearing crosses and those relieved from them, that they must without fail sail for the Holy Land, as they had pledged themselves to do, in the next fleet; and in the Register of Carcassonne the injunction of the crusade is of frequent occurrence. With the disastrous result of the ventures of St. Louis and the fall of the Kingdom of Jerusalem this form of penance gradually diminished, but it continued to be occasionally prescribed. As late as 1321 we find Guillem Garric condemned to go beyond seas with the next convoy and remain until recalled by the inquisitor; if legitimately impeded (which was likely, as he was an old man who had rotted in a dungeon for thirty years) he could replace himself with a competent fighting-man, and if he neglected to do so, he was condemned to perpetual prison. This sentence, moreover, affords one of the rare instances of banishment, for Guillem, besides furnishing a substitute, is ordered to expatriate himself to such place as shall be designated, during the pleasure of the inquisitor.*

These penances did not interfere with the social position and self-respect of the penitent. Far heavier was the apparently sim-

---

* Wadding. Annal. ann. 1238, No. 7.—Concil. Narbonn. ann. 1244 c. 2.— Concil. Biterrens. ann. 1246, Append. c. 26, 29.—Berger, Les Registres d'Innocent IV. No. 3508, 3677, 3866.—Coll. Doat, XXXI. 17.—Vaissette, III. Pr. 468.—MSS. Bib. Nat., fonds latin, nouv. acq. 139, fol. 8.—Molinier, L'Inq. dans le midi de la France, pp. 408-9.—Lib. Sententt. Inq. Tolos. pp. 284-5.—Coll. Doat, XXI. 185, 186, 217.

ple penalty of wearing the crosses, which was known as a *pœna confusibilis*, or humiliating punishment. We have seen that already, in 1208, St. Dominic orders his converted heretic to wear two small crosses on the breast in sign of his sin and repentance. It seems a contradiction that the emblem of the Redemption, so proudly worn by the crusader and the military orders, should be to the convert an infliction almost unbearable, but when it became the sign of his sin and disgrace there were few inflictions which might not more readily be borne. The two little crosses of St. Dominic grew to conspicuous pieces of saffron-colored cloth, of which the arms were two and a half fingers in breadth, two and a half palms in height, and two palms in width, one sewed on the breast and the other on the back, though occasionally one on the breast sufficed. If the convert during his trial had committed perjury, a second transverse arm was added at the top; and if he had been a "perfected" heretic, a third cross was placed upon the cap. Another form was that of a hammer, worn by prisoners temporarily liberated on bail; and we have seen the red tongues fastened on false-witnesses, and the symbol of a letter inflicted on a forger, while other emblematical forms were prescribed, as the fancy of the inquisitor might dictate. They were never to be laid aside, in doors or out, and when worn out the penitent was obliged to renew them. During the latter half of the thirteenth century those who went beyond seas might abandon their crosses during their crusade, but were obliged to reassume them on returning. In the earlier days of the Inquisition a term ranging from one year to seven or eight was usually prescribed, but in the later period it was always for life, unless the inquisitor saw fit, as a reward of good behavior, to remit it. Thus in the *auto de fé* of 1309 Bernard Gui permitted Raymonde, wife of Étienne Got, to remove the crosses which she had been condemned to wear, some forty years before, by Pons de Poyet and Étienne de Gâtine.*

---

* C. Biterrens. ann. 1246, Append. c. 26.—Lib. Sententt. Inq. Tolosan. pp. 8, 13, 130, 228.

In Italy the crosses appear to be of red cloth (Archiv. di Firenze, Prov. S. Maria Novella, 31 Ott. 1327).

At an early period there is a single allusion to another "*pœna confusibilis*" in the shape of a wooden collar or yoke worn by the penitent. This occurs at La Charité, in 1233, and I have not met with it elsewhere (Ripoll, I. 46).

The Council of Narbonne, in 1229, prescribed the wearing of these crosses by all converts who voluntarily abandoned heresy and returned to the faith of their own free will, as an evidence of their detestation of their former errors. Apparently the penance was found hard to bear, and efforts were made to escape it, for the statutes of Raymond, in 1234, and the Council of Béziers of the same year, threaten confiscation for all who refuse to wear them, or endeavor to conceal them. Subsequent councils renewed and extended the obligation on all who were reconciled to the Church; and that of Valence, in 1248, decreed that all who disobeyed should be forced without mercy to resume them, and that abandoning them after due monition should be visited, like jail-breaking, with the full penalties of impenitent heresy. In a case recorded in 1251, a penitent preparing for a crusade seems to have thought himself authorized to abandon the crosses before starting, and was sentenced to come to Carcassonne on the first Sunday of every month until his departure, barefooted and in shirt and drawers, and visit every church in the city, with a rod, to undergo scourging.*

Though this penance was regarded as merciful in comparison with imprisonment, it was not easily endurable, and we can readily understand the sharp penalties required to enforce obedience. In the sentences of Pierre Cella it is only prescribed in aggravated cases, and then merely for from one to five years, though subsequently it grew to be universal, and without a limit of time. The unfortunate penitent was exposed to the ridicule and derision of all whom he met, and was heavily handicapped in every effort to earn a livelihood. Even in the earlier time, when a majority of the population of Languedoc were heretics, and the cross-wearers were so numerous that their presence in Palestine was dreaded, the Council of Béziers, in 1246, feels obliged to warn the people that penitents should be welcomed and their cheerful endurance of penance should be a subject of gratulation for all the faithful, and therefore it strictly forbids ridicule of those who wear crosses, or refusal to transact business with them. Though penitents were

---

* Concil. Narbonn. ann. 1229 c. 10.—Statut. Raymondi ann. 1234 (Harduin. VII. 205).—Concil. Biterrens. ann. 1234 c. 4.—Concil. Tarraconens. ann. 1242.— Concil. Narbonn. ann. 1244 c. 1.—Concil. Valentin. ann. 1248 c. 13.—Concil. Albiens. ann. 1254 c. 4.—MSS. Bib. Nat., fonds latin, nouv. acq. 139, fol. 2.

under the special protection of the Church, it had too zealously preached detestation of heresy to be able to control the feelings of the population towards those whom it thus saw fit to stigmatize. A slight indication of this is seen in the case of Raymonde Manifacier, who, in 1252, was cited before the Inquisition of Carcassone for abandoning the crosses, when she urged in extenuation that the one on her cloak had been torn and she was too poor to replace it, while as regards that on her cape, her mistress, whom she served as nurse, had forbidden her to wear it and had given her a cape without one. A stronger case is that already cited of Arnaud Isarn, who found, after a year's experience, that he could not earn a living while thus bearing the marks of his degrada-tion.*

The Inquisition recognized the intolerable hardships to which its penitents were exposed, and sometimes in mercy mitigated them. Thus, in 1250, at Carcassonne, Pierre Pelha receives permission to lay aside the crosses temporarily during a voyage which he is obliged to make to France. Bernard Gui assures us that young women were frequently excused from wearing them, because with them they would be unable to find husbands; and among the formulas of his "*Practica*" one which exempts the penitent from crosses enumerates the various reasons usually assigned, such as the age or infirmity of the wearer (presumably rendering him a safe object of insult) or on account of his children, whom he may not otherwise be able to support, or for the sake of his daughters, whom he cannot marry. Still more suggestive are formulas of proclamations threatening to prosecute as impeders of the Inquisition and to impose crosses on those who ridicule such penitents or drive them away or prevent them from following their callings; and the insufficiency of this is shown by still other formulas of orders addressed to the secular officials, who are required to see that no such outrages are perpetrated. Sometimes monitions of this kind formed part of the regular proceedings of the *autos de fé*. The wearing of the symbol of Christianity was evidently a punishment of no slight character. The well-known *sanbenito* of the modern Spanish Inquisition was de-

---

* Coll. Doat, XXI. 185 sqq. — Concil. Biterrens. ann. 1246 c. 6. — Molinier, L'Inquis. dans le midi de la France, p. 412.—Lib. Sententt. Inq. Tolosan. p. 350.

rived from the scapular with saffron-colored crosses which was worn by those condemned to imprisonment, when on certain feast-days they were exposed at the church doors, that their misery and humiliation might serve as a warning to the people.*

It will be remembered that at the outset there was some discussion as to whether it should be competent for the inquisitors to inflict the pecuniary penance of fines. The voluntary poverty and renunciation of money of the Mendicants, to whom the Holy Office was confided, had not yet become so obsolete that the incongruity could be overlooked of their using their almost limitless discretion in levying fines and handling the money thence accruing. That they commenced it early is shown by a sentence of 1237, already quoted, in which Pons Grimoardi, a voluntary convert, is required to pay to the order of the inquisitor ten livres Morlaas, while in 1245, in Florence, one rendered by the indefatigable inquisitor, Ruggieri Calcagni, shows that already fines were habitual there. It was not without cause, therefore, that the Council of Narbonne, in 1244, in its instructions to inquisitors, ordered them to abstain from pecuniary penances both for the sake of the honor of their Order and because they would have ample other work to do. The Order itself felt this to be the case, and as inquisitors were not yet, at least in theory, emancipated from the control of their superiors, already, in 1242, the Provincial Chapter of Montpellier had endeavored to enforce the rules of the Order by strictly prohibiting them from inflicting pecuniary penances for the future, or from collecting those which had already been imposed. How little respect was shown to these injunctions is visible from a bull of Innocent IV., in 1245, in which, to preserve the reputation of the inquisitors, he orders all fines paid over to two persons selected by the bishop and inquisitor, to be expended in building prisons and in supporting prisoners, in compliance with which the Council of Béziers, in 1246, abandoned the position taken by the Council of Narbonne, and agreed that the fines should be employed on the prisons, and in defraying the neces-

* Molinier, op. cit. p. 404, 414–15.—Bernard. Guidon. Gravamina (Doat, XXX. 115). — Ejusd. Practica P. II. (Doat, XXIX. 75).—Arch. de l'Inq. de Carc. (Doat, XXXVII. 107, 135, 149).—Eymeric. Direct. Inq. pp. 496–99.

sary expenses of the Inquisition, possibly because the good bishops found that they themselves were expected to meet these demands as appertaining to the episcopal jurisdiction. In an inquisitorial manual of the period this is specified as the destination of the fines, but the power was speedily abused, and in 1249 Innocent IV. sternly rebuked the inquisitors in general for the heavy exactions which they wrung from their converts, to the disgrace of the Holy See and the scandal of the faithful at large. This apparently had no effect, and in 1251 he prohibited them wholly from levying fines if any other form of penance could be employed. Yet the inquisitors finally triumphed and won the right to inflict pecuniary penances at discretion. These were understood to be for pious uses, in which term were included the expenses of the Inquisition; and as they were payable to the inquisitors themselves, they doubtless were so expended—it is to be hoped in accordance with the caution of Eymerich, "decently and without scandal to the laity." In the sentences of Frà Antonio Secco on the peasants of the Waldensian valleys in 1387, the penance of crosses is usually accompanied with a fine of five or ten florins of pure gold, payable to the Inquisition, nominally to defray the expenses of the trial. An attempt of the State to secure a share was defeated by a council of experts assembled at Piacenza in 1276 by the Lombard inquisitors, Frà Niccolò da Cremona and Frà Daniele da Giussano. A more decent use of the power to inflict money payments was one which Pierre Cella, the first inquisitor of Toulouse, frequently employed, by adding to the pilgrimages or other penances imposed the obligation of maintaining a priest or a poor man for a term of years or for life.*

In the later period of the Inquisition it was argued that fines were inadmissible, because if the accused were a heretic all his property disappeared in confiscation, while if he were not he

---

* Vaissette, III. Pr. 386.—Lami, Antichità Toscane, p. 560.—Concil. Narbonn. ann. 1244 c. 17. — Innoc. PP. IV. Bull. *Quia te*, 19 Jan. 1245 (Doat, XXXI. 71).— Molinier, op. cit. pp. 23, 390. — Concil. Biterrens. ann. 1246, Append. c. 27.—Practica super Inquisit. (MSS. Bib. Nat., fonds latin, No. 14930, fol. 222).—Innoc. PP. IV. Bull. *Cum a quibusdam*, 14 Mai. 1249 (Doat, XXXI. 81, 116). — Coll. Doat, XXXIII. 198. — Ripoll, I. 194. — Eymeric. Direct. Inq. pp. 648-9, 653. — Zanchini Tract. de Hæret. c. xix., xx., xli.—Archivio Storico Italiano, No. 38, pp. 27, 42.— Campi, Dell' Hist. Eccles. di Piacenza, P. II. p. 309.—Coll. Doat, XXI. 185 sqq.

should not be punished, but the inquisitors responded that, although this was true, there were fautors and defenders of heresy, and those whose heresy consisted merely in a thoughtless word, all of whom could legitimately be fined; and the profitable abuse went on.*

Scarcely separable from the practice of fines was that of commuting penances for money. When we remember how extensive and lucrative was the custom of commuting the vows of crusaders, it was inevitable that a similar abuse should flourish in the Church's dealings with the penitents whom the Inquisition had placed within its power. A ready excuse was found in the proviso that the sums thence arising should be spent in pious uses—and no use could be more pious than that of ministering to the wants of those who were zealously laboring for the purity of the faith. In this the Holy See set the example. We have seen how, in 1248, Algisius, the papal penitentiary, ordered the release, by authority of Innocent IV., of six prisoners who had confessed heresy, alleging as a reason the satisfactory contributions which they had made to the Holy Land. The same year Innocent formally authorized Algisius to commute the penalties of certain heretics, without regard to the inquisitors, and he further empowered the Archbishop of Ausch to transmute into subsidies the penances imposed on reconciled heretics. Raymond was preparing for his crusade, and the excuse was a good one. The heretics were eager to escape by sacrificing their substance, and the project promised to be profitable. In 1249, accordingly, Algisius was sent to Languedoc armed with power to commute all inquisitorial penances into fines to be devoted to the needs of the Church and of the Holy Land, and to issue all necessary dispensations notwithstanding the privileges of the Inquisition. It is not to be supposed that the example was lost upon the inquisitors. Naturally enough, the cases which have reached us usually specify some pious work to which the funds were to be devoted, as when, in 1255, the inquisitors of Toulouse allowed twelve of the principal citizens of Lavaur to commute their penances into money to be contributed to building the church which was afterwards the Cathedral of Lavaur; and in 1258 they assisted the church of Najac in the same way by

---

* Bernardi Comens. Lucerna Inquisit. s. v. *Pœnam.*

allowing a number of the inhabitants to redeem their penalties for its benefit. The public utility of bridges caused them to be included in the somewhat elastic term of pious uses. Thus, in 1310, at Toulouse, Mathieu Aychard is released from wearing crosses and performing certain pilgrimages on condition of contributing forty livres Tournois to a new bridge then under construction at Tonneins; and in a formula for such transactions given by Bernard Gui, absolution and dispensation from pilgrimages and other penances are said to be granted in consideration of the payment of fifty livres for the building of a certain bridge, or of a certain church, or "to be spent in pious uses at our discretion." This last clause shows that commutations were by no means always thus liberally disposed of, and in fact they often inured to the benefit of those imposing them. We have a specimen of this in letters of the Inquisitor of Narbonne in 1264, granting absolution to Guillem du Puy in consideration of his giving one hundred and fifty livres Tournois to the Inquisition. The magnitude of these sums shows the eagerness of the penitents to escape, and the enormous power of extortion wielded by the inquisitor. If he was a man of integrity he could doubtless resist the temptation, but to the covetous and self-indulgent the opportunity of oppressing the helpless was almost unlimited. The system was kept up to the end. Under Nicholas V. Fray Miguel, the Inquisitor of Aragon, gave mortal offence to some high dignitaries in following certain papal instructions, whereupon they maltreated him and kept him in prison for nine months. It was a flagrant case of impeding the Inquisition, and in 1458 Pius II. ordered the Archbishop of Tarragona to dig up the bones of one of the offenders who had died, and to send the rest to the Holy See for judgment—but he added that the archbishop might, at his discretion, substitute a mulct for the war against the Turks, to be transmitted to the papal camera. It goes without saying that the death-penalty could never legally be commuted.*

---

* Arch. de l'Inq. de Carcassonne (Doat, XXXI. 152).—Archives Nationales de France, J. 430, No. 1. — Berger, Les Registres d'Innoc. IV. No. 4093. — Vaissette, III. 460, 462.—Molinier, op. cit. pp. 173, 283-4, 391, 396, 397.—Lib. Sententt. Inq. Tolos. p. 40.—Bern. Guidon. Practica (Doat, XXIX. 83).—Coll. Doat, XXXI. 292. —Arch. de l'Inq. de Carcassonne (Doat, XXXV. 192).—Zanchini Tract. de Hæret. c. xix.

Penitents who died before fulfilling their penance afforded a specially favorable opportunity for such transactions as these. Death, as we have seen, afforded no immunity from the jurisdiction of the Inquisition and in no wise abated its energy of prosecution. There might be a distinction drawn in practice between those who were taken off while humbly performing the penance assigned to them, but before its completion, and those who had wilfully neglected its commencement; but legally the non-fulfilment of penance entailed condemnation for heresy whether in the dead or living. In 1329, for instance, the Inquisition of Carcassonne ordered the exhumation and cremation of the bones of seven persons declared to have died in heresy for not having fulfilled the penance enjoined on them, which of course carried with it the confiscation of their property and the subjection of their descendants to the usual disabilities. The Councils of Narbonne and Albi directed the inquisitors to exact satisfaction at discretion from the heirs of those who had died before judgment, if they would have been condemned to wear crosses, as well as those who had confessed and been sentenced, and who had not lived, whether to commence or to complete their penance. Gui Foucoix expresses his belief that in these cases the penitent is admitted to purgatory, and he decides that nothing should be demanded from his heirs; but even his authority did not overcome the more palatable doctrine of the councils, and a contemporary manual directs the inquisitor to exact a "congruous satisfaction." There is something peculiarly repulsive in the rapacity which thus followed beyond the grave those who had humbly confessed and repented and were received into the bosom of the Church, but the Inquisition was unrelenting and exacted the last penny. For instance, the Inquisitor of Carcassonne had prescribed five years' pilgrimage to the Holy Land for Jean Vidal, who died before performing it. March 21, 1252, his heirs, under citation, swore that his whole estate was worth twenty livres, and gave security to obey the decision of the inquisitor, which was announced the following August, and proved to be a demand for twenty livres—the entire value of his property. In another case, Raymonde Barbaira had died before accomplishing some pilgrimages with crosses to which she had been sentenced. An inventory of her property showed it to consist of some bedding, clothing, a chest, a few cattle, and four sous in money, which had been divided up among her kindred, and from this pitiful inheritance the inquisitor, on March 7, 1256, demanded forty sous, for the payment of which by Easter the heirs had to give security. Such petty and vulgar details as these give us a clearer insight into the spirit and working of the Inquisition, and of the grinding oppression which it exercised on the subject populations. Even in the case of fautors who were not heretics, the heirs were obliged to perform any pecuniary penance which had been inflicted upon them.*

A more legitimate source of income, but yet one which opened the door to grave abuses, was the custom of taking bail, which of course was liable to forfeiture, serving, in such cases, as an irregular form of commutation. This custom dated from the inception of the Inquisition, and was practised at every stage of the proceedings, from the first citation to the final sentence, and even afterwards, when prisoners were sometimes liberated temporarily on giving security for their return. The convert who was absolved on abjuring was also required to give security that he would not relapse. Thus, in 1234, we see Lantelmo, a Milanese noble, ordered to give bail in two thousand lire, and two Florentine merchants bailed by their friends in two thousand silver marks. So, in 1244, the Baroni, of Florence, gave bail in one thousand lire to obey the mandates of the Church; and in 1252 a certain Guillem Roger pledged one hundred livres that he would go beyond seas by the next fleet and serve there for two years. The security was always to be pecuniary, and the inquisitor was warned not to take it of heretics, for their offence implied confiscation, but this was not strictly observed, as in special cases friends were found who furnished the necessary pledges. Forfeited bail was payable to the inquisitor, sometimes directly, and sometimes through the hands of the bishops, and was to be used for the expenses of the Inquisition. The usual form of bond pledged all the property of the principal and that of two sureties, jointly and severally; and as a general rule bail may be said to have been universal, except

---

* Arch. de l'Inq. de Carcassonne (Doat, XXVII. 236).—Concil. Narbonn. ann. 1244 c. 19. — Concil. Albiens. ann. 1254 c. 25. — Guid. Fulcod. Quæst. VII.— Practica super Inquisit. (MSS. Bib. Nat., fonds latin, No. 14930 fol. 221-2).— Molinier, op. cit. pp. 365, 392.—Bernardi Comens. Lucerna Inquisit. s. v. *Inquisitores*, No. 18.

in cases where the offence was regarded as too serious to admit of it, or when the offender could not procure it.*

It was impossible that these methods of converting the sentences of the Inquisition into current coin could flourish without introducing widespread corruption. Admission to bail might be the result of favoritism or degenerate into covert bribery. The discretion of the inquisitor was so wide that bribery itself could be safely indulged in. A crime necessarily so secret as this form of extortion cannot be expected to leave traces behind it, except in those cases in which it proved a failure, but sufficient instances of the latter are on record to show that the tribunals were surrounded by men who made a trade of their influence, real or presumed, with the judges. When these were incorruptible the business was suppressed with more or less success, but when they were acquisitive, they had ample field for unhallowed gain, to be wrung without stint or check from the subject populations both by bribery and extortion. Considering that every one above the age of seven was liable to the indelible suspicion of heresy by the mere fact of citation, it will be seen what an opportunity lay before the inquisitor and his spies and familiars to practise upon the fears of all, to sell exemptions from arrest, as well as to bargain for liberation. That these fruitful sources of gain were not abundantly worked would be incredible even in the absence of proof, but proof sufficient exists. In 1302 Boniface VIII. wrote to the Dominican Provincial of Lombardy that the papal ears had been lacerated with complaints of the Franciscan inquisitors of Padua and Vicenza, whose malicious cupidity had wronged many men and women by exacting from them immense sums and inflicting on them all manner of injuries. When the pope naïvely adduces in cumulation of their

---

* Concil. Narbonn. ann. 1244 c. 17.—C. Biterrens. ann. 1246, Append. c. 15.— Innoc. PP. IV. Bull. *Cum venerabilis*, 29 Jan. 1253; Bull. *Cum per nostras*, 30 Jan. 1253; Bull. *Super extirpatione*, 30 Mai. 1254.—Alex. PP. IV. Bull. *Super extirpatione*, 13 Nov. 1258, 20 Sept. 1259; Bull. *Ad audientiam*, 23 Jan. 1260.— Berger, Les Registres d'Innoc. IV. No. 3904.—Ripoll, I. 69, 71, 223-4, 247.— Lami, Antichità Toscane, p. 576.—MS. Bib. Nat., fonds latin, nouv. acquis. 139 fol. 43.—Eymeric. Direct. Inquis. p. 638.—Zanchini Tract. de Hæret. c. xix.— Bern. Guidon. Practica P. v. (Doat, XXX.).—Albert. Repert. Inq. s. v. *Cautio*.

The right to offer bail, except in capital offences, was one thoroughly recognized by the secular law. See, for instance, Isambert, Anc. Loix Franç. III. 57.

villainy that these wrong-doers had not employed the illicit gains for the benefit of the Holy Office, or of the Roman Church, or even of their own Order, he affords ground for the suspicion that a judicious distribution of the spoils secured silent condonation of such offences in many cases. He had sent Gui, Bishop of Saintes, to investigate these complaints, who reported them well founded, and he orders the provincial to replace the delinquents with Dominicans. The change brought little relief, for the very next year Mascate de' Mosceri, a jurist of Padua, appealed to Benedict from the new Dominican inquisitor, Frà Benigno, who was vexing him with prosecutions in order to extort money from him; and in 1304 Benedict was obliged to address to the inquisitors of Padua and Vicenza a grave warning as to the official complaints which still arose about their fraudulent prosecution of good Catholics by means of false witnesses. It is easy to understand the complaint made by the stricter Franciscans that the inquisitors of their Order rode around in state in place of walking barefoot as was prescribed by the rule. At this very time, moreover, the Dominicans of Languedoc were the subject of precisely similar arraignment on the part of the communities subjected to them. Redress in this case was long in coming, but at last the investigation set on foot by Clement V. convinced him of the truth of the facts alleged, and at the Council of Vienne, in 1311, he caused the adoption of canons, embodied in the Corpus Juris, which placed on record conspicuously his conviction that the inquisitorial office was frequently abused by the extortion of money from the innocent and the escape of the guilty through bribery. The remedy which he devised, of *ipso facto* excommunication in such cases, was complained of by Bernard Gui on the ground that it would invalidate the rightful acts, as well as the evil ones, of the wrong-doer; which only serves to show the vicious circle in which the whole business moved. Yet neither the hopes of Clement nor the fears of Bernard were justified by the result. The inquisitors continued to enrich themselves and the people to suffer untold miseries. In 1338 a papal investigation was made of a transaction by which the city of Albi purchased, by the payment of a sum of money to the Inquisitor of Carcassonne, the liberation of some citizens accused of heresy. In 1337 Benedict XII. ordered his nuncio in Italy, Bertrand, Archbishop of Embrun, to investigate the complaints which came from all parts of Italy that the inquisitors extorted money, received presents, allowed the guilty to escape, and punished the innocent, through hatred or avarice, and empowered him to make removals in consequence; and the exercise of this power shows that the complaints were well founded. The effects of the measure, however, were evanescent. In 1346 the whole republic of Florence rose against their inquisitor, Piero di Aquila, for various abuses, among which figured extortion. He fled and refused to return during the investigation which followed, in spite of the offer of a safe-conduct. A single witness swore to sixty-six cases of extortion, and in a partial list of them which has been preserved the sums exacted vary from twenty-five to seventeen hundred gold florins, showing how unlimited were the profits which tempted the unscrupulous. Villani tells us that in two years he had thus amassed more than seven thousand florins, an enormous sum in those days; that there were no heretics in Florence at the time, and that the offences which thus proved so lucrative to him consisted of usury and thoughtless blasphemy. As for usury, Alvaro Pelayo tells us that at that time the bishops of Tuscany set the example by habitually so employing the church funds, but the inquisitors did not meddle with the prelates. As for blasphemy, the subtle refinements which converted simple blasphemous expressions into heresy, as set forth by Eymerich, show how readily a skilful inquisitor could speculate on idle oaths. Boccaccio doubtless had Frà Piero in memory when he described the recent inquisitor of Florence who, like all his brethren, had an eye as keen to discover a rich man as a heretic, and who extracted a heavy *douceur* from a citizen for boasting in his cups that he had wine so good that Christ would drink it. The keenness which thus made profitable business for the Holy Office, when heresy was declining, is illustrated by the case of Marie du Canech, a money-changer of Cambrai, in 1403. In a case before the Ordinary she incautiously expressed the opinion that when under oath she was not bound to give evidence against her own honor and interest. For this the deputy inquisitor, Frère Nicholas de Péronne, prosecuted her and condemned her to various penances, including nine years' abstention from business and eighty gold crowns for expenses.*

---

* Molinier, op. cit. pp. 299-302.—Arch. de l'Inq. de Carcassonne (Doat,

These abuses continued to the last. Cornelius Agrippa tells us that it was customary for inquisitors to convert corporal punishments into pecuniary ones and even to exact annual payments as the price of forbearance. When he was in the Milanese, about 1515, there was a disturbance caused by their secretly extorting large sums from women of noble birth, whose husbands at length discovered it, and the inquisitors were glad to escape with their lives.*

I have dwelt at some length upon this feature of the Inquisition because it is one which has rarely received attention, although it inflicted misery and wrong to an almost unlimited extent. The stake consumed comparatively few victims. While the horrors of the crowded dungeon can scarce be exaggerated, yet more effective for evil and more widely exasperating was the sleepless watchfulness which was ever on the alert to plunder the rich and to wrench from the poor the hard-earned gains on which a family

---

XXXIV. 5. It is perhaps worthy of note that Ripoll, in printing this bull of Boniface VIII., T. II. p. 61, discreetly suppresses the details of inquisitorial wrong-doing).—Grandjean, Registres de Benoît XI. No. 169, 509.—Chron. Girardi de Fracheto Contin. ann. 1303 (D. Bouquet, XXI. 22–3).—Articuli Transgressionum (Archiv. für Litt.- u. Kirchengeschichte, 1887, p. 104).—C. 1, § 4, c. 2 Clement. v. 3.—Bernard. Guidon. Gravamina (Doat, XXX. 118–19).—Coll. Doat, XXXV. 113.—Ripoll, VII. 61.—Archivio di Firenze, Riformagioni, Classe XI. Distinz. I. No. 39.—Villani, Cronica, xii. 58.—Alvar. Pelag. de Planct. Eccles. Lib. ii. art. vii.—Eymeric. Direct. Inq. p. 332.—Decamerone, Giorn. I. Nov. 6.—Archives administratives de Reims, III. 641.

The strictness with which the canons against usury were construed is illustrated in a case decided by the University of Paris in 1490. The Faculty of Theology was consulted as to the righteousness of a contract under which a certain church had bought for three hundred livres an annual rent of twenty livres arising from certain lands, with the right of recalling the purchase-money after two months' notice; while by a separate agreement the land-owner had the right of redemption for nine years. This is doubtless a specimen of the means adopted of evading the prohibition of interest payment, which must have grown frequent with the development of commerce and industry. The contract ran for twenty-six years before it was questioned and referred to the University. A commission of twelve doctors of theology was appointed, who discussed the subject thoroughly, and reported, eleven to one, that the contract was usurious, and that the annual payments must be computed as partial payments on account of the purchase-money (D'Argentré, Collect. Judic. de nov. Error. I. ii. 323).

* Cornel. Agrippa de Vanitate Scientiar. cap. xcvi.

depended for support. It was only in rare cases that the victims
dared to raise a cry, and rarer still were those in which that cry
was heard; but sufficient instances have reached us to prove what
a scourge was the institution, in this aspect alone, on all the populations cursed by its presence. At a very early period the wealthy
already recognized that well-timed liberality was advisable towards
those who held such power in the hollow of their hands. In 1244
the Dominican Chapter of Cahors lifted a warning voice and ordered inquisitors not to allow their brethren to receive presents
which would expose the whole Order to disrepute; but this scru-
pulousness wore off, and even a man of high character like Eymerich could argue that inquisitors may properly be the recipients of
gifts, though he dubiously adds that they ought to be refused from
those under trial, except in special circumstances. As the accounts
of the Inquisition were rendered only to the papal camera, it will
be seen how little the officials had to dread investigation and ex-
posure. As little had they to fear the divine wrath, for their very
functions, while thus engaged, insured them plenary indulgence for
all sins confessed and repented. Thus secure, here and hereafter,
they were virtually relieved from all restraint.*

There was one purely temporal penalty which came within the
competence of the Inquisition—the designation of the houses which
were to be destroyed in consequence of the contamination of heresy.
The origin of this curious practice is not readily traced. Under
the Roman law, buildings in which heretics held their conventicles
with the owner's consent were not torn down, but were forfeited to
the Church. Yet as soon as heresy began to be formidable we
find their destruction commanded by secular rulers with singular
unanimity. The earliest provision I have met with occurs in the
assizes of Clarendon in 1166, which order the razing of all houses
in which heretics were received. The example was followed by
the Emperor Henry VI. in the edict of Prato, in 1194, by Otho IV.
in 1210, and by Frederic II. in the edict of Ravenna, in 1232, as
an addition to his coronation - edict of 1220, from which it had
been omitted. It had already been adopted in the code of Verona
in 1228 in all cases in which the owner, after eight days' notice,

---

* Molinier, op. cit. p. 307.—Eymeric. Direct. Inq. p. 650, 685.

neglected to expel heretic occupants ; it is found in the statutes of Florence a few years later, and is included in the papal bulls defining the procedure of the Inquisition. In France the Council of Toulouse, in 1229, decreed that any house in which a heretic was found was to be destroyed, and this was given the force of secular law by Count Raymond in 1234. It naturally forms a feature of the legislation of the succeeding councils which regulated the inquisitorial proceedings, and was adopted by St. Louis. Castile, in fact, seems to be the only land in which the regulation was not observed, owing doubtless to the direct derivation of its legislation from the Roman law, for, in the Partidas, houses in which heretics were sheltered are ordered to be given to the Church. Elsewhere such dwellings were razed to the ground, and the site, as accursed, was to remain forever a receptacle for filth and unfit for human habitation; yet the materials could be employed for pious uses unless they were ordered to be burned by the inquisitor who rendered the sentence. This sentence was addressed to the parish priest, with directions to publish it for three successive Sundays during divine service.*

In France the royal officials in charge of the confiscations came at length to object to this destruction of property, which was sometimes considerable, as the castle of the seigneur was as liable to it as the cabin of the peasant. In 1329 it forms one of the points for which the Inquisitor of Carcassonne, Henri de Chamay, asked and obtained the confirmation of Philippe de Valois, and the same year he had the satisfaction, in an *auto* held in September, to order the destruction of four houses, and a farm, whose owners had been hereticated in them on their death-beds. Some fifty years later, however, a quarrel on the subject between the king's representatives and the inquisitors of Dauphiné resulted differently. Charles le Sage, after consulting with the pope, issued letters of

---

* Constt. v., VIII. § 3, Cod. I. v.—Assis. Clarendon. Art. 21.—Lami, Antichità Toscane, p. 124.—Hist. Diplom. Frid. II. T. IV. pp. 299-300.—Lib. Juris Civilis Veronæ c. 156 (Ed. 1728, p. 117).—Alex. PP. IV. Bull. *Ad extirpanda*, § 21.—Concil. Tolosan. ann. 1229 c. 6.—Statut. Raymondi ann. 1234 (Harduin. VII. 203).— Vaissette, III. Pr. 370-1.—Concil. Biterrens. ann. 1246, Append. c. 35.—Concil. Albiens. ann. 1254 c. 6.—Établissements, Liv. I. c. 36.—Siete Partidas, P. VII. Tit. xxvi. l. 5.—Bern. Guidon. Practica (Doat, XXIX. 89).—Lib. Sententt. Inq. Tolosan. pp. 4, 80-1, 168.

October 19, 1378, ordering that the penalty should no longer be enforced. The independent spirit of northern Germany manifested itself in the same manner, and in the Sachsenspiegel there is a peremptory command that no houses shall be destroyed except for rape committed within them. In Italy the custom continued, as there the confiscations did not inure to the sovereign, but it was held that if the owner had no guilty knowledge of the use made of his house he was entitled to keep it. Lawyers disputed, however, as to the perpetuity of the prohibition to build on the spot, some holding that possession by a Catholic for forty years conferred a right to erect a new house, which others denied, arguing that a perpetual and imprescriptible servitude had been created. The inquisitors, in process of time, arrogated to themselves the power to issue licenses to build anew on these sites, and this right they exercised, doubtless, to their own profit, though they might not have found it easy to cite authority for it.*

Another temporal penalty may be alluded to as illustrating the unlimited discretion enjoyed by the inquisitors in imposing penance. When, in 1321, the town of Cordes made humble submission for its long-continued insubordination to its bishop and inquisitor, the penance assigned to the community by Bernard Gui and Jean de Beaune was the construction of a chapel of such size as might be ordered, in honor of St. Peter Martyr, St. Cecilia, St. Louis, and St. Dominic, with the statues of those saints in wood or stone above the altar; and, to complete the humiliation of the community, the portal was to be adorned with statues of the bishop and of the two inquisitors, the whole to be finished within two years, under a penalty of five hundred livres Tournois, which was to be doubled for a delay of another two years. Doubtless the people of Cordes built the chapel without delay, but they hesitated at this glorifying of their oppressors, for, twenty-seven years afterwards, in 1348, we find the municipal authorities summoned before the Inquisition of Toulouse and compelled to give pledges that the portal shall forthwith be completed and the inquisitorial effigies be erected.†

---

* Isambert, Anc. Loix Françaises, IV. 364; V. 491.—Ripoll, I. 252.—Arch. de l'Inq. de Carcassonne (Doat, XXVII. 248).—Sachsenspiegel, Buch III. Art. I.—Zanchini Tract. de Hæret. c. xxxix., xl.

† Lib. Sententt. Inq. Tolosan. 280.—Arch. de l'Inq. de Carc. (Doat, XXXV. 122).

The severest penance the inquisitor could impose was incarceration. It was, according to the theory of the inquisitors, not a punishment, but a means by which the penitent could obtain, on the bread of tribulation and water of affliction, pardon from God for his sins, while at the same time he was closely supervised to see that he persevered in the right path and was segregated from the rest of the flock, thus removing all danger of infection. Of course it was only used for converts. The defiant heretic who persisted in disobedience, or who pertinaciously refused to confess his heresy and asserted his innocence, could not be admitted to penance, and was handed over to the secular arm.*

In the bull *Excommunicamus* of Gregory IX., in 1229, all who after arrest were converted to the faith through fear of death were ordered to be incarcerated for life, thus to perform appropriate penance. The Council of Toulouse almost simultaneously made the same regulation, and manifested its sense of the real value of the involuntary conversions by adding the caution that they be prevented from corrupting others. The Ravenna decree of Frederic II., in 1332, adopted the same rule and made it settled legal practice. The Council of Arles, in 1234, called attention to the perpetual backsliding of those converted by force, and ordered the bishops to enforce strictly the penance of perpetual prison in all such cases. As yet the relapsed were not considered as hopeless, and were not abandoned to the secular court, or "relaxed," but were similarly imprisoned for life.†

The Inquisition at its inception thus found the rule established, and enforced it with the relentless vigor which it manifested in all its functions. It was represented as a special mercy shown to those who had forfeited all claims on human compassion. There were to be no exemptions. The Council of Narbonne, in 1244,

---

* Zanchini Tract. de Hæret. c. x.

† Gregor. PP. IX. Bull. *Excommunicamus*, 20 Aug. 1229.—Concil. Narbonn. ann. 1229 c. 9.—Hist. Diplom. Frid. II. T. IV. p. 300.—Concil. Arelatens. ann. 1234 c. 6.—Vaissette, III. Pr. 314.

Gregory's bull, as inserted in the canon law, provides perpetual imprisonment for those who "*redire noluerint*" (C. 15, § 1, Extra v. vii.), which is self-evidently an error for "*voluerint*," as the previous section directs that persistent heretics are to be handed over to the secular arm. Besides, Frederic's Ravenna decree, issued soon after, in prescribing lifelong imprisonment for converts, speaks of this being in accordance with the canons.

specifically declared that, except when special indulgence could be procured from the Holy See, no husband was to be spared on account of his wife, or wife on account of her husband, or parent in consideration of helpless children; neither sickness nor old age should claim mitigation. Every one who did not come forward within the time of grace and confess and denounce his acquaintances was liable to this penance, which in all cases was to be lifelong; but the prevalence of heresy in Languedoc was so great, and the terror inspired by the activity of the inquisitors grew so strong, that those who had allowed the allotted period to elapse flocked in, begging for reconciliation, in such multitudes that the good bishops declare not only that funds for the support of such crowds of prisoners were lacking, but even that it would be impossible to find stones and mortar sufficient to build prisons for them. The inquisitors are therefore instructed to delay incarceration in these cases, unless impenitence, relapse, or flight, is to be apprehended, until the pleasure of the pope can be learned. Apparently Innocent IV. was not disposed to leniency, for in 1246 the Council of Béziers sternly orders the imprisonment of all who have overstayed the time of grace, while counselling commutation when it would entail evident peril of death on parents or children. Imprisonment thus became the usual punishment, except of obstinate heretics, who were burned. In a single sentence of Feburary 19, 1237, at Toulouse, some twenty or thirty penitents are thus condemned, and are ordered to confine themselves in a house until prisons can be built. In a fragment which has been preserved of the register of sentences in the Inquisition of Toulouse from 1246 to 1248, comprising one hundred and ninety-two cases, with the exception of forty-three contumacious absentees, the sentence is invariably imprisonment. Of these, one hundred and twenty-seven are perpetual, six are for ten years, and sixteen for an indefinite period, as may seem expedient to the Church. It apparently was not till a later period that the order of the Council of Narbonne was obeyed, and the sentence always was for life. In the later periods this proportion will not hold good, for all inquisitors were not like the fierce Bernard de Caux, who then ruled the Holy Office in Toulouse; but perpetual imprisonment remained to the last the principal penance inflicted on penitents, although the decrees of Frederic and the canons of the councils of Toulouse and Narbonne were not held to apply to those who abjured heartily after arrest.*

In the later sentences which have reached us it is often not easy to guess why one prisoner is incarcerated and another let off with crosses, when the offences enumerated as to each would seem to be indistinguishable. The test between the two probably was one which does not appear on the record. All alike were converts, but he whose conversion appeared to be hearty and spontaneous was considered to be entitled to the easier penance, while the harsher one was inflicted when the conversion seemed to be enforced and the result of fear. Yet how relentlessly a man like Bernard Gui, who represents the better class of inquisitors, could enforce the strict measure of the law is seen in the case of Pierre Raymond Dominique, who had been cited to appear in 1309, had fled and incurred excommunication, had consequently, in 1315, been condemned as a contumacious heretic, and in 1321 had voluntarily come forward and surrendered himself on a promise that his life should be spared. His acts of heresy had not been flagrant, and he pleaded as an excuse for his contumacy his wife and seven children, who would have starved had they been deprived of his labor, but in spite of this he was incarcerated for life. Even the stern Bernard de Caux was not always so merciless. In 1246, we find him, in sentencing Bernard Sabbatier, a relapsed heretic, to perpetual imprisonment, adding that as the culprit's father is a good Catholic and old and sick, the son may remain with him and support him as long as he lives, meanwhile wearing the crosses.†

There were two kinds of imprisonment, the milder, or "*murus largus*," and the harsher, known as "*murus strictus*" or "*durus*" or "*arctus*." All were on bread and water, and the confinement, according to rule, was solitary, each penitent in a separate cell, with no access allowed to him, to prevent his being corrupted or corrupting others; but this could not be strictly enforced, and about 1306 Geoffroi d'Ablis stigmatizes as an abuse the visits of

---

* Concil. Tarraconens. ann. 1242.—Concil. Narbonn. ann. 1244 c. 9, 19.—Concil. Biterrens. ann. 1246, Append. c. 20.—Coll. Doat, XXI. 152.—MSS. Bib. Nat., fonds latin, No. 9992.—Bern. Guidon. Practica P. IV. (Doat, XXX.).

† Lib. Sententt. Inq. Tolos. *passim*, pp. 347-9.—Eymeric. Direct. Inq. p. 507.—MSS. Bib. Nat., fonds latin, No. 9992.—Practica super Inquisit. (MSS. Bib. Nat., fonds latin, No. 14930, fol. 222).

clergy, and laity of both sexes, permitted to prisoners. Husband and wife, however, were allowed access to each other if either or both were imprisoned; and late in the fourteenth century Eymerich agrees that zealous Catholics may be admitted to visit prisoners, but not women and simple folk who might be perverted, for converted prisoners, he adds, are very liable to relapse, and to infect others, and usually end with the stake.*

In the milder form, or "*murus largus*," the prisoners apparently were, if well behaved, allowed to take exercise in the corridors, where· sometimes they had opportunities of converse with each other and with the outside world. This privilege was ordered to be given to the aged and infirm by the cardinals who investigated the prison of Carcassonne and took measures to alleviate its rigors. In the harsher confinement, or "*murus strictus*," the prisoner was thrust into the smallest, darkest, and most noisome of cells, with chains on his feet—in some cases chained to the wall. This penance was inflicted on those whose offences had been conspicuous, or who had perjured themselves by making incomplete confessions, the matter being wholly at the discretion of the inquisitor. I have met with one case, in 1328, of aggravated false-witness, condemned to "*murus strictissimus*," with chains on both hands and feet. When the culprits were members of a religious order, to avoid scandal the proceedings were usually held in private, and the imprisonment would be ordered to take place in a convent of their own Order. As these buildings, however, usually were provided with cells for the punishment of offenders, this was probably of no great advantage to the victim. In the case of Jeanne, widow of B. de la Tour, a nun of Lespenasse, in 1246, who had committed acts of both Catharan and Waldensian heresy, and had prevaricated in her confession, the sentence was confinement in a separate cell in her own convent, where no one was to enter or see her, her food being pushed in through an opening left for the purpose—in fact, the living tomb known as the "*in pace*."†

---

* Arch. de l'Inq. de Carcassonne (Doat, XXXIII. 143).—Concil. Biterrens. ann. 1246 c. 23, 25.—Eymeric. Direct. Inq. p. 507.

† Arch. de l'hôtel-de-ville d'Albi (Doat, XXXIV. 45).—Bern. Guidon. Gravam. (Doat, XXX. 100).—Lib. Sententt. Inq. Tolos. pp. 32, 200, 287.—Arch. de l'Inq. de Carcassonne (Doat, XXVII. 136, 156).—MSS. Bib. Nat., fonds latin, No. 9992.

The cruelty of the monastic system of imprisonment known as *in pace*, or

I have already alluded to the varying treatment designedly practised in the detentive imprisonment of those who were under trial. When there was no special object to be attained by cruelty, this probably was as mild as could reasonably be expected. From occasional indications in the trials, it would seem that considerable intercourse was allowed with the outside world, as well as between the prisoners themselves, though watchful care was enjoined to prevent communication of any kind which might tend to harden the prisoner against a full confession of his sins.*

The prisons themselves were not designed to lighten the penance of confinement. At best the jails of the Middle Ages were frightful abodes of misery. The seigneurs-justiciers and cities obliged to maintain them looked upon the support of prisoners as a heavy charge of which they would gladly relieve themselves. If a debtor was thrust into a dungeon, although the law limited his confinement to forty days and ordered him to be comfortably fed, these prescriptions were customarily eluded, for the worse he was treated the greater effort he would make to release himself. As for criminals, bread and water were their sole diet, and if they perished through neglect and starvation it was a saving of expense. The prisoner who had money and friends could naturally obtain better treatment by liberal payment; but this alleviation was not often to be looked for in the case of heretics whose property had been confiscated, and with whom sympathy was dangerous.†

_____

vade in pacem, was such that those subjected to it speedily died in all the agonies of despair. In 1350 the Archbishop of Toulouse appealed to King John to interfere for its mitigation, and he issued an *Ordonnance* that the superior of the convent should twice a month visit and console the prisoner, who, moreover, should have the right twice a month to ask for the company of one of the monks. Even this slender innovation provoked the bitterest resistance of the Dominicans and Franciscans, who appealed to Pope Clement VI., but in vain. — Chron. Bardin, ann. 1350 (Vaissette, IV. Pr. 29).

The hideous abuse of keeping a prisoner in chains was forbidden by the contemporary English law (Bracton, Lib. III. Tract. i. cap. 6).

* Lib. Sententt. Inq. Tolos. pp. 102, 153, 231, 252–4, 301. — Muratori Antiq. Dissert. LX. (T. XII. p. 519).—Bern. Guidon. Practica P. v. (Doat, XXX.).—Arch. de l'Inq. de Carcassonne (Doat, XXVII. 7).

† Beaumanoir, Coutumes du Beauvoisis, cap. 51, No. 7. — G. B. de Lagrèze, La Navarre Française, II. 339.

The enormous number of captives resulting from the vigorous operations of the Inquisition in Languedoc had rendered the question as to the duty of building and maintaining prisons one of no little magnitude. It unquestionably rested with the bishops, whose laches in persecuting heresy were only made good by the inquisitors, and the bishops, at the Council of Toulouse, in 1229, had admitted this, only excepting that when the heretic had property those to whom the confiscations inured should provide for him. The burden, however, proved unexpectedly large, and we find them, in the Council of Narbonne, in 1244, trying to shift their responsibility by suggesting that the penitents who, but for the recent papal command, would be sent on crusades, should be utilized in building prisons and furnishing them with necessaries, "lest the prelates be overburdened with the poor converts, and be unable to provide for them on account of their multitude." Two years later, at Béziers, they declared that provision for both construction and maintenance ought to be made by those who profited by the confiscations, to which might be added the fines imposed by the inquisitors, which was not unreasonable; but in 1249 Innocent IV. still asserted that it was their business, and scolded them for not attending to it, and ordered that they be compelled to do it. At length, in 1254, the Council of Albi definitely decided that the holders of confiscated property should make provision for the imprisonment and maintenance of its former owners, and that, when heretics had nothing to confiscate, the cities or lords on whose lands they were captured should be responsible for them, and should be compelled by excommunication to attend to it. Still, the responsibility of the bishops was so self-evident that some zealous inquisitors talked of prosecuting them as fautors of heresy for neglecting to provide prisons, but Gui Foucoix discreetly advises against this, and recommends that such cases should be referred to the Holy See.*

In the accounts of the Sénéchausseé of Toulouse for 1337 there is an item of twenty sols expended in Nov., 1333, for straw for the prisoners to lie on, lest they should perish with cold during the winter. Other items, amounting to eighty-three sols eleven deniers, for the repairs of the fetters and shackles which they wore shows the rigor of their confinement.—Vaissette, Éd. Privat, X. Pr. 798-99.

* Concil. Tolosan. ann. 1229 c. 11.—Concil. Valentin. ann. 1234 c. 5.—Concil. Narbonn. ann. 1244 c. 4. — Coll. Doat, XXXI. 157. — Concil. Biterrens. ann.

The fate of the unfortunate captives was evidently most precarious while their oppressors and despoilers were thus squabbling as to the cost of keeping them in jail and providing them with bread and water. There was evident fitness that those who profited by the enormous confiscations resulting from persecution should at least provide prisons and maintenance for the unhappy victims of fanaticism and greed; and St. Louis, to whom the chief profits came as suzerain of the territories ceded at the Treaty of Paris, recognized in part his responsibility. In 1233 he undertook to provide prisons in Toulouse, Carcassonne, and Béziers. In 1246 he ordered his seneschal to provide for the inquisitors competent prisons in Carcassonne and Béziers, and to furnish daily bread and water for the prisoners. In 1258 we find him ordering his seneschal of Carcassonne to bring to speedy completion those which had been commenced; he assumes that the prelates and barons on whose lands heretics are captured should provide for their maintenance; but, in order to avoid trouble, he is willing that expenditures for this purpose shall be made from the royal funds, to be subsequently collected from the seigneurs. With the death of Alfonse and Jeanne of Toulouse, in 1272, all the territories lapsed to the crown, and, with insignificant exceptions, all the confiscations fell to the king. Henceforth the maintenance of prisons and prisoners, and the wages of jailers and attendants, were defrayed by the crown, except perhaps at Albi, where the bishop shared in the spoils, and seems to have been held to a portion of the expenses. Among the requests of Henri de Chamay, granted in 1329 by Philippe de Valois, is that the inquisitorial prison at Carcassonne shall be repaired by the king, and that all who have shared in the confiscations shall be made to contribute *pro rata*. Thereupon the seneschal assessed the Count of Foix to the extent of three hundred and two livres eleven sols nine deniers, which the latter refused to pay, and appealed to the king, with what result is not known. From a decision of the Parlement of Paris in 1304 it appears that the royal allowance for maintenance was three deniers per diem for each convicted prisoner, which would seem liberal enough, though Jacques de Polignac,

---

1246, Append. c. 23, 27.—Innoc. PP. IV. Bull. *Cum sicut*, 1 Mart. 1249 (Doat, XXXI. 114).—Conc^{il} Albiens. ann. 1254 c. 24.—Guid. Fulcod. Quæst. x.

who had charge of the prison at Carcassonne, and who was punished for his frauds, made out his accounts at the rate of eight deniers. This extravagance was not a precedent, and in 1337 we find the accounts still made out at the old rate of three deniers. For the accused detained and awaiting trial the Inquisition itself presumably had to provide. In Italy, where the confiscations, as we shall see, were divided into thirds, the Inquisition was self-supporting. In Naples the royal prisons were employed, and a royal order was required for incarceration.*

While the penance prescribed was a diet of bread and water, the Inquisition, with unwonted kindness, did not object to its prisoners receiving from their friends contributions of food, wine, money, and garments, and among its documents are such frequent allusions to this that it may be regarded as an established custom. Collections were made among those secretly inclined to heresy to alleviate the condition of their incarcerated brethren, and it argues much in favor of the disinterested zeal of the persecuted that they were willing to incur the risk attendant on this benevolence, for any interest shown towards these poor wretches exposed them to accusation to fautorship.†

The prisons were naturally built with a view to economy of construction and space rather than to the health and comfort of the captives. In fact the papal orders were that they should be constructed of small, dark cells for solitary confinement, only taking care that the "*enormis rigor*" of the incarceration should not extinguish life. M. Molinier's description of the Tour de l'Inquisition at Carcassonne, which was used as the inquisitorial prison, shows how literally these instructions were obeyed. It was a horrible place, consisting of small cells, deprived of all light and ventilation, where through long years the miserable inmates endured

---

* Molinier, op. cit. p. 435.—Vaissette, III. Pr. 536.—Vaissette, Éd. Privat. VIII. 1206.—Arch. de l'hôtel-de-ville d'Albi (Doat, XXXIV. 45).—Bern. Guidon. Gravam. (Doat, XXX. 109). — Isambert. Anc. Loix Françaises, IV. 364. — Vaissette, Éd. Privat, X. Pr. 693–4, 813–14.—Les Olim, III. 148.—Hauréau, Bernard Délicieux, p. 19.—Archivio di Napoli, Reg. 113, Lett. A, fol. 385 ; Reg. 154, Lett. C, fol. 81 ; MSS. Chioccorello, T. VIII.

† Arch. de l'Inq. de Carcassonne (Doat, XXVII. 14, 16). — Muratori Antiq. Dissert. LX. (T. XII. pp. 500, 507, 529, 535).—Lib. Sententt. Inq. Tolos. pp. 252–4, 307.—Tract. de Hæres. Paup. de Lugd. (Martene Thesaur. V. 1786).

a living death far worse than the short agony of the stake. In these abodes of despair they were completely at the mercy of the jailers and their servants. Complaints were not listened to; if a prisoner alleged violence or ill-treatment his oath was contemptuously refused, while that of the prison officials was received. A glimpse into the discipline of these establishments is afforded by the instructions given, in 1282, by Frère Jean Galande, Inquisitor of Carcassonne, to the jailer Raoul and his wife Bertrande, whose management had been rather lax. Under pain of irrevocable dismissal he is prohibited in future from keeping scriveners or horses in the prison; from borrowing money or accepting gifts from the prisoners; from retaining the money or effects of those who die; from releasing prisoners or allowing them to go beyond the first door, or to eat with him; from employing the servants on any other work or sending them anywhere, or gambling with them, or permitting them to gamble with each other.*

Evidently a prisoner who had money could obtain illicit favors from the honest Raoul; but these injunctions make no allusion to one of the most crying abuses which disgraced the establishments —the retention by the jailers of the moneys and provisions placed in their hands by the friends of the imprisoned. Frauds of all kinds naturally grew up among all who were concerned in dealing with these helpless creatures. In 1304 Hugolin de Polignac, the custodian of the royal prison at Carcassonne, was tried on charges of embezzling a part of the king's allowance, of carrying the names of prisoners on the rolls for years after their death, and of retaining the moneys contributed for them by their friends; but the evidence was insufficient to convict him. The cardinals whom Clement V. commissioned soon after to investigate the abuses of the Inquisition of Languedoc intimate broadly the nature of the frauds habitually practised, when they required the new jailers whom they appointed to swear to deliver to each captive without diminution the provisions supplied by the king, as well as those furnished by friends—an intimation confirmed by the decretals of Clement V. Their report shows that they were horror-struck with what they saw. At Carcassonne they took the control of

---

* Practica super Inquisit. (MSS. Bib. Nat., fonds latin, No. 14930, fol. 222).— Molinier, op. cit. p. 449. — Arch. de l'Inq. de Carcassonne (Doat, XXXII. 125; XXXVII. 83).

the prison wholly from the inquisitor, Geoffroi d'Ablis, and placed it in the hands of the bishop, ordering the upper cells to be repaired at once, in order that the aged and sick should be transferred to them; at Albi they struck the chains off the prisoners, commanded the cells to be lighted and new and better ones built within a month; at Toulouse things were equally bad. Everywhere there was complaint of lack of food and of beds, as well as of frequent torture. Their measures for reformation consisted in dividing the responsibility between bishop and inquisitor, whose concurrence was requisite to a sentence of imprisonment, and each of whom should appoint a jailer, while each jailer should have a key to each cell, and swear never to speak to a prisoner except in presence of his colleague. This insufficient remedy was adopted by Clement, and can hardly be imagined to have worked much improvement. Bernard Gui bitterly complained of the infamy cast on the Inquisition by the papal assertion of fraud and ill-treatment in the management of its prisons, and he pronounced the new regulations impracticable. Slender as was the restraint which they imposed on the inquisitors, we may feel sure that it was not long submitted to. In a few years Bernard Gui, in his Practica, assumes that the power of imprisoning lies wholly with the inquisitor; he contemptuously cites the Clementine canon by its title only, and proceeds to quote a bull of Clement IV. as if still in force, giving the authority to the inquisitor, and making no mention of the bishop. In fact, before the century was out, Eymerich considered the Clementine canons on this subject not worth inserting in his work, because, as he tells us, they were nowhere observed in consequence of their cost and inconvenience. About 1500, however, Bernardo di Como admits that the Clementine rule may be observed in punitive confinement after sentence, but holds that the inquisitor has sole control of the detentive prisons used before and during trial.*

---

* Les Olim, III. 148.—Archives de l'hôtel-de-ville d'Albi (Doat, XXXIV. 45). — Bern. Guidon. Gravam. (Doat, XXX. 105–8). — Ejusd. Practica P. IV. c. 1.— Eymeric. Direct. Inq. p. 587.—Bernardi Comens. Lucerna Inquisit. s. v. *Carcer.*

The passage in the *Practica* alluded to occurs in MSS. Bib. Nat., fonds latin, No. 14579, fol. 258. The allusion to the Clementines is not in the MS. printed by Douais, Paris, 1885, p. 179.

In 1325 Bishop Richard Ledred of Ossory availed himself of the Clementine

With such jailers it is probably rather to their corruption than to any lack of strength in the buildings that we may attribute the occasional escape of the inmates, which appears to have been by no means an infrequent occurrence. Even those who were confined in chains sometimes effected their liberation. More sufficient, however, as a means of release from the horrors of these foul dungeons was the excessive mortality caused by their filthy and unventilated squalor. Occasionally, as we have seen, the unfortunate were unlucky enough to live through protracted confinement, and there is one case in which a woman was graciously discharged, with crosses, in view of her having been for thirty-three years in the prison of Toulouse. As a rule, however, we may conclude that the expectation of life was very short. No records remain, if any were kept, to show the average term of those condemned to lifelong penance; but in the *autos de fé* there occur sentences pronounced upon prisoners who had died before their cases were ended, which show how large was the death-rate. These cases were despatched in batches. In the *auto* of 1310, at Toulouse, there are ten, who had died after confessing their heresy and before receiving sentence; in that of 1319 there are eight. The prison of Carcassonne seems to have been almost as deadly. In the *auto* of 1325 we find a lot of four similar cases, and in that of 1328 there are five. It is only under these peculiar circumstances that we have any chance of guessing at the deaths which occurred in prison, and from these scattered indications we can assume that the insanitary condition of the jails worked its inevitable result without human interference.*

Imprisonment was naturally the most frequent penance inflicted by the inquisitors. In Bernard Gui's Register of Sentences, comprising his operations between 1308 and 1322, there are six hundred and thirty-six condemnations recorded, which may be thus classified:

---

canon to claim supervision over the imprisonment of William Outlaw, whom he threw into the Castle of Kilkenny on a charge of fautorship of sorcerers—there being, apparently, no episcopal jail.—Wright's Proceedings against Dame Alice Kyteler, Camden Soc. 1843, p. 31.

* Lib. Sententt. Inq. Tolos. pp. 8, 13, 14, 19, 25, 26, 29, 158–62, 246–8, 255–61.—Arch. de l'Inq. de Carcassonne (Doat, XXVII. 7, 131; XXVIII. 164).

Delivered to the secular court and burned............................	40
Bones exhumed and burned..	67
Imprisoned...	300
Bones exhumed of those who would have been imprisoned....	21
Condemned to wear crosses..	138
Condemned to perform pilgrimages......................................	16
Banished to Holy Land...	1
Fugitives..	36
Condemnation of the Talmud..	1
Houses to be destroyed...	16
	636

and this may presumably be taken as a fair measure of the comparative frequency of the several punishments in use.

One peculiarity of the inquisitorial sentence remains to be noted. It always ended with a reservation of power to modify, to mitigate, to increase, and to reimpose at discretion. As early as 1244 the Council of Narbonne instructed the inquisitors always to reserve this power, and it became established as an invariable custom. Even without its formal expression, Innocent IV., in 1245, conferred on the inquisitors, acting with the advice and consent of the bishop of the penitent, authority to modify the penance imposed. The bishop, in fact, usually concurred in these alterations of sentences, but Zanchini informs us that though his assent should be asked, it was not essential, except in the case of clerks. The inquisitor, however, had no power to grant absolute pardons, which was reserved exclusively to the pope. The sin of heresy was so indelible that no authority short of the vicegerent of God could wash it out completely.*

This power to mitigate sentences was frequently exercised. It served as a stimulus to the penitents to give evidence by their deportment of the sincerity of their conversion, and, perhaps, also, it was occasionally of benefit as a means of depleting overcrowded jails. Thus in Bernard Gui's Register of Sentences there occur one hundred and nineteen cases of release from prison, with the obligation to wear the crosses, and of these fifty-one were subse-

* Concil. Narbonn. ann. 1244 c. 7. — Innoc. PP. IV. Bull. *Ut commissum*, 20 Jan. 1245 (Doat, XXXI. 68). — Vaissette, III. Pr. 468. — Concil. Biterrens. ann. 1246, Append. c. 20.—Zanchini, Tract. de Hæret. c. xxi., xxxviii.

quently relieved from the crosses. Besides these latter, there are also eighty-seven cases in which those originally condemned to crosses were permitted to lay them aside. This mercy was not peculiar to the Inquisition of Toulouse. In 1328, in a single sentence, twenty-three persons were released from the prison of Carcassone, their penance being commuted to crosses, pilgrimages, and other observances. What the measure of mercy was in such cases may be guessed from another sentence of commutation at Carcassonne in 1329, liberating ten penitents, among them the Baroness of Montréal. They were required to wear the yellow crosses for life and to perform twenty-one pilgrimages, embracing shrines as distant as Rome, Compostella, Canterbury, and Cologne. They were to hear mass every Sunday and feast-day during life, and present themselves with rods to the officiating priest and receive the discipline in the face of the congregation; and also to accompany all processions and be similarly disciplined at the final station. Existence under such conditions might well be regarded as a doubtful blessing.*

These mitigatory sentences, moreover, like the original ones, strictly reserved the power of alteration and reimposition, with or without cause. When the Inquisition once laid hands upon a man it never released its hold, and its utmost mercy was merely a ticket-of-leave. Just as no verdict of acquittal ever was issued, so the Council of Béziers, in 1246, and Innocent IV., in 1247, told the inquisitors that when they liberated a prisoner he was to be warned that the slightest cause of suspicion would lead him to be punished without mercy, and that they must retain the right to incarcerate him again without the formality of a fresh trial or sentence if the interest of the faith required. These conditions were observed in the formularies and enjoined in the manuals of practice. The penitent was made to understand fully that whatever liberty he enjoyed was subject to the arbitrary discretion of his judge, who could recall him to dungeon or fetters at any moment, and in his oath of abjuration he pledged his person and all his property to appear at once whenever he might be summoned. If Bernard Gui in his Formulary gives a draft of pardon for person and property and disabilities of heirs, he adds a caution that it is

---

* Arch. de l'Inq. de Carcassonne (Doat, XXVII. 2, 192).

never, or most rarely, to be used. When some great object was to be attained, such as the capture of a prominent heretic teacher, the inquisitors might stretch their authority and hold out promises of this kind to his disciples to induce them to betray him—promises which, it is pleasant to say, were almost universally spurned. If special penances had been imposed, on their fulfilment the inquisitor, if he saw fit, might declare the penitent to be a man of good character, but this did not alter the reservation in the original sentence. The mercy of the Inquisition did not extend to a pardon, but only to a reprieve, *dum bene se gesserit*, and the man who had once undergone a sentence never knew at what moment he might not be summoned to hear of its reimposition or even of a harsher one. Once a delinquent, his fate forever after was in the hands of the silent and mysterious judge who need not hear him nor give any reason for his destruction. He lived forever on the verge of ruin, never knowing when the blow might fall, and utterly powerless to avert it. He was always a subject to be watched by the universal police of the Inquisition — the parish priest, the monks, the clergy, nay, the whole population—who were strictly enjoined to report any neglect of penance or suspicious conduct, when he was at once liable to the awful penalties of relapse. Nothing was easier for a secret enemy than to destroy him, safe that his name would never be mentioned. We may pity the victims of the stake and the dungeon, but their fate was scarce harder than that of the multitudes who were the objects of the Inquisition's apparent mercy, but whose existence from that hour was one of endless, hopeless anxiety.*

The same implacability manifested itself after death. Allusion has frequently been made to the exhumation of the bones of those who by opportunely dying had seemed to exchange the vengeance of man for that of God, and it is only necessary to mention here that the fate of the dead was harder than that of the living. If he had died after confession and repentance, it is true, his punish-

---

* Lib. Sententt. Inq. Tolosan. pp. 40, 118, 122, 137, 139, 146, 147.—Bern. Guidon. Practica (Doat, XXIX. 85).—Ejusd. P. v. (Doat, XXX.).—Concil. Biterrens. ann. 1246, Append. c. 21, 22. — Vaissette, III. Pr. 467. — Practica super Inquisit. (MSS. Bib. Nat., fonds latin, No. 14930, fol. 222, 224).—Pegnæ Comment. in Eymeric. p. 509.—Zanchini Tract. de Hæret. c. xx.

ment was only that which he would have received if alive, the digging up replacing imprisonment, and his heirs being forced to perform or compound for any lighter penance; but if he had not confessed and there was evidence of heresy he was classed with the impenitent heretics, his remains were delivered to the secular arm, and his property hopelessly confiscated. This will account for the large number of these executions as shown in the records quoted above. If the secular authorities hesitated to perform the task of exhumation, they were coerced with excommunication.*

The same spirit pursued the descendants. In the Roman law the crime of treason was pursued with merciless vindictiveness, and its provisions are constantly quoted by the canon lawyers as precedents for the punishment of heresy, with the addition that treason to God is far more heinous than that to an earthly sovereign. It was, perhaps, natural that the churchman, in his eagerness to defend the kingdom of God, should follow and surpass the example of the emperors, and this will explain, if it may not justify, much that is abhorrent in the inquisitorial procedure. In the Code of Justinian, treason is made especially odious by inflicting on the sons disability to hold office and to succeed to collateral estates. By the Council of Toulouse, in 1229, even spontaneously converted heretics were declared ineligible to public office. It was natural, therefore, that Frederic II. should apply the Roman practice to heresy, and should extend its provision to grandchildren. This, like the rest of his legislation, was eagerly adopted and enforced by the Church. Alexander IV., however, in a bull of 1257, repeatedly reissued by his successors, explained that this did not apply in cases where the culprit had made amends and performed penance, and this was still further lightened by Boniface VIII., who removed the incapacity from grandchildren by the female ·line of those who had died in heresy. In this form it remained permanently in the canon law.†

---

* Concil. Arelatens. ann. 1234 c. 11. — Concil. Albiens. ann. 1254 c. 26. — Lib. Sententt. Inq. Tolosan. pp. 162–7, 203, 246–7, 251–2.—Zanchini Tract. de Hæret. c. xxvii.

† Const. 5 Cod. IX. viii.— Concil. Tolosan. ann. 1229 c. 10.—Hist. Diplom. Frid. II. T. IV. pp. 8, 302.— Innoc. PP. IV. Bull. *Ut commissum,* 21 Jun. 1254.— Alex. PP. IV. Bull. *Quod super nonnullis,* 9. Dec. 1257 (Doat, XXXI. 244).—Ray-

The Inquisition depended so much upon secular officials for assistance that there was some justification in its seeking to prevent those who might be suspected of sympathizing with heresy from holding office in which they could thwart its plans and aid the offender.   Yet as there was no prescription of time as to proceedings against the dead, so was there none in invoking disabilities against their descendants, and the records of the Inquisition were an inexhaustible treasury of torment for those who were in any way connected with heresy.   No one, in fact, could feel sure that evidence might not at any moment be discovered or manufactured against some long-deceased parent or grandparent, which would ruin his career, and that some industrious searcher into the archives might not find some blot on his genealogical tree.   In 1288 Philippe le Bel writes to the Seneschal of Carcassonne that Raymond Vitalis of Avignon is exercising the office of notary in Carcassonne, though his maternal grandfather, Roger Isarn, is said to have been burned for heresy.   If this is the fact, the seneschal is ordered to deprive him of the position.   In 1292 Guiraud d'Auterive, a sergeant-at-arms of the king, was proceeded against on the same grounds, and we find Guillem de S. Seine, the Inquisitor of Carcassonne, furnishing to the royal procureur evidence that, in 1256, Guiraud's father and mother had confessed to acts of heresy, and that, in 1276, his uncle, Raymond Carbonnel, had been burned as a perfected heretic.   In these cases we see the royal power invoked for the dismissal of the official, but in the perfected theory of the Inquisition the inquisitor had the power to deprive of office any one whose father or grandfather had been a heretic or defender of heretics.   In order to avoid questions like these, when a penitent had fulfilled his penance, prudent children would take out letters declaratory of the fact, so as to have evidence of capacity to hold office.   In special cases the inquisitor had power to relieve descendants of these disabilities, and this was occasionally done; but, like the remission of penance, this relief was only a suspension, liable at any moment to forfeiture on the slightest manifestation of heretical tendencies.*

---

nald. ann. 1258, No. 23. — Potthast No. 17745, 18396. — Eymeric. Direct. Inq. p. 123. — C. 15, Sexto v. ii.

* Eymeric. Direct. Inquis. p. 571. — Arch. de l'Inq. de Carcassonne (Doat,

Underlying all these sentences was another on which they, and, indeed, the whole power of the Inquisition, were based in last resort —the sentence of excommunication. Theoretically the censures of the Inquisition might be the same as those of any other ecclesiastics authorized to cut men off from salvation, but the latter had so habitually abused their functions that the anathema, in the mouth of priests who were neither feared nor respected, lost, at times at least, its awe-inspiring authority. The censures of the Inquisition were in the hands of a smaller body of men, selected for their implacable vigor, and no one ever disregarded them with impunity. The secular authorities, moreover, were bound to put to the ban and confiscate the property of any one whom the inquisitor might excommunicate for heresy or fautorship. In fact, as the inquisitors were fond of boasting, their curse was stronger in four ways than that of the secular clergy. They could coerce the temporal government to outlaw the excommunicate; they could force it to confiscate his property; they could condemn any one remaining under excommunication for a year; and they could inflict the major excommunication upon any one communicating with their excommunicates.* Thus they enforced obedience to their citations and submission to their penances. Thus they made the secular power execute their sentences; thus they swept aside the statutes that interfered with their proceedings; thus they proved that the kingdom of God which they represented was superior to the kingdoms of earth. Of all excommunications that of the inquisitor worked the speediest vengeance and inspired the sharpest terror, and the boldest shrank from provoking it.

XXXII. 156).—Regist. Curiæ Franciæ de Carcassonne (Doat, XXXII. 241).— Bernardi Comens, Lucerna Inquisit. s. v. *Inquisitores*, No. 19.—Lib. Sententt. Inq. Tolosan. Index.—Wadding. Regest. Nich. PP. III. No. 10.

* Ripoll, I. 208, 394. — Tractatus de Inquisitione (Doat, XXXVI.). — Bern. Guidon. Practica P. IV. (Doat, XXX.).—Eymeric. Direct. Inquis. 360-1.

CHAPTER VII.

CONFISCATION.

ALTHOUGH, for the most part, as we shall see, confiscation was technically not the work of the Inquisition, the distinction was rather nominal than real. Even in times and places in which the inquisitor did not pronounce the sentence of confiscation, it was the accompaniment of the sentence which he did pronounce. It was, therefore, one of the most serious of the penalties at his disposal, and the largeness of the results effected by it give it an importance worthy a somewhat minute examination.

For the source of this, as of so much else, we must look to the Roman law. It is true that, cruel as were the imperial edicts against heresy, they did not go to the length of thus indirectly punishing the innocent. Even when the detested Manichæans were mercilessly condemned to death, their property was confiscated only when their heirs were likewise heretics. If the children were orthodox they succeeded to the estate of the heretic parent, who could not execute a will and disinherit them. It was otherwise with crime. Any conviction involving deportation or the mines carried with it confiscation, though the wife could reclaim her dower and any gifts made to her before the commission of the offence, and so could children emancipated from the *patria potestas*. All else inured to the fisc. In *majestas*, or treason, the offender was liable to condemnation after death, involving the confiscation of his estate, which was held to have lapsed to the fisc at the time when he first conceived the crime. These provisions furnished the armory whence pope and king drew the weapons which rendered the pursuit of heresy attractive and profitable.*

King Roger, who occupied the throne of the Two Sicilies during the first half of the twelfth century, seems to have been the

---

* Constt. 13, 15, 17 Cod. I. v.; 2, 3, 4, 7, 8, 9 Cod. IX. xlix.; 5, 6 Cod. IX. viii.

first to apply the Roman practice by decreeing confiscation for all
who apostatized from the Catholic faith—whether to the Greek
Church, to Islam, or to Judaism does not appear. Yet the Church
cannot escape the responsibility of naturalizing this penalty in
European law as a punishment for spiritual transgressions. The
great Council of Tours, held by Alexander III., in 1163, commanded all secular princes to imprison heretics and confiscate their
property. Lucius III., in his Verona decretal of 1184, sought to
obtain for the Church the benefit of the confiscation which he
again declared to be incurred by heresy. One of the earliest acts
of Innocent III., in his double capacity of temporal prince and
head of Christianity, was to address a decretal to his subjects of
Viterbo, in which he says,

"In the lands subject to our temporal jurisdiction we order the property of
heretics to be confiscated; in other lands we command this to be done by the
temporal princes and powers, who, if they show themselves negligent therein,
shall be compelled to do it by ecclesiastical censures. Nor shall the property of
heretics who withdraw from heresy revert to them, unless some one pleases to
take pity on them. For as, according to the legal sanctions, in addition to capital punishment, the property of those guilty of *majestas* is confiscated, and life
simply is allowed to their children through mercy alone, so much the more
should those who wander from the faith and offend the Son of God be cut off
from Christ and be despoiled of their temporal goods, since it is a far greater
crime to assail spiritual than temporal majesty."*

This decretal, which was adopted into the canon law, is important as embodying the whole theory of the subject. In imitation
of the Roman law of *majestas*, the property of the heretic was forfeited from the moment he became a heretic or committed an act

---

* Constt. Sicular. Lib. I. Tit. 3.—Concil. Turon. ann. 1163 c. 4.—Lucii PP.
III. Epist. 171.—Innoc. PP. III. Regest. II. 1.—Cap. 10 Extra v. 7.

It was probably in obedience to the canon of Tours that, in 1178, the property of Pierre Mauran of Toulouse was declared forfeited to the count, and he
was allowed to redeem it with a fine of five hundred pounds of silver (Roger.
Hoveden. Annal. ann. 1178).

The decree of Alonso II. of Aragon against the Waldenses, in 1194, referred
to above (p. 81) (Pegnæ Comment. 39 in Eymeric. p. 281), inflicts confiscation
on all who favor the heretics, but there are no traces of its enforcement, or of the
subsequent canons of the Council of Girona in 1197 (Aguirre V. 102–3). The
same may be said of the edicts of Henry VI., in 1194, repeated by Otho IV. in
1210 (Lami, Antichità Toscane, p. 484).

of heresy. If he recanted, it might be restored to him purely in mercy. When the ecclesiastical tribunals declared him to be, or to have been, a heretic, confiscation operated itself; the act of seizing the property was a matter for the secular power to whom it inured, and the mercy which might spare it could only be shown by that power. All this it is requisite to keep in mind if we would correctly appreciate some points which have frequently been misunderstood.

Innocent's decretal further illustrates the fact that at the commencement of the struggle with heresy the chief difficulty encountered by the Church in relation to confiscation was to persuade or coerce the temporal rulers to do what it held to be their duty in taking possession of heretical property. This was one of the principal offences which Raymond VI. of Toulouse expiated so bitterly, as explained to him by Innocent in 1210. His son proclaimed it as the law in his statutes of 1234, and included in its provisions, in accordance with the Ordonnance of Louis VIII., in 1226, and that of Louis IX., in 1229, all who favored heretics in any way or refused to aid in their capture; but his policy did not always comport with its enforcement, and he sometimes had to be sternly rebuked for non-feasance. After all danger of armed resistance had disappeared, however, sovereigns, as a rule, eagerly welcomed the opportunity of recruiting their slender revenues, and the confiscation of the property of heretics and of fautors of heresy was generally recognized in European law, although the Church was occasionally obliged to repeat its injunctions and threats, and though there were some regions in which they were slackly obeyed.*

---

* Innoc. PP. III. Regest. xɪɪ. 154 (Cap. 26 Extra v. xl.).—Isambert, Anc. Loix Françaises I. 228, 232.—Harduin. VII. 203–8.—Vaissette, III. Pr. 385.—Concil. Albiens. ann. 1254 c. 26.—Innoc. PP. IV. Bull. *Cum fratres*, ann. 1252 (Mag. Bull. Roman. I. 90).

Confiscation was an ordinary resource of mediæval law. In England, from the time of Alfred, property, as well as life, was forfeited for treason (Alfred's Dooms 4—Thorpe I. 63), a penalty which remained until 1870 (Low and Pulling's Dictionary of English History, p. 469). In France murder, false-witness, treachery, homicide, and rape were all punished with death and confiscation (Beaumanoir, Coutumes du Beauvoisis xxx. 2–5). By the German feudal law the fief might be forfeited for a vast number of offences, but the distinction was drawn that, if the offence was against the lord, the fief reverted to him; if simply a

The relation of the Inquisition to confiscation varied essentially with time and place. In France the principle derived from the Roman law was generally recognized, that the title to property devolved to the fisc as soon as the crime had been committed. There was therefore nothing for the inquisitor to do with regard to it. He simply ascertained and announced the guilt of the accused and left the State to take action. Thus Gui Foucoix treats the subject as one wholly outside of the functions of the inquisitor, who at most can only advise the secular ruler or intercede for mercy; while he holds that those only are legally exempt from forfeiture who come forward spontaneously and confess before any evidence has been taken against them. In accordance with this, there is, as a rule, no allusion to confiscation in the sentences of the French Inquisition, though in one or two instances chance has preserved for us, in the accounts of the *procureurs des encours,* or royal stewards of the confiscations, evidence that estates were sold and covered into the fisc in cases in which the forfeiture is not specified in the sentence. In condemnations of absentees and of the dead, confiscation is occasionally declared, as though in these the State might need some guidance, but even here the practice is not uniform. In a sentence issued by Guillem Arnaud and Étienne de S. Thibery, November 24, 1241, on two absentees, their estates are adjudged to whom it may concern. In the Register of Bernard de Caux (1246–1248), in thirty-two cases of contumacious absentees confiscation is included in the sentence, and in nine similar ones it is omitted, as well as in one hundred and fifty-nine condemnations to prison in which it was undoubtedly operative. In the Inquisition of Carcassonne, a sentence of December 12, 1328, on five deceased persons, who would have been imprisoned had they lived, ends with "*et consequenter bona ipsorum dicimus confiscanda,*" while a previous sentence, February 24, 1325, identical in character, on four defunct culprits, has no such corollary appended. In fact, strictly speaking, it was recognized that the in-

---

crime, it descended to the heirs (Feudor. Lib. I. Tit. xxiii.–iv.). In Navarre, confiscation formed part of the penalties of suicide, murder, treason, and even of blows or wounds inflicted where the queen or royal children were dwelling. There is a case in which confiscation was enforced on a man because he struck another at Olite, which was within a league of Tafalla, where the queen chanced to be staying at the time (G. B. de Lagrèze, La Navarre Française II. 335).

quisitor had no power to remit confiscations without permission from the fisc, and the custom of extending mercy to those who came forward voluntarily and confessed was founded upon a special concession to that effect granted by Raymond of Toulouse to the Inquisition in 1235. As soon as a suspected heretic was cited or arrested the secular officials sequestrated his property and notified his debtors by proclamation. No doubt, when condemnation took place, the inquisitor communicated the result to the proper officials, but as a rule no record of the fact seems to have been kept in the archives of the Holy Office, although an early manual of practice specifies it as part of his duty to see that the confiscation was enforced. At a later period, in 1328, in a record of an assembly of experts held at Pamiers, the presence is specified of Arnaud Assalit, royal *procureur des encours* of Carcassonne, so that probably by this time it had become customary for that official to attend these deliberations and thus obtain early notice of the sentences to be passed.*

In Italy it was long before any settled practice was established. In 1252 a bull of Innocent IV. directs the rulers of Lombardy, Tarvisina, and Romagna to confiscate without fail the property of all who were excommunicated as heretics, or as receivers, defenders, or fautors of heretics, thus recognizing confiscation as a matter belonging to the secular power. Yet soon the papal authority succeeded in obtaining a share of the spoils, even beyond the limits of the States of the Church, as is seen in the bulls *Ad extirpanda* of Innocent IV. and Alexander IV., and the matter thus became one in which the Inquisition had a direct interest. The indifference which so well became the French tribunals was therefore not readily maintained, and the share of the inquisitor in the results led him to participate in the process of securing them. Yet there

---

* Guid. Fulcod. Quæst. xv.—Coll. Doat, XXI. 154; XXXIII. 207; XXXIV. 189; XXXV. 68.—MSS. Bib. Nat., fonds latin, No. 9992.—Coll. Doat, XXVIII. 131, 164.—Responsa Prudentum (Doat, XXXVII. 83).—Grandes Chroniques, ann. 1323.—Les Olim, T. I. p. 556.—Guill. Pelisso Chron. Ed. Molinier, p. 27.—Practica super Inquisit. (MSS. Bib. Nat., fonds latin, No. 14930, fol. 224).—Coll. Doat, XXVII. fol. 118.

In 1460, when the nearly extinct French Inquisition was resuscitated to punish the sorcerers of Arras, confiscation formed part of the sentence.—Mémoires de Jacques du Clercq, Liv. IV. ch. 4.

were variations in practice. Zanghino tells us that formerly confiscations were decreed in the States of the Church by the ecclesiastical judges and elsewhere by the secular power, but that in his time (circa 1320) they were everywhere (in Italy) included in the jurisdiction of the episcopal and inquisitorial courts, and the secular authorities had nothing to do with them; but he adds that confiscation is prescribed by law for heresy, and that the inquisitor has no discretion to remit it, except in the case of voluntary converts with the assent of the bishop. Yet though the forfeiture occurs *ipso facto* by the commission of the crime, it requires a declaratory sentence of confiscation. This consequently was expressed in the most formal manner in the condemnation of the accused by the Italian Inquisition, and the secular authorities were told not to interfere unless called upon.*

At a very early period in some places the Italian inquisitors seem to have undertaken not only to decree but to control the confiscations. About 1245 we find the Florentine inquisitor, Ruggieri Calcagni, sentencing a Catharan named Diotaiuti, for relapse, with a fine of one hundred lire. Ruggieri acknowledges the receipt of this, to be applied to the pope, or to the furtherance of the faith, and formally concedes the rest of the heretic's estate to his wife Jacoba, thus exercising ownership over the whole. Yet this was not maintained, for in 1283 there is a sentence of the Podestà of Florence, reciting that the inquisitor Frà Salomone da Lucca had notified him that the widow Ruvinosa, lately deceased, had died a heretic, and that her property was to be confiscated; whereupon he orders it to be seized and sold, and the proceeds divided according to the papal constitutions. At length, however, the inquisitors assumed and exercised full control over the handling of the confiscations. In the conveyance of a confiscated house by the municipal authorities of Florence, in 1327, to the Dominicans, the deed is careful to assert that it is made with the assent of the inquisitor. Even in Naples we see King Robert, in 1324, ordering the inquisitors to pay out of the royal share of the confiscations fifty ounces of gold to the Prior of the Church of San Domenico of Naples, to aid in its completion.†

---

* Coll. Doat, XXXI. 175.—Zanchini Tract. de Hæret. c. xviii., xxv., xxvi., xli. —Archivio Storico Italiano, No. 38, p. 29.

† Lami, Antichità Toscane, 560, 588-9.—Zanchini Tract. de Hæret. c. xxvi.—

In Germany the Diet of Worms, in 1231, indicates the confusion existing in the feudal mind between heresy and treason by allowing the allodial lands and personal property of the condemned to descend to the heirs, while fiefs were confiscated to the suzerain. If he was a serf, his goods inured to his master; but from all personal property was deducted the cost of burning its owner and the *droits de justice* of the seigneur-justicier. Two years later, in 1233, the Council of Mainz protested against the injustice, which quickly showed itself in Germany as elsewhere, of assuming guilt as soon as a man was accused, and treating his property as though he were convicted. It directed that the estates of those on trial should remain untouched until sentence was rendered, and any one who meanwhile should plunder or partition them should be excommunicated until he made restitution and rendered satisfaction. Finally, however, when the Emperor Charles IV. endeavored to introduce the Inquisition into Germany, in 1369, he adopted the Italian custom and ordered one third of the confiscations to be made over to the inquisitors.*

The exact degree of criminality which entailed confiscation is not capable of very rigid definition. Even in states where the inquisitor nominally had no control over it, the arbitrary discretion lodged with him as to the fate of the accused placed the matter practically in his hands, and his notification to the secular authorities would be a virtual sentence. It is probable that custom varied with time and with the temper of the inquisitor. We have seen that Innocent III. commanded it for all heretics, but what constituted technical heresy was not so easily determined. The statutes of Raymond decreed it not only for heretics, but for those who showed them favor. The Council of Béziers, in 1233, demanded it for all reconciled converts not condemned to wear crosses, and those of Béziers, in 1246, and Albi, in 1254, prescribed it for all whom the inquisitors should penance with imprisonment. Still, in a sentence of February 19, 1237, in which the inquisitors

---

Archiv. di Firenze, Prov. S. Maria Novella, Nov. 18, 1327.—Archivio di Napoli, Regist. 253, Lett. A, fol. 63.

* Hist. Diplom. Frid. II. T. III. p. 466.—Kaltner, Konrad v. Marburg u. die Inquisition, Prag, 1882, p. 147.—Mosheim de Beghardis, p. 347.

of Toulouse condemn some twenty or thirty penitents to perpetual imprisonment, confiscation is only threatened as an additional punishment in case they do not perform the penance. Imprisonment, however, finally was admitted by legists as the invariable test; although St. Louis, when in 1259 he mitigated his Ordonnance of 1229, ordered confiscation not only for those who were condemned to prison, but for those who contumaciously refused obedience to citations and those in whose houses heretics were found, his officials being instructed to ascertain from the inquisitors in all cases, while pending, whether the accused deserved imprisonment, and if so, to retain the sequestrated property. When he further provided, as a special grace, that the heirs should be restored to possession in cases where the heretic had offered himself for conversion before citation, had entered a religious order, and had worthily died there, he shows how universal confiscation had previously been and how ruthlessly the principle had been enforced that a single act of heresy forfeited all ownership. In fact, even at the close of the fifteenth century, the rule was laid down that confiscation was a matter of course, while restoration of property to a reconciled penitent required an express declaration.*

According to the most lenient construction of the law, therefore, the imprisonment of a reconciled convert carried with it the confiscation of his property, and as imprisonment was the ordinary penance, confiscation was general. There may possibly have been exceptions. The six prisoners released in 1248 by Innocent IV. had been in jail for some time—some of them for four years and more after confessing heresy — and yet the liberal contributions to the Holy Land which purchased their pardon show that they or their friends must have had control of property — unless, indeed, the money was raised on a pledge of the estates to be restored. So when Alaman de Roaix was condemned to imprisonment by Bernard de Caux, in 1248, the sentence provided for an annuity to be paid to a person designated, and for compensation to be made for the rapine which he had committed, which would look as though

---

* Harduin. VII. 203. —Concil. Biterrens. ann. 1233 c. 4; ann. 1246, Append. c. 35. — Concil. Albiens. ann. 1254 c. 26. — Coll. Doat, XXI. 151. — Guid. Fulcod. Quæst. xv. — Isambert Anc. Loix Françaises, I. 257. — Arch. de l'Inq. de Carcassonne (Doat, XXXI. 263).—Bernardi Comens. Lucerna Inquisit. s. v. *Filii.*

property were left to him; but as he had for ten years been a contumacious and proscribed fugitive, these fines must have been taken out of his estate in the hands of the State. Apparent exceptions such as these can be accounted for, and the proceedings of the Inquisition as a whole indicate that imprisonment and confiscation were inseparable. Sometimes, even, it is stated in sentences passed upon the dead that they are pronounced worthy of imprisonment in order to deprive the heirs of succession to the estates. At a later date, indeed, Eymerich, who dismisses the whole matter briefly as one with which the inquisitor has no concern, speaks as though confiscation only took place when a heretic did not repent and recant before sentence, but his commentator, Pegna, easily proves this to be an error. Zanghino assumes as a matter of course that property is forfeited by the act of heresy; and he points out that pecuniary penances cannot be imposed because the whole estate is gone, although there may be mercy shown at discretion with the assent of the bishop, and simple suspicion is not subject to confiscation.*

In the early zeal of persecution everything was swept away in wholesale seizure, but, in 1237, Gregory IX. assumed that the dowers of Catholic wives ought to be exempt in certain cases, and in 1247 Innocent IV. erected it into a rule that such dowers should be restored to the wives and should not be included in future forfeitures, although heresy would not justify divorce, and, in 1258, St. Louis accepted this rule. It was subject to serious limitations, however, since under the canon law the wife could not claim it if she had been cognizant of the husband's heresy when she married, and, according to some authorities, if she had lived with him after ascertaining it, or even if she had failed to inform against him within forty days after discovering it. As the children were incapable of inheritance, she only held the dower for life, after which it fell into the fisc.†

---

* Archives de l'Inq. de Carcassonne (Doat, XXXI. 152).—Berger, Registres d'Innoc. IV. No. 1844.—MSS. Bib. Nat., fonds latin, No. 9992.—Lib. Sententt. Inq. Tolosan. pp. 158–62.—Arch. de l'Inq. de Carcassonne (Doat, XXVII. 98).—Eymeric. Direct. Inquis. pp. 663–5.—Zanchini Tract. de Hæret. c. xviii., xix., xxv.

† Archives de l'Évêché de Béziers (Doat, XXXI. 35).—Potthast No. 12743.—Isambert, I. 257.—C. 14 Sexto v. 2.—Zanchini Tract. de Hæret. c. xxv.—Livres de Jostice et de Plet, Liv. I. Tit. iii. § 7.

Although in principle confiscation was an affair of the State, the division of the spoils did not follow any invariable rule. Before the organization of the Inquisition, when the Waldenses of Strassburg were burned, it is mentioned that their forfeited property was equally divided between the Church and the secular authorities. Lucius III., as we have just seen, endeavored to turn the forfeitures to the benefit of the Church. In the papal territory there could be little question as to this, and Innocent IV., in his bull *Ad extirpanda* of 1252, showed disinterestedness in devoting the whole proceeds to the stimulation of persecution. One third was given to the local authorities, one third to the officials of the Inquisition, and one third to the bishop and inquisitor, to be expended in the assault on heresy — provisions which were retained in the subsequent recensions of the bull by Alexander IV. and Clement IV., while forfeited bail went exclusively to the inquisitor. Yet this was speedily held to refer only to the independent states of Italy, for, in 1260, we find Alexander IV. ordering the inquisitors of Rome and Spoleto to sell the confiscated estates of heretics and pay over the proceeds to the pope himself; and a transaction of 1261 shows Urban IV. collecting three hundred and twenty lire from some confiscations at Spoleto.*

At length, both in the Roman province and elsewhere throughout Italy, the custom settled down to a tripartite division between the local community, the Inquisition, and the papal camera, the reason for the latter, as given by Benedict XI., being that the bishops appropriated to themselves the share intrusted to them for the persecution of heresy. In Florence a transaction of 1283 shows this to be the received regulation; and documents of various dates during the next half-century indicate that it was the custom of the republic to appoint attorneys or trustees to take seisin of confiscated property in the name of the city, which in 1319 liberally granted its share for the next ten years to the construction of the church of Santa Reparata. That the amounts were not small may be guessed from a petition of the inquisitors to the republic in 1299, setting forth that the Holy Office must have funds wherewith

---

* Hoffmann, Geschichte der Inquisition, II. 370. — Lucii PP. III. Epist. 171. — Innoc. PP. IV. Bull. *Ad extirpanda*, § 34.—Ejusd. Bull. *Super extirpatione*, 30 Mai. 1254 (Ripoll, I. 247). — Alex. PP. IV. Bull. *Discretioni* (Mag. Bull. Rom. I. 120). — Potthast No. 18200.

to pay its stipendiary officials, and therefore praying leave to invest in real estate the sums accruing to the Inquisition from this source—showing accumulations prudently garnered for the future. The request was granted to the extent of one thousand lire, with the proviso that none of the city's share be taken. This latter precaution would seem to argue no great confidence in the integrity of the inquisitors, nor was the insinuation uncalled for. By this time the money-changers had fairly occupied the Temple, and, as we have seen in the last chapter, it seemed almost impossible to preserve official honesty when persecution had become almost as much a financial speculation as a matter of faith. That plain-spoken Franciscan, Alvaro Pelayo, Bishop of Silva, writing about the year 1335, bitterly reproaches those of his brethren who act as inquisitors with their abuse of the funds accruing to the Holy Office. The papal division into thirds he declares was generally disregarded; the inquisitors monopolized the whole and spent it on themselves or enriched their kindred at their pleasure. Chance has preserved in the Florentine archives some documents confirmatory of this accusation. It seems that in 1343 Clement VI. obtained evidence that the inquisitors of both Florence and Lucca were habitually defrauding the papal camera of its third of the fines and confiscations, and accordingly he sent to Pietro di Vitale, Primicerio of Lucca, authority to collect the sums in arrears and to prosecute the embezzlers. How it fared with them we have no means of knowing, but the camera seems not to have gained much. In filling the vacancies thus occasioned Pietro di Aquila, a Franciscan of high standing, was appointed in Florence, who fell at once into the same evil ways, and within two years was obliged to fly from a prosecution by the primicerio, in addition to the charges of extortion brought against him by the republic.*

In Naples, under the Angevines, when the Inquisition was first introduced, Charles of Anjou monopolized the confiscations with the same rapacity that was customary in France. As early as March, 1270, we find him writing to his representatives in the Principato Ultra that three heretics had recently been burned at

---

* Nich. PP. IV. Bull. *Habet vestræ*, 3 Oct. 1290.—Raynald. ann. 1438, No. 24.—Lami, Antichità Toscane, pp. 588-9.—Alv. Pelag. de Planctu Eccles. Lib. II. art. 67.—Archivio di Firenze, Riformagioni, Classe v. No. 110; Classe XI. Distinz. 1, No. 39.

Benevento, whose estates he orders looked after and accounted for in detail. In 1290, however, Charles II. ordered the fines and confiscations to be divided into thirds, of which one should inure to the royal fisc, one be used for the promotion of the faith, and one be given to the Inquisition. Feudal lands, however, were to revert to the crown or to the immediate lord as the case might require.*

In Venice the compromise reached in 1289 between the signiory and Nicholas IV., whereby the republic permitted the introduction of the Inquisition, provided that all receipts of the Holy Office should be for the benefit of the State, and this arrangement seems to have been maintained. In Piedmont the confiscations were divided between the State and the Inquisition until, in the latter half of the fifteenth century, Amedeo IX. took the whole, allowing to the Holy Office only the expenses of the proceedings.†

In the other Italian states the papal curia grew dissatisfied with its share, when there was no longer a necessity of purchasing the co-operation of the civil power with a third of the spoils. It is a disputed point with the jurists when and how the change was effected, but in the first quarter of the fourteenth century the Church succeeded in grasping the whole of the confiscations, which were divided equally between the Inquisition and the papal camera. The rapacity with which this source of income was exploited is illustrated in a case occurring at Pisa in 1304. The inquisitor Angelo da Reggio had condemned the memory of a deceased citizen, Loterio Bonamici, and confiscated his property, part of which he then gave away and part he sold at prices which the papal curia esteemed too low. Benedict XI. thereupon ordered the Bishop of Ostia not to punish the inquisitor, but to use freely the censures of the Church in hunting up the assets in the hands of the holders and to take it from them. Finally, in 1438, Eugenius IV. generously handed back to the bishops the share of the papal camera in order to stimulate their slackness in persecution, and, where the bishop was also the temporal lord of his see, the confiscations were to be equally divided between him and the Inquisition. Bernardo di Como, however, writing about the year 1500, asserts that the

---

* Archivio di Napoli, Registro 9, Lett. C, fol. 90; Regist. 51, Lett. A, fol. 9; Reg. 98, Lett. B, fol. 13; Reg. 113, Lett. A, fol. 194; MSS. Chioccorelli, T. VIII.

† Albizio, Risposto al P. Paolo Sarpi, p. 25.—Sclopis, Antica Legislazione del Piemont, p. 485.

whole confiscations inure to the inquisitor to be expended at his discretion; but he subsequently admits that the subject is confused and uncertain, owing to contradictory papal decisions and conflicting jurisdictions in different territories.*

In Spain the rule was laid down that if the heretic were a clerk, or a lay vassal of the Church, the confiscation went to the Church; if otherwise, to the temporal seigneur.†

This greed for the plunder of the wretched victims of persecution is peculiarly repulsive as exhibited by the Church, and may to some extent palliate the similar action by the State in countries where the latter was strong enough to seize and retain it. The threats of coercion, which at first were necessary to induce the temporal princes to confiscate the property of their heretical subjects, soon became superfluous, and history has few displays of man's eagerness to profit by his fellow's misfortunes more deplorable than that of the vultures which followed in the wake of the Inquisition to batten on the ruin which it wrought.

In Languedoc at first the Inquisition endeavored to control the confiscations for the purpose of building prisons and maintaining prisoners, but these pretensions received no attention. Under the feudal system, the confiscations were for the benefit of the seigneur haut-justicier. The rapid extension of the royal jurisdiction, in the second half of the thirteenth century in France, ended by practically placing them in the hands of the king, but during the earlier and more profitable period there were quarrels over the spoils. After the treaty of Paris, in 1229, St. Louis, in granting fiefs in the newly-acquired territories, seems to have endeavored to provide for these questions by reserving the confiscations for heresy. The prudence

---

* Zanchini Tract. de Hæret. c. xix., xxvi., xli. Cf. Pegnæ Comment. in Eymeric. p. 659.—Grandjean, Registre de Benoît XI. No. 299.—Raynald. ann. 1438, No. 24. —Bernardi Comens. Lucerna Inquis. s. v. *Bona hæreticorum*, No. 6, 8. As early as 1387, in the sentences of Antonio Secco on the Waldenses of the Alpine valleys, the confiscations are declared to be solely for the benefit of the Inquisition (Archivio Storico Italiano, No. 38, pp. 29, 36, 50).

It must be placed to the credit of Benedict XI. that, in 1304, he authorized Frà Simone, Inquisitor of Rome, to restore confiscations unjustly made by his predecessors and to moderate punishments inflicted by them if he considered them too severe (Grandjean, No. 474).

† Alonsi de Spina Fortalicii Fidei, Lib. II. Consid. xi. (fol. 74 Ed. 1594).

of this is shown by the suit brought by the Maréchaux de Mirepoix
—one of the few families founded by the adventurers who accompanied de Montfort—who claimed the movables of all heretics captured in their lands, even if the goods were in the lands of the
king—a demand which was rejected by the Parlement of Paris,
in 1269. The bishops put in a claim to the confiscations of all real
and personal property of heretics living under their jurisdiction,
and at the Council of Lille (Comtat Venaissin) in 1251, they
threatened with excommunication any one who should dispute it.
The groundlessness of this claim is seen in an agreement made under the auspices of the Legate Romano in December, 1229, between
the Bishop of Béziers and the king, in which the royal right to the
confiscations is recognized as incontestable, and the bishop only
stipulates that in case of fiefs they shall, if granted, be held subject
to his seignorial rights, or if the king retains them some compensation shall be made for the loss of the suzerainty. This indicates
a source of reasonable complaint, for, in the annexation of fiefs to
the crown, the bishops found themselves losing in place of profiting
by persecution. Various efforts were made to adjust these conflicting claims over the spoil. By a transaction of 1234 we see
that the king had subjected himself to the stipulation of parting
with all confiscated property within a year and a day. The Council of Béziers, in 1246, adopted a canon on the subject, but it could
not be enforced, and at length, about 1255, St. Louis agreed upon
a compromise, whereby all confiscated lands subject to the bishops
were equally divided, with a right on the part of the prelates to
buy out, within two months, the royal share at a price fixed by
arbitration; if this right was not exercised the king was bound,
within a year and a day, to pass the lands out of his hands into
those of a person of the same condition as the former owner, to be
held under the same terms of service or villeinage; but all movables were declared to belong unreservedly to the crown. Under
this arrangement the temporalities of the sees grew rapidly. We
have seen the apostolic poverty which afflicted the bishops of Toulouse prior to the crusades: during the succeeding century the
whole land was impoverished and the cities suffered especially, yet
when, in 1317, John XXII. carved six new bishoprics out of the see
of Toulouse, his reason was found in the excessive revenues of the
bishop, amounting to forty thousand livres Tournois per annum, al-

though it had already been shorn of nearly half of its territory by Boniface VIII. to form the see of Pamiers.*

The bishops of Albi were especially active and fortunate in this saturnalia of plunder. During the confusion of the wars and the settlement they assumed rights, including *haute justice* and the confiscations, which led to contests with the representatives of the crown, lasting for thirty years. They were specially active in the pursuit of heretics, which they thus found profitable as well as praiseworthy. In 1247 Bishop Bertrand procured from Innocent IV. a special deputation of inquisitorial power, probably to strengthen his claims, and the next year he drove a thriving business in selling commutations for confiscation to condemned and repentant heretics—an expedient more lucrative than regular, for when Alphonse of Poitiers, in 1253, endeavored to speculate in the confiscations in the same way, he was compelled to desist by the Archbishop of Narbonne and the Bishop of Toulouse, who declared that it would lead to the scandal of the faithful and the destruction of religion. Finally, to settle the claims of the bishop on the confiscations, St. Louis, in December, 1264, made with Bernard de Combret, the incumbent of the see, a convention, promptly confirmed by Urban IV., by which the prelate was entitled to one half of all confiscations of realty and personalty within the diocese, with the further advantage that the king's share of the real estate passed into possession of the bishop if it was not sold within a twelvemonth, and became his absolute property if not sold within

---

* MSS. Bib. Nat., fonds latin, No. 14930, fol. 224.—Livres de Jostice et de Plet, Liv. I. Tit. iii. § 7.—Vaissette, III. 391.—Les Olim, I. 317.—MSS. Bib. Nat., fonds latin, No. 11847.—Concil. Insulan. ann. 1251 c. 3.—Teulet, Layettes, II. 165.—Concil. Biterrens. ann. 1246 c. 4.—Vaissette, Éd. Privat, VIII. 975.—Baluz. Concil. Narbonn. Append. pp. 96-99.—Coll. Doat, XXXV. 48. Cf. Berger, Registres d'Innoc. IV. No. 3543-4, 1547-8.—Vaissette, IV. 170.—Baudouin, Lettres inédites de Philippe le Bel, Paris, 1886, p. xl.

In spite of the general sense of equity manifested by St. Louis, he was by no means indifferent to acquisitions justified by the spirit of the age. In 1246 there seems to have been a raid made upon the Jews of Carcassonne, who were thrown into prison. In July St. Louis writes to his seneschal that he wants to get from them all that he can; they are, therefore, to be held in strict duress, while the amount which they can be made to pay is to be reported to him. In August he writes that the sum proposed is not satisfactory, and the seneschal is instructed to extort all that he can.—Vaissette, Éd. Privat, VIII. 1191-2.

three years. Accordingly in the accounts of the royal *procureurs des encours* of Carcassonne we constantly find the confiscations in Albi shared with the bishop. Although between St. John's day 1322 and 1323 this share in money amounted only to one hundred and sixty livres, there were times when it was much greater. About the year 1300 Bishop Bernard de Castanet generously gave to the Dominican Church of Albi his portion of the estates of two citizens, Guillem Aymeric and Jean de Castanet, condemned after death, which amounted to more than one thousand livres. It can readily be imagined that this arrangement with the crown gave rise to constant quarrels. In vain Philippe le Bel, in 1307, ordered the observance of the agreement with restitution for any infractions. In 1316 we find the bishop claiming properties which had not been sold within the three years, and Arnaud Assalit, the *procureur*, arguing that he had been prevented from effecting sales by just and legitimate causes, when the seneschal, Aymeric de Croso, decided that the impediments had been legitimate, and that the rights of the king were not forfeited.*

These were not the only questions arising from this wholesale spoliation which afforded an ample harvest to the legal profession. A suit brought by the bishops of Rodez for some lands held by the crown as heretic confiscations dragged on for thirty years until it reached the Parlement of Paris, which coolly annulled all the proceedings on the ground that those who had acted for the crown had lacked the requisite authority. Almost equally protracted and confused was a suit between Eleanor de Montfort, Countess of Vendôme, and the king over the lands of Jean Baudier and Raymond Calverie. The confiscations occurred in 1300; in 1327 the suit was still pursuing its weary way, to be finally compromised in 1335.†

All prelates were not as rapacious as those of Albi, one of whom we find still, in 1328, complaining of the evasions resorted to by the victims to save a fragment of their property for their

---

* A. Molinier (Vaissette, Éd. Privat, VII. 284–94; VIII. 919).—Coll. Doat, XXXIV. 131, 135, 189; XXXV. 93.—Urbani PP. IV. Epist. 62 (Martene Thesaur. II. 94).—Bern. Guidon. Hist. Conv. Albiens.—Vaissette, III. Pr. 467, 500.—Arch. de l'Inq. de Carcass. (Doat, XXXI. 143, 146).

† C. Molinier, L'Inquisition dans le midi de la France, p. 101.—Les Olim, III. 1126–9, 1440–2. See also I. 920.

families; but the princes and their representatives were relentless in grasping all that they could lay their hands on. I have mentioned that as soon as a suspect was cited before the Inquisition his property was sequestrated to await the result, and proclamation was made to all his debtors and those who held his effects to bring everything to the king. Charles of Anjou carried this practice to Naples, where a royal order, in 1269, to arrest sixty-nine heretics contains instructions to seize simultaneously their goods, which are to be held for the king. So assured were the officials that condemnation would follow trial that they frequently did not await the result, but carried out the confiscation in advance. This abuse was coeval with the founding of the Inquisition. In 1237 Gregory IX. complained of it and forbade it, but to little purpose, for in 1246 the Council of Béziers again prohibited it, unless, indeed, the offender had knowingly adhered to those who were known to be heretics, in which case, apparently, it was sanctioned. When, in 1259, St. Louis mitigated the rigors of confiscation, he indirectly forbade this wrong by instructing his officials that, when the accused was not condemned to imprisonment, they should give him or his heirs a hearing to reclaim the property; but, if there was any suspicion of heresy, it was not to be restored without taking security that it should be surrendered if anything was proved within five years, during which period it was not to be alienated. Yet still the outrage of confiscation before conviction continued with sufficient frequency to induce Boniface VIII. to embody its prohibition in the canon law. Even this did not put a stop to it. The Inquisition had so habituated men's minds to the belief that no one escaped who had once fallen into its hands, that the officials considered themselves safe in acting upon the presumption. By an unusual coincidence we have the data from various sources in a single case of this kind which is doubtless the type of many others. In the prosecutions at Albi in 1300, a certain Jean Baudier was first examined January 20, when he acknowledged nothing. At a second hearing, February 5, he confessed to acts of heresy, and he was condemned March 7. Yet his confiscated property was sold January 29, not only before his sentence, but before his confession. Guillem Garric, charged with complicity in the plot to destroy the inquisitorial records of Carcassonne in 1284, was not sentenced until 1319, but in 1301 we find the Count of Foix and the royal officials quarrelling over his confiscated castle of Monteirat.*

The ferocious rapacity with which this process of confiscation was carried on may be conceived from a report made by Jean d'Arsis, Seneschal of Rouergue, to Alphonse of Poitiers, about 1253, as an evidence of the zeal with which he was guarding the interests of his suzerain. The Bishop of Rodez was conducting a vigorous episcopal inquisition, and at Najac had handed over a certain Hugues Paraire as a heretic, whom the seneschal burned "incontinently" and collected over one thousand livres Tournois from his estate. Hearing, subsequently, that the bishop had cited before him at Rodez six other citizens of Najac, d'Arsis hastened thither to see that no fraud was practised on the count. The bishop told him that these men were all heretics, and that he would make the count gain one hundred thousand sols from their confiscations, but both he and his assessors begged the seneschal to forego a portion to the culprits or their children, which that loyal servitor bluntly refused. Then the bishop, following evil counsel, and in fraud of the rights of the count, endeavored to elude the forfeiture by condemning the heretics to some lighter penance. The seneschal, however, knew his master's rights and seized the property, after which he allowed some pittance to the penitents and their children, reporting that in addition to this he was in possession of about one thousand livres; and he winds up by advising the count, if he wishes not to be defrauded, to appoint some one to watch and supervise the further inquisitions of the bishop. On the other hand the bishops complained that the officials of Alphonse permitted heretics, for a pecuniary consideration, to retain a part or the whole of their confiscated property, or else condemned to the flames those who did not deserve it in order to seize their estates. These frightful abuses grew so unbearable that, in 1254, the officials of Alphonse, including Gui Foucoix, endeavored to reform them by issuing general regulations on the subject, but the matter was one

---

* Archives de l'Évêché d'Albi (Doat, XXXV. 83).—Les Olim, I. 556.—Archivio di Napoli, Regist. 4, Lett. B, fol. 47.—Archives de l'Évêché de Béziers (Doat, XXXI. 35).—Concil. Biterrens. ann. 1246 c. 3.—Isambert, Anc. Loix Françaises, I. 257.—C. 19 Sexto v. 2.—MSS. Bib. Nat., fonds latin, No. 11847.—Collect. Doat, XXXV. 68.—Molinier, L'Inq. dans de midi de la France, p. 102.—Vaissette, Éd. Privat, X. Pr. 370 sqq.

which in its inherent nature scarce admitted of reform. Yet Alphonse, with all his greed, was not unwilling to share the plunder with those who secured it for him, and several of his not wholly disinterested liberalities of this kind are on record. In 1268 we have a letter of his assigning to the Inquisition a revenue of one hundred livres per annum on the confiscated estate of a heretic; and in 1270 another, confirming the foundation of a chapel from a similar source.*

Nothing could exceed the minute thoroughness with which every fragment of a confiscated estate was followed up and seized. The account of the collections of confiscated property from 1302 to 1313 by the *procureurs des encours* of Carcassone is extant in MS., and shows how carefully the debts due to the condemned were looked after, even to a few pence for a measure of corn. In the case of one wealthy prisoner, Guillem de Fenasse, the estate was not wound up for eight or ten years, and the whole number of debts collected foots up to eight hundred and fifty-nine, in amounts ranging from five deniers upward. As the collectors never credit themselves with amounts paid in discharge of debts due by these estates, it is evident that the rule that a heretic could give no valid obligations was strictly construed and that creditors were shamelessly cheated. In this seizure of debts the nobles asserted a right to claim any sums due by debtors who were their vassals, but Philippe de Valois, in 1329, decided that when the debts were payable at the domicile of the heretic they inured to the royal fisc, irrespective of the allegiance of the debtor. Another illustration of the remorseless greed which seized everything is found in a suit decided by the Parlement of Paris in 1302. On the death of the Chevalier Guillem Prunèle and his wife Isabelle, the guardianship of their orphans would legally vest in the next of kin, the Chevalier Bernard de Montesquieu, but he had been burned some years before for heresy, and his estate, of course, confiscated. The Seneschal of Carcassonne insisted that the guardianship which thus subsequently fell in formed part of the assets of the estate, and he accordingly assumed it, but a nephew, an Esquire Bernard de

---

* Boutaric, Saint Louis et Alphonse de Poitiers, Paris, 1870, pp. 455-6.—Douais, Les sources de l'histoire de Inquisition (Revue des Questions Historiques, Oct. 1881, p. 436).—Coll. Doat, XXXII. 51, 64.

Montesquieu, contested the matter and finally obtained a decision in his favor.*

Equal care was exercised in recovering alienated property. As, in obedience to the Roman law of *majestas*, forfeiture occurred *ipso facto* as soon as the crime of heresy was committed, the heretic could convey no legal title, and any assignments which he might have made were void, no matter through how many hands the property might have passed. The holder was forced to surrender it, nor could he demand restitution of what he had paid, unless the money or other consideration were found among the goods of the heretic. The eagerness with which, in such cases, the rigor of the law was enforced may be estimated from one occurring in 1272. Charles of Anjou had written from Naples to his viguier and sous-viguier at Marseilles telling them that a certain Maria Roberta, before condemnation to prison for heresy, had sold a house which was subject to confiscation; this he ordered them to seize, to sell by auction, and to report the proceeds; but they neglected to do so. The viguiers were changed, and now the unforgetful Charles writes to the new officials, repeating his orders and holding them personally responsible for obedience. At the same time he writes to his seneschal with instructions to look after the matter, as it lies very near to his heart.†

The cruelty of the process of confiscation was enhanced by the pitiless methods employed. As soon as a man was arrested for suspicion of heresy his property was sequestrated and seized by the officials, to be returned to him in the rare cases in which his guilt might be declared not proven. This rule was enforced in the most rigorous manner, every article of his household gear and provisions being inventoried, as well as his real estate.‡ Thus, whether innocent or guilty, his family were turned out-of-doors to starve or to depend upon the precarious charity of others—a charity

---

* Archives de l'Évêché d'Albi (Doat, XXXIII. 207–72).—Coll. Doat, XXXV. 93.—Les Olim, II. 111.

† Bernardi Comens. Lucerna Inquis. s. v. *Bona hæreticor.*—Archidiac. Gloss. sup. c. 19 Sexto v. 2.—Archivio di Napoli, Regist. 15, Lett. C, fol. 77, 78.

The English law of felony was also retroactive, and all alienations subsequent to the commission of the crime were void (Bracton, Lib. III. Tract. ii. cap. 13, No. 8).

‡ Coll. Doat, XXXII. 309, 316.

chilled by the fact that any manifestation of sympathy was dangerous. It would be difficult to estimate the amount of human misery arising from this source alone.

In this chaos of plunder we may readily imagine that those who were engaged in such work were not over-nice as to securing a share of the spoliations. In 1304 Jacques de Polignac, who had been for twenty years keeper of the inquisitorial jail at Carcassonne, and several of the officials employed on the confiscations, were found to have converted and detained a large amount of valuable property, including a castle, several farms and other lands, vineyards, orchards, and movables, all of which they were compelled to disgorge and to suffer punishment at the king's pleasure.*

It is pleasant to turn from this cruel greed to a case which excited much interest in Flanders at a time when in that region the Inquisition had become so nearly dormant that the usages of confiscation were almost forgotten. The Bishop of Tournay and the Vicar of the Inquisition condemned at Lille a number of heretics, who were duly burned. They confiscated the property, claiming the movables for the Church and the inquisitor, and the realty for the fisc. The magistrates of Lille boldly interposed, declaring that among the liberties of their town was the privilege that no burgher could forfeit both body and goods; and, acting for the children of one of the victims, they took out *apostoli* and appealed to the pope. The counsellors of the suzerain, Philippe le Bon of Burgundy, with a clearer perception of the law, claimed that the whole confiscations inured to him, while the ecclesiastics declared the rule to be invariable that the personalty went to the Church and only the real estate to the fisc. The triangular quarrel threatened long and costly litigation, and finally all parties agreed to leave the decision to the duke himself. With rare wisdom, in 1430, he settled the matter, with general consent, by deciding that the sentence of confiscation should be treated as not rendered, and the property be left to the heirs, at the same time expressly declaring that the rights of Church, Inquisition, city, and state, were reserved without prejudice, in any case that might arise in future, which was, he said, not likely to occur. He did not manifest the same disinterestedness in 1460, however, in the terrible persecution.

---

* Les Olim, II. 147.—Doat, XXVI. 253.

of the sorcerers of Arras, when the movables were confiscated to the episcopal treasury, and he seized the landed property in spite of the privileges alleged by the city.*

In addition to the misery inflicted by these wholesale confiscations on the thousands of innocent and helpless women and children thus stripped of everything, it would be almost impossible to exaggerate the evil which they entailed upon all classes in the business of daily life. All safeguards were withdrawn from every transaction. No creditor or purchaser could be sure of the orthodoxy of him with whom he was dealing; and, even more than the principle that ownership was forfeited as soon as heresy had been committed by the living, the practice of proceeding against the memory of the dead after an interval virtually unlimited, rendered it impossible for any man to feel secure in the possession of property, whether it had descended in his family for generations, or had been acquired within an ordinary lifetime.

The prescription of time against the Church had to be at least forty years—against the Roman Church, a hundred, and this prescription ran, not from the commission of the crime, but from its detection. Though some legists held that proceedings against the deceased had to be commenced within five years after death, others asserted that there was no limit, and the practice of the Inquisition shows that the latter opinion was followed. The prescription of forty years' possession by good Catholics was further limited by the conditions that they must at no time have had a knowledge that the former owner was a heretic, and, moreover, he must have died with an unsullied reputation for orthodoxy—both points which might cast a grave doubt on titles.†

---

* Archives Générales de Belgique, Papiers d'État, v. 405.—Mémoires de Jacques du Clercq, Liv. iv. ch. 4, 14.

In Arras a charter of 1335, confirmed by Charles V. in 1369, protected the burghers from confiscation when condemned for crime by any competent tribunal.—Duverger, La Vauderie dans les États de Philippe le Bon, Arras, 1885, p. 60.

† C. 6, 8, 9, 14, Sexto xii. 26.—Bernardi Comensis Lucerna Inquis. s. v. *Bona hæreticorum.*—Eymeric. Direct. Inquis. pp. 570-2.—Zanchini Tract. de Hæret. c. xxiv.—J. F. Ponzinib. de Lamiis c. 76.

Severe as was the contemporary English law against felony, it had at least

Prosecution of the dead, as we have seen, was a mockery in which virtually defence was impossible and confiscation inevitable. How unexpectedly the blow might fall is seen in the case of Gherardo of Florence. He was rich and powerful, a member of one of the noblest and oldest houses, and was consul of the city in 1218. Secretly a heretic, he was hereticated on his death-bed between 1246 and 1250, but the matter lay dormant until 1313, when Frà Grimaldo, the Inquisitor of Florence, brought a successful prosecution against his memory. In the condemnation were included his children Ugolino, Cante, Nerlo, and Bertuccio, and his grandchildren, Goccia, Coppo, Frà Giovanni, Gherardo, prior of S. Quirico, Goccino, Baldino, and Marco—not that they were heretics, but that they were disinherited and subjected to the disabilities of descendants of heretics. When such proceedings were hailed as pre-eminent exhibitions of holy zeal, no man could feel secure in his possessions, whether derived from descent or purchase.*

An instance of a different character, but equally illustrative, is furnished by the case of Géraud de Puy-Germer. His father had been condemned for heresy in the times of Raymond VII. of Toulouse, who generously restored the confiscated estates. Yet, twenty years after the death of the count, in 1268, the zealous agents of Alphonse seized them as still liable to forfeiture. Géraud there-

---

this concession to justice, that a felon had to be convicted in his lifetime; his death before conviction thus prevented confiscation (Bracton, Lib. III. Tract. ii. cap. 13, No. 17).

* Lami, Antichità Toscane, pp. 497, 536-7.—It is true that when, in 1335, Henri de Chamay, Inquisitor of Carcassonne, sent to the papal court the depositions against the memory of eighteen persons accused of heretical acts committed between 1284 and 1290, and asked for instructions, the decision was that no reliance was to be placed on the testimony of witnesses who mostly contradicted themselves, and who only swore to what they had heard long before. Three previous investigations against the same persons had been held without reaching a conclusion, and the papal advisers assumed that there had been good reasons for dropping the matter.—Vaissette, Éd. Privat, IX. 401.

How the system worked is seen in the complaint made in 1247 to St. Louis, by Guillem Pierre de Vintrou, that the royal seneschal of Carcassonne had seized his property derived through his mother, because his grandfather, seventeen years after death, had been accused of heresy. St. Louis thereupon ordered an examination and report.—Vaissette, Éd. Privat, VIII. 1196.

upon appealed to Alphonse, who ordered an investigation, but with what result does not appear.*

Not only were all alienations made by heretics set aside and the property wrested from the purchasers, but all debts contracted by them, and all hypothecations and liens given to secure loans, were void. Thus doubt was cast upon every obligation that a man could enter into. Even when St. Louis softened the rigor of confiscation in Languedoc, the utmost concession he would make was that creditors should be paid for debts contracted by culprits before they became heretics, while all claims arising subsequently to an act of heresy were rejected. As no man could be certain of the orthodoxy of another, it will be evident how much distrust must have been thrown upon every bargain and every sale in the commonest transactions of life. The blighting influence of this upon the development of commerce and industry can readily be perceived, coming as it did at a time when the commercial and industrial movement of Europe was beginning to usher in the dawn of modern culture. It was not merely the spiritual striving of the thirteenth century that was repressed by the Inquisition; the progress of material improvement was seriously retarded. It was this, among other incidents of persecution, which arrested the promising civilization of the south of France and transferred to England and the Netherlands, where the Inquisition was comparatively unknown, the predominance in commerce and industry which brought freedom and wealth and power and progress in its train.†

The quick-witted Italian commonwealths, then rising into mercantile importance, were keen to recognize the disabilities thus inflicted upon them. In Florence a remedy was sought by requiring the seller of real estate always to give security against possible future sentences of confiscation by the Inquisition—the security in general being that of a third party, although there must have been no little difficulty in obtaining it, and though it might likewise be invalidated at any moment by the same cause.

---

* Vaissette, Éd. Privat, VIII. 1641.

† Zanchini Tract. de Hæret. c. xxvii.—Isambert, Anc. Loix Françaises, I. 257. Yet there is a case in 1269 in which a creditor of two condemned heretics applies to Alphonse of Poitiers to be paid out of the confiscations, and Alphonse orders an inquiry into the circumstances.—Vaissette, Éd. Privat, VIII. 1682.

Even in contracts for personalty, security was also often demanded and given. This was, at least, only replacing one evil by another of scarcely less magnitude, and the trouble grew so intolerable that a remedy was sought for one of its worst features. The republic solemnly represented to Martin IV. the scandals which had occurred and the yet greater ones threatened, in consequence of the confiscation of the real estate of heretics in the hands of *bona-fide* purchasers, and by a special bull of Nov. 22, 1283, the pontiff graciously ordered the Florentine inquisitors in future not to seize such property.*

The princes who enjoyed the results of confiscations recognized that they carried with them the correlative duty of defraying the expenses of the Inquisition; indeed, self-interest alone would have prompted them to maintain in a state of the highest efficiency an instrumentality so profitable. Theoretically, it could not be denied that the bishops were liable for these expenses, and at first the inquisitors of Languedoc sought to obtain funds from them, suggesting that at least pecuniary penances inflicted for pious uses should be devoted to paying their notaries and clerks. This was fruitless, for, as Gui Foucoix (Clement IV.) remarks, their hands were tenacious and their purses constipated, and as it was useless to look to them for resources, he advises that the pecuniary penances be used for the purpose, providing it be done decently and without scandalizing the people. Throughout central and northern Italy, as we have seen, the fines and confiscations rendered the Inquisition fully self-supporting, and the inquisitors were eager to make business out of which they could reap a pecuniary harvest. In Venice the State defrayed all expenses and took all profits. In Naples the same policy was at first pursued by the Angevine monarchs, who took the confiscations and, in addition to maintaining prisoners, paid to each inquisitor one augustale (one quarter ounce of gold) per diem for the expenses of himself and his associate, his notary, and three familiars, with their horses. These stipends were assigned upon the Naples customs on iron, pitch, and salt; the orders for their payment ran usually for six

---

* Lami, Antichità Toscane, p. 593. — Archivio di Firenze, Riformagioni, Classe v. No. 110.

months at a time and had to be renewed; there was considerable delay in the settlements, and the inquisitors had substantial cause of complaint, although the officials were threatened with fines for lack of promptness. In 1272, however, I find a letter issued to the inquisitor, Frà Matteo di Castellamare, providing him with a year's salary, payable six months in advance. When, as mentioned above, Charles II., in 1290, divided the proceeds according to the papal prescription, he liberally continued to contribute to the expenses, though on a somewhat reduced scale. In letters of May 16, 1294, he orders the payment to Frà Bartolomeo di Aquila of four tareni per diem (the tareno was one thirtieth of an ounce of gold), and July 7 of the same year he provides that five ounces per month be paid to him for the expenses of his official family.*

In France there was at first some question as to the responsibility for the charges attendant upon persecution. The duty of the bishops to suppress heresy was so plain that they could not refuse to meet the expenses, at least in part. Before the establishment of the Inquisition this consisted almost wholly in the maintenance of imprisoned converts, and at the Council of Toulouse they agreed to defray this in the case of those who had no money, while those who had property to be confiscated they claimed should be supported by the princes who obtained it. This proposition, like the subsequent one of the Council of Albi, in 1254, was altogether too cumbrous to work. The statutes of Raymond, in 1234, while dwelling elaborately on the subject of confiscation, made no provision for meeting the cost of the new Inquisition, and the matter remained unsettled. In 1237 we find Gregory IX. complaining that the royal officials contributed nothing for the support of the prisoners whose property they had confiscated. When, in 1246, the Council of Béziers was assembled, the Cardinal Legate of Albano reminded the bishops that it was their business to provide for it, according to the instructions of the Council of Montpellier, whose proceedings have not reached us. The good bishops were not disposed to do this. As we have seen, they

---

* MSS. Bib. Nat., fonds latin, No. 14930, fol. 228.—Guid. Fulcod. Quæst. III. —Archivio di Napoli, Regist. 6, Lett. B, fol. 35; Reg. 10, Lett. B, fol. 6, 7, 96; Reg. 11, Lett. C, fol. 40; Reg. 13, Lett. A, fol. 212; Reg. 51, Lett. A, fol. 9; Reg. 71, Lett. M, fol. 382, 385, 440; Reg. 98, Lett. B, fol. 13; Reg. 113, Lett. A, fol. 194; Reg. 253, Lett. A, fol. 63; MSS. Chioccorello, T. VIII.

claimed that prisons should be built at the expense of the recipients of the confiscations, and suggested that the fines should be used for their maintenance and for that of the inquisitors. The piety of St. Louis, however, would not see the good work halt for lack of the necessary means; with a more worldly prince we might assume that he recognized the money spent on inquisitors as profitably invested. In 1248 we find him defraying their expenses in all the domains of the crown, and we have shown above how he assumed the cost of prisons and prisoners; in addition to which, in 1246, he ordered his Seneschal of Carcassonne to pay out of the confiscations ten sols per diem to the inquisitors for their expenses. It may fairly be presumed that Count Raymond contributed with a grudging hand to the support of an institution which he had opposed so long as he dared; but when he was succeeded, in 1249, by Jeanne and Alphonse of Poitiers, the latter politic and avaricious prince saw his account in stimulating the zeal of those to whom he owed his harvest of confiscations. Not only did he defray the cost of the fixed tribunals, but his seneschals had orders to pay the expenses of the inquisitors and their familiars in their movements throughout his territories. He paid close attention to detail. In 1268 we find Guillem de Montreuil, Inquisitor of Toulouse, reporting to him the engagement of a notary at six deniers per diem and of a servitor at four, and Alphonse graciously ordering the payment of their wages. Charles of Anjou, who was equally greedy, found time amid his Italian distractions to see that his Seneschal of Provence and Forcalquier kept the Inquisition supplied on the same basis as did the king in the royal dominions.*

Large as were the returns to the fisc from the industry of the Inquisition, the inquisitors were sometimes disposed to presume upon their usefulness, and to spend money with a freedom which

---

* Concil. Tolosan. ann. 1229 c. 9. — Concil. Albiens. ann. 1254 c. 24. — Harduin. VII. 415. — Archives de L'Évêché de Béziers (Doat, XXXI. 35). — Concil. Biterrens. ann. 1246 c. 22. — D. Bouquet, T. XXI. pp. 262, 264, 266, 278, etc. — Vaissette, Éd. Privat, VIII. 1206, 1573.—Archives de l'Inq. de Carcassonne (Doat, XXXI. 250).—Archivio di Napoli, Regist. 20, Lett. B, fol. 91.

The care with which Alphonse looked after the proceeds of the confiscations is seen in his demand for an account from his seneschal, Jacques du Bois, March 25, 1268 (Vaissette, Éd. Privat, VIII. 1274).

seemed unnecessary to those who paid the bills. Even in the
fresh zeal of 1242 and 1244, before the princes had made provision
for the Holy Office, and while the bishops were yet zealously
maintaining their claims to the fines, the luxury and extravagance
of the inquisitors called down upon them the reproof of their own
Order as expressed in the Dominican provincial chapters of Montpellier and Avignon. It would be, of course, unjust to cast such
reproach upon all inquisitors, but no doubt many deserved it, and
we have seen that there were numerous ways in which they could
supply their wants, legitimate or otherwise. It might, indeed, be
a curious question to determine the source whence Bernard de
Caux, who presided over the tribunal of Toulouse until his death,
in 1252, and who, as a Dominican, could have owned no property,
obtained the means which enabled him to be a great benefactor
to the convent of Agen, founded in 1249. Even Alphonse of Poitiers sometimes grew tired of ministering to the wishes of those
who served him so well. In a confidential letter of 1268 he complains of the vast expenditures of Pons de Poyet and Étienne de
Gâtine, the inquisitors of Toulouse, and instructs his agent to try
to persuade them to remove to Lavaur, where less extravagance
might be hoped for. He offered to put at their disposal the castle
of Lavaur, or any other that might be fit to serve as a prison; and
at the same time he craftily wrote to them direct, explaining that,
in order to enable them to extend their operations, he would place
an enormous castle in their hands.*

Some very curious details as to the expenses of the Inquisition,
thus defrayed from the confiscations, from St. John's day, 1322, to
1323, are afforded by the accounts of Arnaud Assalit, *procureur
des encours* of Carcassonne and Béziers, which have fortunately
been preserved. From the sums thus coming into his hands the
procureur met the outlays of the Inquisition to the minutest item
—the cost of maintaining prisoners, the hunting up of witnesses,
the tracking of fugitives, and the charges for an *auto de fé,* including the banquets for the assembly of experts and the saffron-colored cloth for the crosses of the penitents. We learn from this

* Molinier, L'Inquisition dans le midi de la France, p. 308. — Bern. Guidon.
Fundat. Convent. Prædicat. (Martene Thesaur. VI. 481).—Boutaric, Saint Louis
et Alphonse de Poitiers, pp. 456-7.

that the wages of the inquisitor himself were one hundred and fifty livres per annum, and also that they were very irregularly paid. Frère Otbert had been appointed in Lent, 1316, and thus far had received nothing of his stipend, but now, in consequence of a special letter from King Charles le Bel, the whole accumulation for six years, amounting to nine hundred livres, is paid in a lump. Although by this time persecution was slackening for lack of material, the confiscations were still quite profitable. Assalit charges himself with two thousand two hundred and nineteen livres seven sols ten deniers collected during the year, while his outlays, including heavy legal expenses and the extraordinary payment to Frère Otbert, amounted to one thousand one hundred and sixty-eight livres eleven sols four deniers, leaving about one thousand and fifty livres of profit to the crown.*

Persecution, as a steady and continuous policy, rested, after all, upon confiscation. It was this which supplied the fuel to keep up the fires of zeal, and when it was lacking the business of defending the faith languished lamentably. When Catharism disappeared under the brilliant aggressiveness of Bernard Gui, the culminating point of the Inquisition was passed, and thenceforth it steadily declined, although still there were occasional confiscated estates over which king, prelate, and noble quarrelled for some years to come. The Spirituals, Dulcinists, and Fraticelli were Mendicants, who held property to be an abomination; the Waldenses were poor folk—mountain shepherds and lowland peasants—and the only prizes were an occasional sorcerer or usurer. Still, as late as 1337 the office of bailli of the confiscations for heresy in Toulouse was sufficiently lucrative to be worth purchasing under the prevailing custom of selling all such positions, and the collections for the preceding fiscal year amounted to six hundred and forty livres six sols.†

The intimate connection between the activity of persecuting zeal and the material results to be derived from it is well illus-

---

* Coll. Doat, XXXIV. 189.—In 1317 the result had been much less. We have the receipt of the royal treasurer of Carcassonne, Lothaire Blanc, to Arnaud Assalit, dated Sept. 24, 1317, for collections during the year ending the previous St. John's day, amounting to four hundred and ninety-five livres six sols eleven deniers, being the balance after deducting wages and expenses (Doat, XXXIV. 141).

† Doat, XXXV. 79, 100.—Vaissette, Éd. Privat, X. Pr. 705, 777, 788.

trated in the failure of the first attempt to extend the Inquisition into Franche Comté. John, Count of Burgundy, in 1248, represented to Innocent IV. the alarming spread of Waldensianism throughout the province of Besançon and begged for its repression. Apparently the zeal of Count John did not lead him to pay for the purgation of his dominions, and the plunder to be gained was inconsiderable, for, in 1255, Alexander IV. granted the petition of the friars to be relieved from the duty, in which they averred that they had exhausted themselves fruitlessly for lack of money. The same lesson is taught by the want of success which attended all attempts to establish the Inquisition in Portugal. When, in 1376, Gregory XI. ordered the Bishop of Lisbon to appoint a Franciscan inquisitor for the kingdom, recognizing apparently that there would be small receipts from confiscations, he provided that the incumbent should be paid a salary of two hundred gold florins per annum, assessed upon the various sees in the proportion of their forced contributions to the papal camera. The resistance of inertia, which rendered this command resultless, doubtless arose from the objection of the prelates to being thus taxed; and the same may be said of the effort of Boniface IX., when he appointed Fray Vicente de Lisboa as Inquisitor of Spain and ordered his expenses defrayed by the bishops.*

Perhaps the most unscrupulous attempt to provide for the maintenance of the Inquisition was that made by the Emperor Charles IV. when, in 1369, he endeavored to establish it in Germany on a permanent basis. Heretics were neither numerous nor rich, and little could be gained from their confiscations to sustain the zeal of Kerlinger and his brethren; and we shall see hereafter how the houses of the orthodox and inoffensive Beghards and Beguines were summarily confiscated in order to provide domiciles and prisons for the inquisitors, while the cities were invited to share in the spoils in order to enlist popular support for the odious measure; we shall see also how it failed in consequence of the steady repugnance of prelates and people for the Holy Office.†

Eymerich, writing in Aragon, about 1375, says that the source

---

* Potthast No. 13000, 15995.—Monteiro, Historia da Santo Inquisição, P. I. Lib. ii. c. 34, 35.

† Mosheim de Beghardis pp. 356-63.

whence the expenses of the Inquisition should be met is a question which has been long debated and never settled. The most popular view among churchmen was that the burden should fall on the temporal princes, since they obtained the confiscations and should accept the charge with the benefit; but in these times, he sorrowfully adds, there are few obstinate heretics, fewer still relapsed, and scarce any rich ones, so that, as there is little to be gained, the princes are not willing to defray the expenses. Some other means ought to be found, but of all the devices which have been proposed each has its insuperable objection; and he concludes by regretting that an institution so wholesome and so necessary to Christendom should be so badly provided. *

It was probably while Eymerich was saddened with these unpalatable truths that the question was raising itself in the most practical shape elsewhere. As late as 1337 in the accounts of the Sénéchaussée of Toulouse there are expenditures for an *auto de fé* and for repairs to the buildings and prison of the Inquisition, the salaries of the inquisitor and his officials, and the maintenance of prisoners, but the confusion and bankruptcy entailed by the English war doubtless soon afterwards caused this duty to be neglected. In 1375 Gregory XI. persuaded King Frederic of Sicily to allow the confiscations to inure to the benefit of the Inquisition, so that funds might not be lacking for the prosecution of the good work. At the same time he made a vigorous effort to exterminate the Waldenses who were multiplying in Dauphiné. There were prisons to be built and crowds of prisoners to be supported, and he directed that the expenses should be defrayed by the prelates whose negligence had given opportunity for the growth of heresy. Although he ordered this to be enforced by excommunication, it would seem that the constipated purses of the bishops could not be relaxed, for soon after we find the inquisitor laying claim to a share in the confiscations, on the reasonable ground of his having no other source whence to defray the necessary expenses of his tribunal. The royal officials insisted on keeping the whole, and a lively contest arose, which was referred to King Charles le Sage. The monarch dutifully conferred with the Holy See, and, in 1378, issued an *Ordonnance* retaining the whole of the confiscations and

---

* Eymeric. Direct. Inquis. pp. 652-3.

assigning to the inquisitor a yearly stipend—the same as that paid to the tribunals of Toulouse and Carcassonne—of one hundred and ninety livres Tournois, out of which all the expenses of the Inquisition were to be met; with a proviso that if the allowance was not regularly paid then the inquisitor should be at liberty to detain a portion of the forfeitures. No doubt this agreement was observed for a time, but it lapsed in the terrible disorders which ensued on the insanity of Charles VI. In 1409 Alexander V. left to his legate to decide whether the Inquisitor of Dauphiné should receive three hundred gold florins a year, to be levied on the Jews of Avignon, or ten florins a year from each of the bishops of his extensive district, or whether the bishops should be compelled to support him and his officials in his journeys through the country. These precarious resources disappeared in the confusion of the civil wars and invasion which so nearly wrecked the monarchy. In 1432, when Frère Pierre Fabri, Inquisitor of Embrun, was summoned to attend the Council of Basle, he excused himself on account of his preoccupation with the stubborn Waldenses, and also on the ground of his indescribable poverty, "for never have I had a penny from the Church of God, nor have I a stipend from any other source." *

Of course it would be unjust to say that greed and thirst for plunder were the impelling motives of the Inquisition, though, when complaints were made that the fisc was defrauded of its dues by the immunity promised to those who would come in and confess during the time of grace, and when Bernard Gui met this objection by pointing out that these penitents were obliged to betray their associates, and thus, in the long run, the fisc was the gainer, we see how largely the minds of those who urged on persecution were occupied by its profits.† We therefore are perfectly safe in asserting that but for the gains to be made out of fines and confiscations its work would have been much less thorough, and that it would have sunk into comparative insignifi-

* Vaissette, Éd. Privat, X. Pr. 791-2, 802.—Raynald. ann. 1375, No. 26.—Wadding. ann. 1375, No. 21, 22; 1409, No. 13.—Isambert, Anc. Loix Françaises, V. 491.—Martene Ampl. Collect. VIII. 161-3.

† Bernard. Guidon. Practica P. IV. (Doat, XXX.).

cance as soon as the first frantic zeal of bigotry had exhausted itself. This zeal might have lasted for a generation, to be followed by a period of comparative inaction, until a fresh onslaught would have been excited by the recrudescence of heresy. Under a succession of such spasmodic attacks Catharism might perhaps have never been completely rooted out. By confiscation the heretics were forced to furnish the means for their own destruction. Avarice joined hands with fanaticism, and between them they supplied motive power for a hundred years of fierce, unremitting, unrelenting persecution, which in the end accomplished its main purpose.

CHAPTER VIII.

THE STAKE.

LIKE confiscation, the death-penalty was a matter with which the Inquisition had theoretically no concern. It exhausted every effort to bring the heretic back to the bosom of the Church. If he proved obdurate, or if his conversion was evidently feigned, it could do no more. As a non-Catholic, he was no longer amenable to the spiritual jurisdiction of a Church which he did not recognize, and all that it could do was to declare him a heretic and withdraw its protection. In the earlier periods the sentence thus is simply a condemnation as a heretic, accompanied by excommunication, or it merely states that the offender is no longer considered as subject to the jurisdiction of the Church. Sometimes there is the addition that he is abandoned to secular judgment—"relaxed," according to the terrible euphemism which assumed that he was simply discharged from custody. When the formulas had become more perfected there is frequently the explanatory remark that the Church has nothing left to do to him for his demerits; and the relinquishment to the secular arm is accompanied with the significant addition *"debita animadversione puniendum"* — that he is to be duly punished by it. The adjuration that this punishment, in accordance with the canonical sanctions, shall not imperil life or limb, or shall not cause death or effusion of blood, does not appear in the earlier sentences, and was not universal even at a later period.*

That this appeal for mercy was the merest form is admitted by Pegna, who explains that it was used only that the inquisitors might seem not to consent to the effusion of blood, and thus avoid

---

* Coll. Doat, XXI. 143. — MSS. Bib. Nat., fonds latin, No. 9992. — Doctrina de modo procedendi (Martene Thesaur. V. 1807). — Lami, Antichità Toscane, pp. 557, 559. — Lib. Sententt. Inq. Tolosan. pp. 2, 4, 36, 208, 254, 265, 289, 380. —Eymeric. Direct. Inquis. pp. 510–12.

incurring "irregularity." The Church took good care that the nature of the request should not be misapprehended. It taught that in such cases all mercy was misplaced unless the heretic became a convert, and proved his sincerity by denouncing all his fellows. The remorseless logic of St. Thomas Aquinas rendered it self-evident that the secular power could not escape the duty of putting the heretic to death, and that it was only the exceeding kindness of the Church that led it to give the criminal two warnings before handing him over to meet his fate. The inquisitors themselves had no scruples on the subject, and condescended to no subterfuges respecting it, but always held that their condemnation of a heretic was a sentence of death. They showed this in averting the pollution of a Church by not uttering these sentences within the sacred precincts, this portion of the ceremony of an *auto de fé* being performed in the public square. One of their teachers in the thirteenth century, copied by Bernard Gui in the fourteenth,. argues: " The object of the Inquisition is the destruction of heresy. Heresy cannot be destroyed unless heretics are destroyed: heretics cannot be destroyed unless their defenders and fautors are destroyed, and this is effected in two ways, viz., when they are converted to the true Catholic faith, or when, on being abandoned to the secular arm, they are corporally burned." In the next century, Fray Alonso de Spina points out that they are not to be delivered up to extermination without warning once and again, unless, indeed, their growth threatens trouble to the Church, when they are to be extirpated without delay or examination. Under these teachings the secular powers naturally recognized that in burning heretics they were only obeying the commands of the Inquisition. In a commission issued by Philippe le Bon of Burgundy, November 9, 1431, ordering his officials to render obedience to Friar Kaleyser, recently appointed Inquisitor of Lille and Cambrai, among the duties enumerated is that of inflicting due punishment on heretics " as he shall decree, and as is customary." In the accounts of the royal *procureurs des encours*, the cost of these executions in Languedoc was charged against the proceeds of the confiscations as part of the expenses of the Inquisition, thus showing that they were not regarded as ordinary incidents of criminal justice, to be defrayed out of the ordinary revenues, but as peculiarly connected with and dependent upon the operations of the Inquisition, of which the royal officials only acted as ministers. The Inquisitor Sprenger had no hesitation in alluding to the victims whom he caused to be burned — "*quas incinerari fecimus.*" In fact, how modern is the pretension that the Church was not responsible for the atrocity is apparent when, as late as the seventeenth century, the learned Cardinal Albizio, in controverting Frà Paolo as to the control of the Inquisition by the State in Venice, had no scruple in asserting that " the inquisitors in conducting the trials, regularly came to the sentence, and if it was one of death it was immediately and necessarily put into execution by the doge and the senate." *

We have already seen that the Church was responsible for the enactment of the ferocious laws punishing heresy with death, and that she intervened authoritatively to annul any secular statutes which should interfere with the prompt and effective application of the penalties. In the same way, as we have also seen, she provided against any negligence or laxity on the part of the magistrates in executing the sentences pronounced by the inquisitors. According to the universal belief of the period, this was her plainest and highest duty, and she did not shrink from it. Boniface VIII. only recorded the current practice when he embodied in the canon law the provision whereby the secular authorities were commanded to punish duly and promptly all who were handed over to them by the inquisitors, under pain of excommunication, which became heresy if endured for a twelvemonth, and the inquisitors were rigidly instructed to proceed against all magistrates who proved re-

---

* Pegnæ Comment. xx. in Eymeric. p. 124.—Tract. de Paup. de Lugd. (Martene Thesaur. V. 1792).—S. Thom. Aquinat. Summ. Sec. Sec. Q. xi. Art. 3.—Eymeric. Direct. Inquis. pp. 510–12.—Tract. de Inquisit. (Doat, XXX.).—Bern. Guidon. Practica P. iv. (Doat, XXX.).—A. de Spina Fortalic. Fidei Ed. 1494 fol. 76*a*.— MSS. Bib. Nat., fonds Moreau, No. 444, fol. 10. Cf. Archiv. di Napoli, Reg. 6, Lett. D, fol. 39 ; Reg. 13, Lett. A, fol. 139.—Coll. Doat, XXXIV. 189.—Malleus Maleficarum P. ii. Q. i. c. 2.—Albizio, Risposto al P. Paolo Sarpi, p. 30.

Gregory IX. had no scruple in asserting the duty of the Church to shed the blood of heretics. In a brief of 1234 to the Archbishop of Sens he says, " *nec enim decuit Apostolicam Sedem in oculis suis, cum Madianita coeunte Judeo, manum suam a sanguine prohibere, ne si secus ageret non custodire populum Israel. . . . videretur.*"—Ripoll I. 66.

Friar Heinrich Kaleyser was a celebrated doctor of theology, and was subsequently Inquisitor of Cologne (Nider. Formicar. v. viii.).

calcitrant, while they were at the same time cautioned only to speak of executing the laws without specifically mentioning the penalty, in order to avoid falling into "irregularity," though the only punishment recognized by the Church as sufficient for heresy was burning alive. Even if the ruler was excommunicated and incapable of legally performing any other function, he was not relieved from the obligation of this supreme duty, with which nothing was allowed to interfere. Indeed, authorities were found to argue that if an inquisitor were obliged to execute the sentence himself he would not thereby incur irregularity.*

We are not to imagine, however, from these reduplicated commands that the secular power, as a rule, showed itself in the slightest degree disinclined to perform the duty. The teachings of the Church had made too profound an impression for any doubt in the premises to exist. As has been seen above, the laws of all the states of Europe prescribed concremation as the appropriate penalty for heresy, and even the free commonwealths of Italy recognized the Inquisition as the judge whose sentences were to be blindly executed. Raymond of Toulouse himself, in the fit of piety which preceded his death in 1249, caused eighty believers in heresy to be burned at Berlaiges, near Agen, after they had confessed in his presence, apparently without giving them the opportunity of recanting. From the contemporary sentences of Bernard de Caux, it is probable that, had these unfortunates been tried before that ardent champion of the faith, not one of them would have been condemned to the stake as impenitent. Quite as significant was the suit brought by the Maréchal de Mirepoix against the Seneschal of Carcassonne, because the latter had invaded his right to burn for himself all his subjects condemned as heretics by the Inquisition. In 1269 the Parlement of Paris decided the case in his favor, after which, on March 18, 1270, the seneschal acceded to his demand that the bones of seven men and three women of his ter-

---

* C. 18 Sexto v. 2.—Concil. Albiens. ann. 1254 c. 22.—Eymeric. Direct. Inq. pp. 372, 562.—Pegnæ Comment. in Eymeric. p. 564.—Guid. Fulcod. Quæst. x.—Alex. PP. IV. Bull. *Ad audientiam*, 1260 (Eymeric. Append. p. 34).—Bern. Guidon. Practica P. IV. (Doat, XXX.).—Alex. PP. IV. Bull. *Quæsivisti*, 1260 (Ripoll I. 393).—Wadding. Annal. ann. 1288, No. 20.—Zanchini Tract. de Hæret. c. xviii.—Fortalicii Fidei fol. 74*b*.—Bernardi Comens. Lucerna Inquisit. s. v. *Executio*, No. 1, 8.

ritories, recently burned at Carcassonne, should be solemnly surrendered to him in recognition of his right; or, if they could not
be found and identified, then, as substitutes, ten canvas bags filled
with straw—a ghastly symbolic ceremony which was actually performed two days later, and a formal notarial act executed in attestation of it.   Yet, though the De Levis of Mirepoix rejoiced in
the title of Maréchaux de la Foi, it is not to be assumed that this
eagerness arose wholly from bloodthirsty fanaticism, for there was
nothing to which the seigneur-justicier clung more jealously than
to every detail of his jurisdiction.   A similar dispute arose in 1309,
when the Count of Foix claimed the right to burn the Catharan
heresiarch, Jacques Autier, and a woman named Guillelma Cristola,
condemned by Bernard Gui, because they were his subjects, but the
royal officials maintained their master's privileges in the premises, and the suit thence arising was still pending in 1326.   So at
Narbonne, where there was a long-standing dispute between the
archbishop and the viscount as to the jurisdiction, and where, in
1319, the former in conjunction with the inquisitor Jean de Beaune
relaxed three heretics, he claimed for his court the right to burn
them.   The commune, as representing the viscount, resisted this,
and the hideous quarrel was only settled by the representative of
the king stepping in and performing the act.   In so doing, however, he carefully specified that it was not to work prejudice to
either party, while to the end the archbishop protested against the
intrusion upon his rights.*

If, however, from any cause, the secular authorities were re-
luctant to execute the death-sentence, the Church had little ceremony in putting forth its powers to coerce obedience.   When, for
instance, the first resistance in Toulouse had been broken down
and the Holy Office had been reinstated there, the inquisitors, in
1237, condemned six men and women as heretics; but the viguier
and consuls refused to receive the convicts, to confiscate their
property, and "to do with them what was customary to be done
with heretics"—that is, to burn them alive.   Thereupon the inquisitors, after counselling with the bishop, the Abbot du Mas, the
Provost of St. Étienne, and the Prior of La Daurade, proceeded to

---

* Guill. Pod. Laur. cap. 48.—Les Olim, I. 317.—Vaissette, Éd. Privat, VIII.
1674 · X. Pr. 484, 659.—Baluz. et Mansi, II. 257.

excommunicate solemnly the recalcitrant officials in the Cathedral of St. Étienne. In 1288 Nicholas IV. lamented the neglect and covert opposition with which in many places the secular authorities evaded the execution of the inquisitorial sentences, and directed that they should be punished with excommunication and deprivation of office and their communities be subjected to interdict. In 1458, at Strassburg, the Burgermeister, Hans Drachenfels, and his colleagues refused at first to burn the Hussite missionary Frederic Reiser and his servant Anna Weiler, but their resistance was overcome and they were finally forced to execute the sentence. Thirty years later, in 1486, the magistrates of Brescia objected to burning certain witches of both sexes condemned by the Inquisition, unless they should be permitted to examine the proceedings. This was held to be flat rebellion. Civil lawyers, it is true, had endeavored to prove that the secular authorities had a right to see the papers, but the inquisitors had succeeded in having this claim rejected. Innocent VIII. promptly declared the Venetian demands to be a scandal to the faith, and he ordered the excommunication of the magistrates if within six days they did not execute the convicts, any municipal statutes to the contrary being pronounced null and void—a decision which was held to give the secular courts six days in which to carry out the sentence of condemnation. A more stubborn contest arose in 1521, when the Inquisition endeavored to purge the dioceses of both Brescia and Bergamo of the witches who still infested them. The inquisitor and episcopal ordinaries proceeded against them vigorously, but the Signiory of Venice interposed and appealed to Leo X., who appointed his nuncio at Venice to revise the trials. The latter delegated his power to the Bishop of Justinopolis, who proceeded with the inquisitor and ordinaries to the Valcamonica of Brescia, where the so-called heretics were numerous, and condemned some of them to be relaxed to the secular arm. Still dissatisfied, the Venetian Senate ordered the Governor of Brescia not to execute the sentences or to permit them to be executed, or to pay the expenses of the proceedings, but to send the papers to Venice for revision, and to compel the Bishop of Justinopolis to appear before them, which he was obliged to do. This inflamed the papal indignation to the highest pitch. Leo X. warmly assured the inquisitor and the episcopal officials that they had full jurisdiction over the culprits, that their sentences were to be executed without revision or examination, and that they must enforce these rights with the free use of ecclesiastical censures. The spirit of the age, however, was insubordinate, and Venice had always been peculiarly so in all matters connected with the Holy Office. We shall see hereafter how the Council of Ten undauntedly held its position and asserted the superiority of its jurisdiction in a manner previously unexampled.*

In view of this unvarying policy of the Church during the three centuries under consideration, and for a century and a half later, there is a typical instance of the manner in which history is written to order, in the quiet assertion of the latest Catholic historian of the Inquisition that "the Church took no part in the corporal punishment of heretics. Those who perished miserably were only chastised for their crimes, sentenced by judges invested with the royal jurisdiction. The record of the excesses committed by the heretics of Bulgaria, by the Gnostics and Manichæans, is historical, and capital punishment was only inflicted on criminals confessing to robbery, assassination, and violence. The Albigenses were treated with equal benignity; ... the Catholic Church deplored all acts of vengeance, however great was the provocation given by the ferocity of those factious masses." So completely, in truth, was the Church convinced of its duty to see that all heretics were burned that, at the Council of Constance, the eighteenth article of heresy charged against John Huss was that, in his treatise *de Ecclesia*, he had taught that no heretic ought to be abandoned to secular judgment to be punished with death. In his defence even Huss admitted that a heretic who could not be mildly led from error ought to suffer bodily punishment; and when a passage was read from his book in which those who deliver an unconvicted heretic to the secular arm are compared to the Scribes and Pharisees who delivered Christ to Pilate, the assembly broke out into a storm of objurgation, during which even the sturdy reformer, Cardinal Pierre d'Ailly, was heard to exclaim,

---

* Vaissette, III. 410.—Wadding. Annal. ann. 1288, No. xix.—Hoffmann, Geschichte der Inquisition, II. 391.—Bernardi Comens. Lucerna Inquisit. s. v. *Executio*, No. 6.—Innoc. PP. VIII. Bull. *Dilectus filius*, 1486 (Pegnæ App. ad Eymeric. p. 84).—Leo. PP. X. Bull. *Honestis*, 1521 (Mag. Bull. Rom. I. 617).—Albizio, Risposto al P. Paolo Sarpi. pp. 64–70.

"Verily those who drew up the articles were most moderate, for his writings are much more atrocious." *

The continuous teachings of the Church led its best men to regard no act as more self-evidently just than the burning of the heretic, and no heresy less defensible than a demand for toleration. Even Chancellor Gerson himself could see nothing else to be done with those who pertinaciously adhered to error, even in matters not at present explicitly articles necessary to the faith.† The fact is, the Church not only defined the guilt and forced its punishment, but created the crime itself. As we shall see, under Nicholas IV. and Celestine V., the strict Franciscans were preeminently orthodox; but when John XXII. stigmatized as heretical the belief that Christ lived in absolute poverty, he transformed them into unpardonable criminals whom the temporal officials were bound to send to the stake, under pain of being themselves treated as heretics.

There was thus a universal consensus of opinion that there was nothing to do with a heretic but to burn him. The heretic as known to the laws, both secular and ecclesiastical, was he who not only admitted his heretical belief, but defended it and refused to recant. He was obstinate and impenitent; the Church could do nothing with him, and as soon as the secular lawgivers had provided for his guilt the awful punishment of the stake, there was no hesitation in handing him over to the temporal jurisdiction to endure it. All authorities unite in this, and the annals of the Inquisition can vainly be searched for an exception. Yet this was regarded by the inquisitor as a last resort. To say nothing of the saving of a soul, a convert who would betray his friends was more useful than a roasted corpse, and, as we have seen, no effort was spared to obtain recantation. Experience had shown that such zealots were often eager for martyrdom and desired to be speedily burned, and it was no part of the inquisitor's pleasure to gratify them. He was advised that this ardor frequently gave way under time and suffering, and therefore he was told to keep the obstinate and defiant heretic chained in a dungeon for six

---

* Rodrigo, Historia Verdadera de la Inquisition, Madrid, 1876, I. 176–77.— Von der Hardt, IV. 317–18.

† Von der Hardt, III, 50–1.

months or a year in utter solitude, save when a dozen theologians
and legists should be let in upon him to labor for his conversion,
or his wife and children be admitted to work upon his heart. It
was not until all this had been tried and failed that he was to be
relaxed. Even then the execution was postponed for a day to
give further opportunity for recantation, which, we are told, rarely
happened, for those who went thus far usually persevered to the
end; but if his resolution gave way and he professed repentance,
his conversion was presumed to be the work of fear rather than of
grace, and he was to be strictly imprisoned for life. Even at the
stake his offer to abjure ought not to be refused, though there was
no absolute rule as to this, and there could be little hope of the gen-
uineness of such conversion. Eymerich relates a case occurring
at Barcelona when three heretics were burned, and one of them, a
priest, after being scorched on one side, cried out that he would
recant. He was removed and abjured, but fourteen years later
was found to have persisted in heresy and to have infected many
others, when he was despatched without more ado.*

The obstinate heretic who preferred martyrdom to apostasy
was by no means the sole victim doomed to the stake. The secular lawgiver had provided this punishment for heresy, but had
left to the Church its definition, and the definition was enlarged
to serve as a gentle persuasive that should supplement all deficiencies in the inquisitorial process. Where testimony deemed sufficient existed, persistent denial only aggravated guilt, and the profession of orthodoxy was of no avail. If two witnesses swore to
having seen a man "adore" a perfected heretic it was enough,
and no declaration of readiness to subscribe to all the tenets of
Rome availed him, without confession, abjuration, recantation,
and acceptance of penance. Such a one was a heretic, to be pitilessly burned. It was the same with the contumacious who did
not obey the summons to stand trial. Persistent refusal of the
oath was likewise technical heresy, condemning the recalcitrant to
the stake. Even when there was no proof, simple suspicion be-

* Concil. Arelatens. ann. 1234 c. 6.—Concil. Tarraconens. ann. 1242.—Concil.
Biterrens. ann. 1246, Append. c. 17.—Bern. Guidon. Practica P. iv. (Doat, XXX.).
—Eymeric. Direct. Inquis. pp. 514-16.—Anon. Passaviens. c. ix. (Mag. Bib. Pat.
XIII. 308). — Zanchini Tract. de Hæret. c. xviii. — Lib. Sententt. Inq. Tolosan.
p. 6.

came heresy if the suspect failed to purge himself with conjurators and remained so for a year. In violent suspicion, refusal to
abjure worked the same result in a twelvemonth. A retracted
confession was similarly regarded. In short, the stake supplied
all defects. It was the *ultima ratio*, and although not many
cases have reached us in which executions actually occurred on
these grounds, there is no doubt that such provisions were of the
utmost utility in practice, and that the terror which they inspired
extorted many a confession, true or false, from unwilling lips.*

There was another class of cases, however, which gave the inquisitors much trouble, and in which they were long in settling
upon a definite and uniform course of procedure. The innumerable forced conversions wrought by the dungeon and stake filled
the prisons and the land with those whose outward conformity
left them at heart no less heretics than before. I have elsewhere
spoken of the all-pervading police of the Holy Office and of the
watchfulness exercised over the converts whose liberation at best
was but a ticket-of-leave. That cases of relapse into heresy should
be constant was therefore a matter of course. Even in the jails it
was impossible to segregate all the prisoners, and complaints are
frequent of these wolves in sheep's clothing who infected their
more innocent fellow-captives. A man whose solemn conversion
had once been proved fraudulent could never again be trusted.
He was an incorrigible heretic whom the Church could no longer
hope to win over. On him mercy was wasted, and the stake was
the only resource. Yet it is creditable to the Inquisition that it
was so long in reducing to practice this self-evident proposition.

As early as 1184 the Verona decree of Lucius III. provides
that those who, after abjuration, relapse into the abjured heresy
shall be delivered to the secular courts, without even the opportu.
nity of being heard. The Ravenna edict of Frederic II., in 1232,
prescribed death for all who, by relapse, showed that their conversion had been a pretext to escape the penalty of heresy. In 1244
the Council of Narbonne alludes to the great multitude of such
cases, and, following Lucius III., orders them to be relaxed with-

---

* Concil. Narbonn. ann. 1244 c. 26.—Concil. Biterrens. ann. 1246, App. c. 9.—
Eymeric. Direct. Inquis. pp. 376–77, 521–4. — MSS. Bib. Nat., fonds latin, No
9992.—Lib. Sententt. Inq. Tolos. pp. 379–80.—Zanchini Tract. de Hæret. c. xxiii.

out a hearing. Yet these stern mandates were not enforced. In
1233 we find Gregory IX. contenting himself with prescribing
perpetual imprisonment for such cases, which he speaks of as being already numerous. In a single sentence of February 19, 1237,
the inquisitors of Toulouse condemn seventeen relapsed heretics to
perpetual imprisonment. Raymond de Pennaforte, at the Council of Tarragona, in 1242, alludes to the diversity of opinion on
the subject, and pronounces in favor of imprisonment; and, in 1246,
the Council of Béziers, in giving similar instructions, speaks of
them as being in accordance with the apostolic mandates. Even
this degree of severity was not always inflicted. In 1242 Pierre
Cella only prescribes pilgrimages and crosses for such offenders,
and, in a case occurring in Florence in 1245, Frà Ruggieri Calcagni lets off the culprit with a not extravagant fine.*

What to do with these multitudes of false converts was evidently a question which perplexed the Church no little, and, as
usual, a solution, at least for the time, was found in leaving the
matter to the discretion of the inquisitors. In answer to the inquiries of the Lombard Holy Office, the Cardinal of Albano, about
1245, tells the officials to make use of such penalties as they shall
deem appropriate. In 1248 Bernard de Caux asked the same
question of the Archbishop of Narbonne, and was told that, according to the "apostolic mandates," those who returned to the
Church a second time, humbly and obediently, might be let off
with perpetual imprisonment, while those who were disobedient
should be abandoned to the secular arm. Under these instructions
the practice varied, though it is pleasant to be able to say that, in
the vast majority of cases, the inquisitors leaned to the side of
mercy. Even the ardent zeal of Bernard de Caux allowed him to
use his discretion gently. In his register of sentences, from 1246
to 1248, there are sixty cases of relapse, none of which are punished more severely than by imprisonment, and in some of them
the confinement is not perpetual. The same lenity is observable

---

* Lucii PP. III. Epist. 171. — Hist. Diplom. Frid. II. T. IV. p. 300. — Concil.
Narbonn. ann. 1244 c. 11.—Gregor. PP. IX. Bull. *Ad capiendas* (Vaissette, III. Pr.
364). — Epistt. Sæcul. XIII. No. 514 (Mon. Germ. Hist.). — Ripoll I. 55. — Concil.
Tarraconens. ann. 1242. — Doctrina de modo procedendi (Martene Thesaur. V.
1800). — Concil. Biterrens. ann. 1246, App. c. 20. — Coll. Doat, XXI. 148, 292. —
Lami, Antichità Toscane, p. 560.

in various sentences rendered during the next ten years, both by him and by other inquisitors. Yet, with one exception, the codes of instruction which date about this period assume that relapse is always to be visited with relaxation, and that the offender is to have no hearing in his defence. In the exceptional instance the compiler illustrates the uncertainty which existed by sometimes treating relapse as punishable with imprisonment and sometimes as entailing the stake. Relapse into usury, however, was let off with the lighter alternative. The fact is that in Languedoc, under the Treaty of Paris, as stated above, an oath of abjuration was administered every two years to all males over fourteen and all females over twelve, and any subsequent act of heresy was technically a relapse. This, perhaps, explains the indecision of the inquisitors of Toulouse. It was impossible to burn all such cases.*

Whatever be the cause, there evidently was considerable doubt in the minds of inquisitors as to the penalty of relapse, and it must be recorded to their credit that in this they were more merciful than the current public opinion of the age. Jean de Saint-Pierre, the colleague and successor of Bernard de Caux, followed his example in always condemning the relapsed to imprisonment, and when, after Bernard's death, in 1252, Frère Renaud de Chartres was adjoined to him, the same rule continued to be observed. Frère Renaud found, however, to his horror, that the secular judges disregarded the sentence and mercilessly burned the unhappy victims, and that this had been going on under his predecessors. The civil authorities defended their course by arguing that in no other way could the land be purged of heresy, which was acquiring new force under the mistaken lenity of the inquisitors. Frère Renaud felt that he could not overlook this cruelty in silence as his predecessors had done. He therefore reported the facts to Alphonse of Poitiers, and informed him that he proposed to refer the matter to the pope, pending whose answer he would keep

---

* Arch. de l'Inq. de Carcassonne (Doat, XXXI. 5, 139, 149).—MSS. Bib. Nat., fonds latin, No. 9992.—Martene Thesaur. I. 1045.—Vaissette, III. Pr. 479.—Molinier, L'Inq. dans le midi de la France, pp. 387-8, 418.—Anon. Passaviens. (Mag. Bib. Pat. XIII. 308).—Tract. de Paup. de Lugd. (Martene Thesaur. V.1791).—Doctrina de modo procedendi (Ibid. 1807).—Practica super Inquisit. (MSS. Bib. Nat., fonds latin, No. 14930, fol. 206, 212, 213, 222, 223).—Concil. Biterrens. ann. 1246, App. c. 33.

his prisoners secure from the brutal violence of the secular officials.*

What was the papal response we can only conjecture, but it doubtless leaned rather to the rigorous zeal of Alphonse's officials than to the milder methods of Frère Renaud, for it was about this time that Rome definitely decided for the unconditional relaxation of all who were guilty of relapsing into heresy which had once been abjured. The precise date of this I have not been able to determine. In 1254 Innocent IV. contents himself, in a very aggravated case of double relapse occurring in Milan, with ordering destruction of houses and public penance, but in 1258 relaxation for relapse is alluded to by Alexander IV. as a matter previously irrevocably settled—possibly by the very appeal of Frère Renaud. It seems to have taken the inquisitors somewhat by surprise, and for several years they continued to trouble the Holy See with the pertinent question of how such a rule was to be reconciled with the universally received maxim that the Church never closes her bosom to her wayward children seeking to return. To this the characteristic explanation was given that the Church was not closed to them, for if they showed signs of penitence they might receive the Eucharist, even at the stake, but without escaping death. In this shape the decision was embodied in the canon law, and made a part of orthodox doctrine in the Summa of St. Thomas Aquinas. The promise of the Eucharist frequently formed part of the sentence in these cases, and the victim was always accompanied to execution by holy men striving to save his soul until the last—though it is shrewdly advised that the inquisitor himself had better not exhibit his zeal in this way, as his appearance will be more likely to excite hardening than softening of the heart.†

Although inquisitors continued to assume discretion in these cases and did not by any means invariably send the relapsed to the stake, still relapse became the main cause of capital punishment. Defiant heretics courting martyrdom were comparatively

---

* Boutaric, Saint Louis et Alphonse de Poitiers, pp. 453–4.

† Ripoll I. 254.— C. 4 Sexto v. 2. — Potthast No. 17845.— S. Thom. Aquin. Sec. Sec. Q. xi. Art. 4. — Eymeric. Direct. Inq. p. 331, 512. — Lib. Sententt. Inq. Tolos. p. 36.—Zanchini Tract. de Hæret. c. xvi.

rare, but there were many poor souls who could not abandon con-
scientiously the errors which they had cherished, and who vainly
hoped, after escaping once, to be able to hide their guilt more effectually.* All this gave a fresh importance to the question of
what legally constituted relapse, and led to endless definitions and
subtleties. It became necessary to determine with some precision,
when the offender was refused a hearing, the exact amount of
criminality in both the first and second offences, which would
justify condemnation for impenitent heresy. Where guilt was
ofttimes so shadowy and impalpable, this was evidently no easy
matter.

There were cases in which a first trial had only developed suspicion without proof, and it seemed hard to condemn a man to
death for an assumed second offence when he had not been proved
guilty of the first. Hesitating to do so, the inquisitors applied to
Alexander IV. to resolve their doubts, and he answered in the
most positive manner. When the suspicion had been "violent"
he said, it was "by a sort of legal fiction" to be held as legal
proof of guilt, and the accused was to be condemned. When it
was "light" he was to be punished more heavily than for a first
offence, but not with the full penalty of relapse. Moreover, the
evidence required to prove the second offence was of the slightest;
any communication with or kindness shown to heretics sufficed.
This decision was repeated by Alexander and his successors with a
frequency which shows how doubtful and puzzling were the points
which came up for discussion, but the rule of condemnation was
finally carried into the canon law and became the unalterable
policy of the Church. The authorities, except Zanghino, agree
that in such cases there was no room for mercy.†

Besides these enigmas there were others respecting forms of
guilt which might reasonably be regarded as less deserving of the
last resort. Thus relapse into fautorship gave rise to considerable

---

* Lib. Sententt. Inq. Tolosan. pp. 2–4, 22, 48, 63, 76, 81–90, 122, 142, 149, 150,
198–99, 230, 232, 287–88.

† Alex. PP. IV. Bull. *Quod super nonnullis*, 9 Dec. 1257, 15 Dec. 1258, 10 Jan.
1260.—Urban. PP. IV. Bull. *Quod super nonnullis*, 21 Aug. 1262.—Can. 8 Sexto
v. 2.—Bern. Guidon. Practica P. IV. (Doat, XXX.).—Eymeric. Direct. Inq. p. 331.—
Bernardi Comens. Lucerna Inquis. s. v. *Relapsus.*—Zanchini Tract. de Hæret. c.
xvi.

divergence of views. The Council of Narbonne, in 1244, was of opinion that those guilty of this offence should be sent to the pope for absolution and the imposition of penance—a cumbrous procedure, not likely to find favor. During the middle period of the Inquisition, the authorities, including Bernard Gui, while not prescribing relaxation to the secular arm, suggest that penance be imposed sufficiently severe to inspire wholesome fear in others; while, towards the end of the fourteenth century, Eymerich holds that a relapsed fautor is to be abandoned to secular justice without a hearing. Even those defamed for heresy, if after due purgation they again incur defamation, are strictly liable to the same fate, though this was so hard a measure that Eymerich proposes that such cases should be referred to the pope.*

There was another class of offenders who gave the inquisitors endless trouble, and for whom it was difficult to frame rigid and invariable rules—those who escaped from prison or omitted to fulfil the penances assigned to them. According to theory, all penitents were converts to the true faith who eagerly accepted penance as their sole hope of salvation. To reject it subsequently was therefore an evidence that the conversion had been feigned or that the inconstant soul had reverted to its former errors, as otherwise the loving and wholesome discipline of the benignant Mother Church would not be spurned. From the beginning, therefore, these culprits were classed with the relapsed. In 1248 the Council of Valence ordered them to have the benefit of a warning, after which further persistence in disobedience rendered them liable to the full penalty of obstinate heresy; and this was sometimes provided for in the sentence itself, by a clause which warned them that any disregard of the observances enjoined would expose them to the fate of perjured and impenitent heretics. Yet as late as 1260 Alexander IV. seems at a loss what rule to prescribe in such cases, and merely talks vaguely of excommunication and reimposition of the penalties, with the assistance, if necessary, of the secular authorities. Yet about the same period Gui Foucoix pronounced in favor of the death-penalty for these offenders, arguing that the offence proved impenitent heresy; but Bernard Gui held this to

---

* Concil. Narbonn. ann. 1244 c. 13.—Doctrina de modo procedendi (Martene Thesaur. V. 1802, 1808).—Bern. Guidon. Practica P. IV. (Doat, XXX.).—Eymeric. Direct. Inq. p. 386.

be too severe, and advised leaving them to the discretion of the in-quisitor—a discretion which he himself had no hesitation in exercising. The two most frequent varieties of the offence were laying aside the yellow crosses and prison-breaking. The former was never, so far as I have seen, punished with death, though visited with penalties sufficiently sharp to serve as a deterrent. The latter, according to the later inquisitors, was capital—the escaped prisoner was a relapsed heretic, to be burned without a hearing. Some jurists argued that a failure fully to betray all heretics of whom the convert had knowledge—a pledge to do so forming a necessary part of the oath of abjuration—constituted relapse, but Bernard Gui regards this as unduly harsh. Absolute refusal to perform the penance enjoined was, of course, evidence of obstinate heresy, leading inevitably to the stake. Such cases were naturally rare, for penance was only prescribed for those who had confessed, had professed conversion, and had asked for reconciliation; but there is one on record of a woman, in the latter half of the fifteenth century, before the Inquisition of Cartagena, who was duly abandoned to the secular arm.*

Notwithstanding these extensions of the death-penalty, I am convinced that the number of victims who actually perished at the stake is considerably less than has ordinarily been imagined. The deliberate burning alive of a human being, simply for difference of belief, is an atrocity so dramatic and appeals so strongly to the imagination that it has come to be regarded as the leading feature in the activity of the Inquisition. Yet, frequent as recourse to the stake undoubtedly was, it formed but a comparatively small part of the instrumentalities of repression. The records of those evil days have mostly disappeared, and there is now no possibility of recon-

---

* Concil. Narbonn. ann. 1244 c. 13.—Concil. Biterrens. ann. 1246, Append. c. 33.—Concil. Valentin. ann. 1248 c. 13.—Archives de l'Évêché d'Albi (Doat, XXXV. 69).—Alex. PP. IV. Bull. *Ad audientiam*, 1260 (Mag. Bull. Rom. I. 118).—Guidon. Fulcod. Quæst. XIII.—Bern. Guidon. Practica P. IV. (Doat, XXX.).—Lib. Sententt. Inq. Tolosan. pp. 177, 199, 350, 393.—MSS. Bib. Nat., fonds latin, nouv. acquis. No. 139, fol. 2.—Eymeric. Direct. Inquis. p. 643.—Zanchini Tract. de Hæret. c. x.—Bern. Comens. Lucerna Inquisit. s. v. *Fuga*, No. 5.—Albertini Repertor. Inquisit. s. vv. *Deficiens, Impœnitens*.

structing their statistics, but if this could be done I have no doubt that the actual executions by fire would excite surprise by falling far short of the popular estimate. Imagination has grown inflamed at the manifold iniquities of the Holy Office, and has been ready to accept without examination exaggerations which have become habitual. No one can suspect the learned Dom Brial of prejudice or of ordinary lack of accuracy, and yet in his Preface to Vol. XXI. of the "Recueil des Historiens des Gaules" (p. xxiii.), he quotes as trustworthy an assertion that Bernard Gui, during his service as Inquisitor of Toulouse from 1308 to 1323, put to death no less than six hundred and thirty-seven heretics. Now that, as we have seen, was the total number of sentences uttered by the tribunal during those years, and of these sentences only forty were capital—in addition to sixty-seven dead heretics condemned to be exhumed and burned, for the most part because they were not alive to recant. Again, no inquisitor left behind him a more enviable record for zeal and activity in the relentless persecution of heresy than Bernard de Caux, who labored in the earlier period when the land was yet full of heresy, and heretics had not yet been cowed into submissiveness. Bernard Gui characterizes him as "a persecutor and hammer of heretics, a holy man and full of God, . . . wonderful in his life, wonderful in doctrine, wonderful in extirpating heresy;" he wrought miracles while alive, and in 1281, twenty-eight years after his death, his body was found uncorrupted and perfect, except part of the nose. Such a man is not to be accused of undue tenderness towards heretics, and yet, in his register of sentences from 1246 to 1248, there is not a single case of abandonment to the secular arm, unless we may reckon as such the condemnations of contumacious absentees, who were necessarily declared to be heretics. These, indeed, were liable to be burned by the secular justice, but, in fact, they could always save themselves by submission, and this very register affords a very striking instance in point. There was no more obnoxious heretic in Toulouse than Alaman de Roaix. He belonged to one of the noblest families in the city, and one which furnished many members to the heretic church, of which he himself was suspected of being a bishop. In 1229 the Legate Romano had condemned him and had imposed on him the penance of a crusade to the Holy Land, which he had sworn to perform and never fulfilled. In 1237 the earliest inquisitors, Guillem Arnaud and Étienne de Saint-Thibery, again took up his case, finding him unremittingly active in protecting heretics and disseminating heresy, spoiling, ransoming, wounding, and slaying priests and clerks, and this time they condemned him *in absentia.* He became a *faydit,* or proscribed man, living sword in hand and plundering the orthodox to support himself and his friends. No more aggravated case of obstinate heresy and persistent contumacy can well be imagined, and yet when he acknowledged his errors, January 16, 1248, professed conversion, and asked for penance, a score of years after his first conversion, he was only condemned to imprisonment.*

In fact, as we have already seen, the earnest endeavors of the inquisitors were directed much more to obtaining conversions with confiscations and betrayal of friends than to provoking martyrdoms. An occasional burning only was required to maintain a wholesome terror in the minds of the population. With his forty cases of concremation in fifteen years, Bernard Gui managed to crush the last convulsive struggle of Catharism, to keep the Waldenses in check, and repress the zealous ardor of the Spiritual Franciscans. The really effective weapons of the Holy Office, the real curses with which it afflicted the people, can be looked for in its dungeons and its confiscations, in the humiliating penances of the saffron crosses, and in the invisible police with which it benumbed the heart and soul of every man who had once fallen into its hands.

A few words will suffice as to the repulsive subject of the execution itself. When the populace was called together to view the last agonies of the martyrs of heresy, its pious zeal was not mocked by any ill-advised devices of mercy. The culprit was not, as in the later Spanish Inquisition, strangled before the lighting of the fagots; nor had the invention of gunpowder suggested the somewhat less humane expedient of hanging a bag of that explosive around his neck to shorten his torture when the flames should reach it. He was tied living to a post set high enough over a pile

---

* Bern. Guidon. Fund. Conv. Prædicat. (Martene Thesaur. VI. 481-3).—Coll. Doat, XXI. 143, 146.—MSS. Bib. Nat., fonds latin, No. 9992.—Molinier, L'Inq. dans le midi de la France, pp. 73-4.

of combustibles to enable the faithful to watch every act of the tragedy to its awful end. Holy men accompanied him to the last, to snatch his soul if possible from Satan; and, if he were not a relapsed, he could, as we have seen, save also his body at the last moment. Yet even in these final ministrations we see a fresh illustration of the curious inconsistency with which the Church imagined that it could shirk the responsibility of putting a human creature to death, for the friars who accompanied the victim were strictly warned not to exhort him to meet death promptly or to ascend firmly the ladder leading to the stake, or to submit cheerfully to the manipulations of the executioner, for if they did so they would be hastening his end and thus fall into " irregularity " —a tender scruple, it must be confessed, and one singularly out of place in those who had accomplished the judicial murder. For these occasions a holiday was usually selected, in order that the crowd might be larger and the lesson more effective; while, to prevent scandal, the sufferer was silenced, lest he might provoke the people to pity and sympathy.*

As for minor details, we happen to have them preserved in an account by an eye-witness of the execution of John Huss at Constance, in 1415. He was made to stand upon a couple of fagots and tightly bound to a thick post with ropes, around the ankles, below the knee, above the knee, at the groin, the waist, and under the arms. A chain was also secured around the neck. Then it was observed that he faced the east, which was not fitting for a heretic, and he was shifted to the west; fagots mixed with straw were piled around him to the chin. Then the Count Palatine Louis, who superintended the execution, approached with the Marshal of Constance, and asked him for the last time to recant. On his refusal they withdrew and clapped their hands, which was the signal for the executioners to light the pile. After it had burned away there followed the revolting process requisite to utterly destroy the half-burned body—separating it in pieces, breaking up the bones and throwing the fragments and the viscera on a fresh fire of logs. When, as in the cases of Arnaldo of Brescia, some of the Spiritual Franciscans, Huss, Savonarola, and others, it was

---

* Eymeric. Direct. Inquis. p. 512.—Tract. de Paup. de Lugd. (Martene Thesaur. V. 1792).

feared that relics of the martyr would be preserved, especial care was taken, after the fire was extinguished, to gather up the ashes and cast them in a running stream.*

There is something grotesquely horrible in the contrast between this crowning exhibition of human perversity and the cool business calculation of the cost of thus sending a human soul through flame to its Creator. In the accounts of Arnaud Assalit we have a statement of the expenses of burning four heretics at Carcassonne, April 24, 1323. It runs thus:

For large wood...	55 sols 6 deniers.
For vine-branches..	21 sols 3 deniers.
For straw...	2 sols 6 deniers.
For four stakes...	10 sols 9 deniers.
For ropes to tie the convicts..........................	4 sols 7 deniers.
For the executioner, each 20 sols....................	80 sols.
In all..............................	8 livres 14 sols 7 deniers.

or, a little more than two livres apiece.†

When the heretic had eluded his tormentors by death and his body or skeleton was dug up and burned, the ceremony was necessarily less impressive, but nevertheless the most was made of it. As early as 1237 Guillem Pelisson, a contemporary, describes how at Toulouse a number of nobles and others were exhumed, when "their bones and stinking corpses" were dragged through the streets, preceded by a trumpeter proclaiming "*Qui aytal fara, aytal perira*"—who does so shall perish so—and at length were duly burned "in honor of God and of the blessed Mary His mother, and the blessed Dominic His servant." This formula was preserved to the end, and it was not economical from a pecuniary point of view. In Assalit's accounts we find that it cost five livres nineteen sols and six deniers, in 1323, for labor to dig up the bones of three dead heretics, a sack and cord in which to stow them, and two horses to drag them to the Grève, where they were burned the next day.‡

The agency of fire was also invoked by the Inquisition to rid

---

* Mladenowic Narrat. (Palacky Monument. J. Huss II. pp. 321-4).—Landucci, Diar. Fiorent. p. 178.

† Coll. Doat, XXXIV. 189.

‡ Guillel. Pelisso Chron. Ed. Molinier p. 45.—Coll. Doat, XXXIV 189.

the land of pestilent and heretical writings, a matter not without
interest as signalizing the commencement of its activity in what
subsequently became the censorship of the press.   The burning of
books displeasing to the authorities was a custom respectable by
its antiquity.   Constantine, as we have seen, demanded the surrender of all Arian works under penalty of death.   In 435 Theo-
dosius II. and Valentinian III. ordered all Nestorian books to be
burned, and another law threatens punishment on all who will
not deliver up Manichæan writings for the same fate.   Justinian
condemned the *secunda editio*, in which the glossators agree in
recognizing the Talmud.   During the ages of barbarism which followed there was little to call forth this method of repressing the
human mind, but with the revival of speculation the ancient
measures were speedily again called into use.   When, in 1210, the
University of Paris was agitated with the heresy of Amaury, the
writings of his colleague, David de Dinant, together with the Phys-
ics and Metaphysics of Aristotle, to which it was attributed, were
ordered to be burned.   Allusion has already been made to the
burning of Romance versions of the Scriptures by Jayme I. of Aragon and to the commands of the Council of Narbonne, in 1229,
against the possession of any portion of Holy Writ by laymen, as
well as to the burning of William of St. Amour's book, "*De peri-
culis.*"   Jewish books, however, and particularly the Talmud, on
account of its blasphemous allusions to the Saviour and the Virgin, were the objects of special detestation, in the suppression of
which the Church was unwearying.   In the middle of the twelfth
century Peter the Venerable contented himself with studying the
Talmud and holding up to contempt some of the wild imaginings
which abound in that curious compound of the sublime and the
ridiculous.   His argumentative methods were not suited to the im-
patience of the thirteenth century, which had committed itself to
sterner dealings with misbelievers, and the persecution of Jewish
literature followed swiftly on that of Albigenses and Waldenses.
It was started by a converted Jew named Nicholas de Rupella,
who, about 1236, called the attention of Gregory IX. to the blasphemies with which the Hebrew books were filled, and especially
the Talmud.   In June, 1239, Gregory issued letters to the Kings
of England, France, Navarre, Aragon, Castile, and Portugal, and
to the prelates in those kingdoms, ordering that on a Sabbath in

the following Lent, when the Jews would be in their synagogues, all their books should be seized and delivered to the Mendicant Friars. A report of the examination which ensued in Paris has been preserved, and shows that there was no difficulty in finding in the Jewish writings abundant matter offensive to pious ears, though the Rabbis who ventured to appear in their defence endeavored to explain away the blasphemous allusions to the Christian Messiah, the Virgin, and the saints. The proceedings dragged on for years, and sentence was not finally rendered until May 13, 1248, after which Paris was edified with the spectacle of the burning of fourteen wagon-loads at one time and of six at another. Like the *luz* or *os coccygis*, which the Rabbis held to be indestructible, the Talmud could not be wiped out of existence, and, in 1255, St. Louis, in his instructions to his seneschals in the Narbonnais, again orders all copies to be burned, together with all other books containing blasphemies; while in 1267 Clement IV. (Gui Foucoix) instructed the Archbishop of Tarragona to coerce by excommunication the King of Aragon and his nobles to force the Jews to deliver up their Talmuds and other books to the inquisitors for examination, when, if they contain no blasphemies, they may be returned, but if otherwise they are to be sealed up and securely kept. Alonso the Wise of Castile was wiser, if, as reported, he caused the Talmud to be translated, in order that its errors might be exposed to the public. The passive resistance of the faithful was not to be overcome, and in 1299 Philippe le Bel felt obliged to denounce the persistent multiplication of the Talmud, and to order his judges to aid the Inquisition in its extermination. Ten years later, in 1309, we hear of three large wagon-loads of Jewish books publicly burned in Paris. How fruitless were all these efforts is seen in a formal sentence recited by Bernard Gui in the *auto de fé* of 1319. Under the impulsion of the Inquisition the royal officials had again made diligent perquisition and had collected all the copies of the Talmud on which they could lay their hands. Experts in the Hebrew tongue had then been employed to examine them carefully, and after mature counsel between the inquisitors and the jurists called in to assist, the books were condemned to be carried in two carts through the streets of Toulouse, while the royal officers proclaimed in loud voice that their fate was due to their blasphemies against the Lord Jesus

Christ and his mother the most holy Virgin and the Christian name, after which they were to be solemnly burned. This is the only case of execution occurring during Bernard Gui's term of service as inquisitor, and, from two carts being required to accommodate the obnoxious books, it was probable the result of search continued for a considerable time. That he deemed the matter to require constant vigilance is shown by his including in his collection of forms one which orders all priests for three Sundays to publish an injunction commanding the delivery to the Inquisition, for examination, of all Jewish books, including "Talamuz," under pain of excommunication. The warfare against this specially obnoxious work continued. In the very next year, 1320, John XXII. issued orders that all copies of it should be seized and burned. In 1409 Alexander V. paused in his denunciation of rival popes to order its destruction. The contest is well known which arose over it at the revival of letters, with Pfefferkorn and Reuchlin as the rival champions, and not all the efforts of the humanists availed to save it from proscription. Even as late as 1554 Julius III. repeated the command to the Inquisition to burn it without mercy, and all Jews were ordered, under pain of death, to surrender all books blaspheming Christ—a provision which was embodied in the canon law and remains there to this day. The censorship of the Inquisition was not confined to Jewish errors, but its activity in this direction will be more conveniently considered hereafter.*

---

* Sozomen. H. E. II. 20.—Constt. vi.; xvi. § 1, Cod. I. 5.—Auth. Novell. CXLVI. c. 1.—Rigord. de Gest. Phil. Aug. ann. 1210.—Petri Venerab. Tract. contra Judæos c. iv.—D'Argentré, Collect. Judicior. de nov. Erroribus I. I. 132, 146–56, 349.—Potthast. No. 10759, 10767, 11376.—Ripoll, I. 487–88.—Pelayo, Heterodoxos Españoles, I. 509.—Coll. Doat, XXXVII. 125, 246.—Harduin. Concil. VII. 485.—S. Martial. Chron. ann. 1309 (Bouquet, XXI. 813).—Lib. Sententt. Inq. Tolos. pp. 273–4.—Bern. Guidon. Practica (Doat, XXIX. 246).—Raynald. ann. 1320, No. 23.—Wadding. ann. 1409, No. 12.—C. 1 in Septimo v. 4.

In the Paris condemnation of 1248 the Talmud only is specified, though in the examination mention is made of the Gloss of Solomon of Troyes, and of a work which from its description would seem to be the Toldos Jeschu, or history of Jesus, which so excited the ire of the Carthusian, Ramon Marti, in his *Pugio Fidei*, and of all subsequent Christians (cf. Wagenseilii Tela Ignea Satanæ, Altdorfi, 1681). No one can read its curious account of the career of Christ from a Jewish standpoint without wondering that a single copy of it was allowed to reach modern times.

This is not the place for us to consider the influence of the Inquisition in all its breadth, but while yet we have its procedure in view it may not be amiss to glance cursorily at some of the effects immediately resulting from its mode of dealing with those whom it tried and condemned or absolved.

On the Church the processes invented and recommended to respect by the Inquisition had a most unfortunate effect. The ordinary episcopal courts employed them in dealing with heretics, and found their arbitrary violence too efficient not to extend it over other matters coming within their jurisdiction. Thus the spiritual tribunals rapidly came to employ inquisitorial methods. Already, in 1317, Bernard Gui speaks of the use of torture being habitual in them; and in complaining of the Clementine restrictions, he asks why the bishops should be limited in applying torture to heretics, while they could employ it without limit in everything else.*

Thus habituated to the harshest measures, the Church grew harder and crueller and more unchristian. The worst popes of the twelfth and thirteenth centuries could scarce have dared to shock the world with such an exhibition as that with which John XXII. glutted his hatred of Hugues Gerold, Bishop of Cahors. John was the son of an humble mechanic of Cahors, and possibly some ancient grudge may have existed between him and Hugues. Certain it is that no sooner did he mount the pontifical throne than he lost no time in assailing his enemy. May 4, 1317, the unfortunate prelate was solemnly degraded at Avignon and condemned to perpetual imprisonment. This was not enough. On a charge of conspiring against the life of the pope he was delivered to the secular arm, and in July of the same year he was partially flayed alive and then dragged to the stake and burned.†

This hardening process went on until the quarrels of the loftiest prelates were conducted with a savage ferocity which would have shamed a band of buccaneers. When, in 1385, six cardinals were accused of conspiring against Urban VI. the angry pontiff had them seized as they left the consistory and thrust into an

---

* Bern. Guidon. Gravam. (Doat, XXX. 101).

† Extrav. Commun. Lib. v. Tit. viii. c. 1.—Amalrici Augerii Vit. Pontif. ann. 1316–17.—Bern. Guidon. Vit. Joann. XXII.

abandoned cistern in the castle of Nocera, where he was staying, so restricted in dimensions that the Cardinal di Sangro, who was tall and portly, could not stretch himself at full length. The methods taught by the inquisitors were brought into play. Subjected to hunger, cold, and vermin, the accused were plied by the creatures of the pope with promises of mercy if they would confess. This failing, torture was used on the Bishop of Aquila and a confession was procured implicating the others. They still refused to admit their guilt, and they were tortured on successive days. All that could be obtained from the Cardinal di Sangro was the despairing self-accusation that he suffered justly in view of the evil which he had wrought on archbishops, bishops, and other prelates at Urban's command. When it came to the turn of the Cardinal of Venice, Urban intrusted the work to an ancient pirate, whom he had created Prior of the Order of St. John in Sicily, with instructions to apply the torture till he could hear the victim howl; the infliction lasted from early morning till the dinner-hour, while the pope paced the garden under the window of the torture-chamber, reading his breviary aloud that the sound of his voice might keep the executioner reminded of the instructions. The strappado and rack were applied by turns, but though the victim was old and sickly, nothing could be wrenched from him save the ejaculation, "Christ suffered for us!" The accused were kept in their foul dungeon until Urban, besieged in Nocera by Charles of Durazzo, managed to escape and dragged them with him. In the flight the Bishop of Aquila, weakened by torture and mounted on a miserable hack, could not keep up with the party, when Urban ordered him despatched and left his corpse unburied by the wayside. The six cardinals, less fortunate, were carried by sea to Genoa, and kept in so vile a dungeon that the authorities were moved to pity and vainly begged mercy for them. Cardinal Adam Aston, an Englishman, was released on the vigorous intercession of Richard II., but the other five were never seen again. Some said that Urban had them beheaded; others that when he sailed for Sicily he carried them to sea and cast them overboard; others, again, that a trench was dug in his stable in which they were buried alive with a quantity of quicklime, to hasten the disappearance of their bodies. Urban's competitor, known as Clement VII., was no less sanguinary. When, as Cardinal Robert of

Geneva, he exercised legatine functions for Gregory XI., he led a band of Free Companions to vindicate the papal territorial claims. The terrible cold-blooded massacre of Cesena was his most conspicuous exploit, but equally characteristic of the man was his threat to the citizens of Bologna that he would wash his hands and feet in their blood. Such was the retroactive influence of the inquisitorial methods on the Church which had invented them to plague the heretic. If Bernabo and Galeazzo Visconti caused ecclesiastics to be tortured and burned to death over slow fires, they were merely improving on the lessons which the Church itself had taught.*

On secular jurisprudence the example of the Inquisition worked even more deplorably. It came at a time when the old order of things was giving way to the new — when the ancient customs of the barbarians, the ordeal, the wager of law, the wer-gild, were growing obsolete in the increasing intelligence of the age, when a new system was springing into life under the revived study of the Roman law, and when the administration of justice by the local feudal lord was becoming swallowed up in the widening jurisdiction of the crown. The whole judicial system of the European monarchies was undergoing reconstruction, and the happiness of future generations depended on the character of the new institutions. That in this reorganization the worst features of the imperial jurisprudence — the use of torture and the inquisitorial process — should be eagerly, nay, almost exclusively, adopted, should be divested of the safeguards which in Rome had restricted their abuse, should be exaggerated in all their evil tendencies, and should, for five centuries, become the prominent characteristic of the criminal jurisprudence of Europe, may safely be ascribed to the fact that they received the sanction of the Church. Thus recommended, they penetrated everywhere along with the Inquisition; while most of the nations to whom the Holy Office was unknown maintained their ancestral customs, developing into various

---

* Theod. a Niem de Schismate Lib. I. c. 42, 45, 48, 50, 51, 52, 56, 57, 60.— Gobelin. Personæ Cosmodrom. Aet. VI. c. 78.—Chronik des J. v. Königshofen (Chron. der Deutschen Städte, IX. 598). — Raynald. ann. 1362, No. 13; 1372, No. 10.—Poggii Hist. Florentin. Lib. II. ann. 1376.

forms of criminal practice, harsh enough, indeed, to modern eyes, but wholly divested of the more hideous atrocities which characterized the habitual investigation into crime in other regions.*

Of all the curses which the Inquisition brought in its train this, perhaps, was the greatest—that, until the closing years of the eighteenth century, throughout the greater part of Europe, the inquisitorial process, as developed for the destruction of heresy, became the customary method of dealing with all who were under accusation; that the accused was treated as one having no rights, whose guilt was assumed in advance, and from whom confession was to be extorted by guile or force. Even witnesses were treated in the same fashion; and the prisoner who acknowledged guilt under torture was tortured again to obtain information about any other evil-doers of whom he perchance might have knowledge. So, also, the crime of "suspicion" was imported from the Inquisition into ordinary practice, and the accused who could not be convicted of the crime laid to his door could be punished for being suspected of it, not with the penalty legally provided for the offence, but with some other, at the fancy and discretion of the judge. It would be impossible to compute the amount of misery and wrong, inflicted on the defenceless up to the present century, which may be directly traced to the arbitrary and unrestricted methods introduced by the Inquisition and adopted by the jurists who fash-

---

* I have treated this subject at some length in an essay on torture (Superstition and Force, 3d Edition, 1878), and need not here dwell further on its details. The student who desires to see the shape which the inquisitorial process assumed in later times can consult Brunnemann (Tractatus Juridicus de Inquisitionis Processu, Ed. octava, Francof. 1704), who attributes its origin to the Mosaic law (Deut. XIII. 12; XVII. 4), and vastly prefers it to the proceeding *per accusationem.* Indeed, a case in which *accusatio* failed or threatened to fail could be resumed or continued by *inquisitio* (op. cit. Cap. I. No. 2, 15–18). It supplied all deficiencies and gave the judge almost unlimited power to convict.

The manner in which the civil power was led to adopt the abuses of the Inquisition is well illustrated in a Milanese edict of 1393, where the magistrates, in proceedings against malefactors, are ordered to employ the inquisitorial process "*summarie et de plano sine strepitu et figura juditii,*" and to supply all defects of fact "*ex certa scientia*" (Antiq. Ducum Mediolan. Decreta. Mediolani, 1654, p. 188). A comparison of this with the Milanese jurisprudence of sixty years earlier, quoted above (p. 401), will show how rapidly in the interval force had usurped the place of justice.

ioned the criminal jurisprudence of the Continent. It was a system which might well seem the invention of demons, and was fitly characterized by Sir John Fortescue as the Road to Hell.*

---

* Fortescue de Laudibus Legum Angliæ cap. xxii.—As late as 1823 there is a case in which a court in Martinique condemned a man to the galleys for life for " vehement suspicion " of being a sorcerer (Isambert. Anc. Loix Françaises, XI. 253).

INDEX